Labor Markets and Social Policy

I N

Central and Eastern Europe

To the memory of
Ralph W. Harbison,
our inspiration and friend

Labor Markets and Social Policy

— I N —

Central and Eastern Europe

The Accession and Beyond

Edited by Nicholas Barr

THE WORLD BANK
Washington, D.C.

ISBN 0-8213-6119-8

Library of Congress Cataloging-in Publication Data

Labor markets and social policy in Central and Eastern Europe: the accession and beyond / Nicholas Barr, ed.
    p. cm.
   Includes bibliographical references and index.
   ISBN 0-8231-6119-8 (pbk.)
   1. Labor market—Europe, Eastern. 2. Labor Market—Europe, Central. 3. Europe, Eastern—Social policy. 4. Europe, Central—Social policy. 5. Europe, Eastern—Economic conditions—1989- 6. Europe, Central—Economic conditions. 7. European Union—Europe, Eastern. 8. European Union—Europe, Central. I. Barr, N. A.

HD5764.7.A6L28 2005
331.1'0943—dc22

                         2005042058

Cover illustration, "Handshake over Chasm," © Images.com/CORBIS

Cover and interior design by Circle Graphics

CONTENTS

PREFACE

In 1994 many of the authors of this book wrote its predecessor, on labor markets and social policy in Central and Eastern Europe during the early transition. The driving force for that book was Ralph W. Harbison, then Chief of the Human Resources Operations Division in the World Bank's Europe and Central Asia Region. He was our boss, our friend, and our partner in crime (the crime being mainly that results on the ground took priority over internal Bank process). Ralph's passion was to get it right for the large numbers of people going through times of great hope (whose fulfilment we discuss in this book), but also a time of emerging unemployment, rising poverty, and increased uncertainty—thus the opening chapter of that first book was titled 'Hopes, Tears and Transformation'. In pursuit of that passion he drove all of us hard and himself even harder—"It's *all* a priority," he would say. But through that came the benefits of friendship and the shared feeling that we were doing something helpful at a time of huge historical change (in November 1989, the main employment office in Warsaw had five unemployed people on its books, a year later unemployment in Poland was over one million). It was also under Ralph's aegis that we got together for two weeks in the icy blasts of Brighton, UK in January 1993 to write the first draft of the book, going from first draft to printed volume in just over 1½ years.

Ralph died suddenly in February 2002, and the idea of this book emerged spontaneously when a group of his friends met after one of several hugely attended memorial meetings for him. Its purpose is to commemorate him and his work by taking forward to EU accession the story of social policy developments in the countries in which we all worked. The authors all share the strong link that Ralph was our boss, our co-author, or both.

The book—like the work of Ralph's division—covers large parts of social policy over the period from pre-transition to post-accession, aiming to show the linkages between the different parts of social policy and to explain the historical continuum over which the reforms took place. The price of this breadth is that people with deep expertise in a particular field might find the chapter in his or her field less satisfying than (we hope) the other chapters.

The book is aimed at readers interested in social policy, and particularly in the process of post-communist transition, in EU accession, and in future social policy challenges for the wider Europe. Thus it should be of interest to academics in departments of economics, social policy, political economy and political science, and to policy makers, including government advisers and civil servants.

Our debts are many and great, though none of the people named below should be implicated in the result, for which we take full responsibility. Our first and major debt, is to our Advisory Committee: Andris Bērziņš, Antonia Bullard, Giovanni Andrea Cornia, Saul Estrin, Robert Holzmann, János Kornai, Julian Schweitzer, and Igor Tomes, who all commented robustly but supportively on drafts of the book as a whole or on particular chapters.

Particular thanks are due to Antonia Bullard for the enormous help she gave us in shaping the writing as we recrafted draft chapters to create the first draft of the book as a whole; to Anton Dobrogonov, on whose work much of Chapter 2 is based; and to Peter Diamond, whose comprehensive trashing of an early draft of Chapter 5 was instrumental in helping to strengthen the arguments.

We are also grateful to others who commented on individual chapters: to Mary Canning, Zsuzsa Ferge, Abby Innes, Claire Gordon, Richard Jackman, Olivia Michell, Waltraud Schelkle, Eugene Smolensky, and Ian Whitman; to participants at a seminar at the European Institute, London School of Economics; and to Peter Costolanski for high-quality research assistance with Chapter 4.

The book would not have been published without the strong support—intellectual support, active encouragement and financial backing—of the Europe and Central Asia Vice-Presidency of the World Bank, for which our particular thanks are due to Shigeo Katsu, Pradeep Mitra, Annette Dixon, Charles Griffin, Arup Banerji, and Mamta Murthi. We are also very grateful to participants at a special session at the World Bank's 2004 Human Development Week, and especially to Mustapha Nabli, whose thorough review helped us to set the arguments in the context of a broader development agenda.

Thanks for the book's readability and appearance are due to the production and editorial team in the World Bank's Office of the Publisher, most particularly Susan Graham and Sherrie M. Brown who worked on a very tight schedule to get the book out in time for the first anniversary of EU accession.

Michal Rutkowski, in piloting the book through the World Bank's internal processes and acting as tireless practical problem solver, fully and seamlessly took over the mantle he inherited from Ralph.

Finally, thanks of a very special sort are due to Irene Harbison, who threw open Ralph's and her rural idyll in Willsboro, New York, to give us the space and time we would not otherwise have had to pull the book together. Brighton in January 1993 to Willsboro in early September 2003 was a long, exciting ride.

Nicholas Barr
London
November 2004

THE AUTHORS

OLUSOJI ADEYI, Coordinator of Global Partnerships for Communicable Diseases; Adjunct Assistant Professor, Johns Hopkins School of Public Health. Formerly Lead Health Specialist, Europe and Central Asia Region, and Health Program Team Leader for Russia, Romania, Bosnia-Herzegovina, and Albania. Co-author of "Trends in Health Status, Services and Finance: The Transition in Central and Eastern Europe" (1996), "Health in Europe and Central Asia: Transition Retrospective and Business Plan" (2003). Lead author of "Averting AIDS Crises in Eastern Europe and Central Asia: A Regional Support Strategy" (2003).

NICHOLAS BARR, Professor of Public Economics, London School of Economics; World Bank Europe and Central Asia Human Resources Operations Division 1990-1992. Editor of *Labor Markets and Social Policy in Central and Eastern Europe: The Transition and Beyond* (1994); principal author, *World Development Report 1996: From Plan to Market*. Other publications include *The Welfare State as Piggy Bank: Information, Risk, Uncertainty and the Role of the State* (2001); and *The Economics of the Welfare State, 4th edition* (2004).

DAVID FRETWELL, Lead Employment and Training Specialist in the Human Development Department of the Europe and Central Asia Region, where he has worked for the last 15 years. He has led the Bank's work on employment and unemployment in ECA since the start of the transition process in 1990, and has also had assignments in Asia, Africa, the Middle East and Latin America. While at the Bank he completed a staff exchange program with the EU European Training Foundation, and an assignment at the World Bank Human Resource Hub in Hungary.

ERIC HANUSHEK, Paul and Jean Hanna Senior Fellow, Hoover Institution, Stanford University; Research Associate, National Bureau of Economic Research; Chairman, Executive Board of Texas Schools Project, University of Texas at Dallas; co-author (with Ralph W. Harbison) *Educational Performance of the Poor: Lessons from Rural Northeast Brazil* (1992).

MICHAEL MERTAUGH, Lead Education Economist, Human Development Department, Europe and Central Asia Region, involving project and analytical work on education in countries including Poland, the Czech Republic, Slovakia, Hungary, Romania, Bulgaria, Bosnia/Herzegovina, FYR Macedonia, Serbia and Montenegro.

ALEXANDER PREKER, Lead Economist, formerly a member of the Human Development Department, Europe and Central Asia Region. He coordinated the team that prepared the World Bank's Sector Strategy for Health, Nutrition and Population in 1997. While working with the World Health Organization in 1999-2000, he was one of the co-authors of the World Health Report 2000 *Health Systems: Measuring Performance*. From 2000-2001 he was a member of Working Group 3 of the WHO Commission on Macro-Economics and Health, chaired by Jeffery Sachs.

MANSOORA RASHID, Sector Manager, Social Protection Unit, South Asia Region, formerly Lead Economist, Human Development Department, Europe, Central Asia Region. Her analytical work has focused on poverty, pensions, safety nets, and labor markets, including *Social Protection Strategy for Eastern Europe and Central Asian Countries* (2003), with the ECA Social Protection Team; *Labor Markets in Transition Countries* (2003), with Jan Rutkowski; *The Financing of Pensions in Central and Eastern Europe* (1996), with Emily Andrews.

DENA RINGOLD, Senior Economist, Human Development Sector Unit, Europe and Central Asia Region. In 2005 Dena was an Ian Axford Fellow in Public Policy based at the Ministry of Mäori Development in Wellington, New Zealand. Her analytical work has focused on poverty and ethnic minorities, particularly the Roma population, social safety nets, and decentralization of social services. Dena is the lead author of *Roma in an Expanding Europe: Breaking the Poverty Cycle* (2005).

JAN RUTKOWSKI, Senior Labor Economist, Human Development Department, Europe and Central Asia Region. He has been involved in labor market reforms in Bulgaria, Croatia, FYR Macedonia, and Serbia, and has done analytical work on labor market performance in transition economies and its contribution to economic growth and poverty reduction.

MICHAL RUTKOWSKI, Director, Human Development Department, Middle East and North Africa Region. Formerly Director, Human Development Department, Europe and Central Asia Region, and Sector Manager, Social Protection, Europe and Central Asia Region. Director of the Office for Pension Reform in Poland, 1996–97; principal author, *World Development Report 1995: Workers in an Integrating World.*

SÁNDOR SIPOS, Sector Manager, Social Protection, Human Development Network. Formerly Lead Social Protection Expert, Human Development Department, Europe and Central Asia Region, and Country Manager for Croatia, Europe and Central Asia Region. Prior to joining the Bank he worked for UNICEF's Innocenti Center setting up the TRANSMONEE social policy monitoring network in the transition countries; principal author of *Children and the Transition to the Market Economy: Safety Nets and Policies in Central and Eastern Europe* (1991).

1

FROM TRANSITION
TO ACCESSION

Nicholas Barr

The communist economic and political system collapsed in Central and Eastern Europe in the summer and autumn of 1989. Three of the authors of this book were citizens of those countries, another three were somewhat startled to find themselves working on social policy in those countries from late-1989 and early 1990 onward, and the rest became involved only slightly later. Given the events of the early transition, it would have been hard to predict that within 15 years many of those countries would be joining the European Union (EU) as full members, with others at an advanced stage of application.

That, however, is exactly what happened. This book—a sequel to an earlier volume (Barr 1994) by many of the same authors—takes the story forward, looking in turn at transition, EU accession, and the post-accession period.

The starting point is the transition from central planning and totalitarian government to a mixed economy and democratic pluralism—its pains, its controversies, and the reasons for its success—and the role of labor market reform and social policy in assisting that process. The main conclusions of the first book were threefold:

First, enhancing these countries' human resources—making labor markets more effective, improving education and training, reducing unemployment and poverty, and promoting better health—is fundamental to the reforms. Second, the state has a diverse and important

> role in these four areas. Third, the reforms will fail unless adequate weight is given to the political and administrative dimensions of policy implementation. (Barr and Harbison 1994, p. 1)

Those conclusions have stood the test of time, as have many of the more specific conclusions. The main strategic change since then is the wide divergence in outcomes between the richest and most advanced reformers, such as the Czech Republic, Hungary, and Slovenia on the one hand, and on the other, the poorer countries in which there has been little or no reform, such as Belarus.

The second topic is EU accession. The objectives here are more modest, with no attempt to analyze the process in depth. Instead, discussion seeks to describe the constraints the accession process imposed on countries' freedom of action, and to set out arguments by different writers about which aspects of accession were helpful to economic, political, and social reform, and which were unhelpful, at least in their timing. These topics are included because they have an important influence on the discussion of the later years of transition and because they partly shape the social policy problems and choices that will continue to challenge both the accession countries and the older members of the EU. These future common challenges—the third topic of the book—include balancing labor protection with economic competitiveness; extending opportunity to socially excluded groups; adjusting old age pensions to accommodate the happy circumstance that people are living longer; ensuring that health care remains affordable while simultaneously addressing the problems of HIV/AIDS and other major threats to health; and adjusting the education system to accommodate rapidly changing labor market needs and diverse cultures.

This chapter sets the scene and poses the issues. Chapter 2 summarizes historical aspects of transition to which later chapters refer. Subsequent chapters discuss in turn labor markets, social safety nets, pensions, health and health care, and education and training. Each chapter has a common structure, discussing the logic of transition, describing the process of EU accession, and setting out the issues that will remain central to the social policy agenda long past accession. Annexes to three of the chapters offer detailed case studies of specific policy areas: active labor market policies; policies to address social exclusion, particularly among the Roma; and financing higher education. Throughout the book, discussion seeks to bring out the most important controversies.

To accommodate such a wide agenda within a relatively short volume, some exclusions are deliberate. First, the chapters are not surveys but intentionally selective, concentrating on central aspects of the reform process—choices with which others might disagree. Second, no attempt is made to set out all the evidence for the arguments; instead a sample is offered with references to the extensive literature. Third, the choice of country coverage is selective, focusing on the eight former communist countries that joined the EU in 2004 (the Czech Republic, Estonia, Hungary, Latvia, Lithuania, Poland, the Slovak Republic, and Slovenia) and the two with a provisional entry date of 2007, Bulgaria and Romania.[1] Finally, such issues as the causes of civil war are not discussed.

THE LOGIC OF TRANSITION

Although it was not apparent in 1989, it is clearer with hindsight why the transition process took its particular shape. The overarching objectives were fairly clear, and the effects of transition and, in consequence, the resulting policy directions followed logically from the nature of the old order. This section deliberately makes some statements sharper than a sophisticated understanding of the facts will bear, to delineate the process clearly.

The objectives of transition

Citizens in Central and Eastern Europe embarked on transition with three explicit objectives:

- Higher living standards, comparable to those of Western Europe
- Greater individual freedom
- A "return to Europe" (see, for example, Davies 1997)

These, however, were not all necessarily objectives in all countries. In some, particularly in the former Soviet Union, reform was not really on the agenda. Nor were they necessarily objectives for everyone. In some countries, although the people wanted higher living standards and greater freedom, the ruling elite may have wanted to restrict freedom and, by rent seeking, to garner most of the gains for themselves. In addition, each of the objectives had different dimensions that were given different weights in different countries. The drive to return to Europe, for example, arose for historical and cultural reasons, out of aspirations to EU living standards and, for security reasons, out of a deep desire to make the break from Soviet power irreversible. Regardless of these differences, the three objectives were at the heart of the transition for the citizens of the EU-aspirant countries.

In pursuing those objectives, policy makers embraced two fundamental policy directions: a move from central planning to a market system, and a move from totalitarian to more democratic forms of government.

Among the profound changes that these moves implied was a need radically to reform the inherited labor markets and social policy institutions. The problem for social policy was how to maintain the best of the old order while adapting it to a new and vastly different economic system; the financial problem was to keep the system going at all when output was falling rapidly and tax revenues even more rapidly.

A central argument in this book is that communist social policy was, by and large, well-adapted to the old economic and political order and—for exactly that reason—was ill-adapted in systematic and predictable ways to the needs of a modern mixed economy in a pluralist society. Thus, the strategic reform directions the book recommends are based not on personal views but are those that follow from the logic of transition.

The old order

The communist system, based on central planning and totalitarian government, is described in box 1.1.

The following stylized facts about the old order should be thought of as a simple model. Like any model, it should not be taken literally, but is useful because it offers insights into the shape of transition and the resulting directions for reform, and hence explains the structure of subsequent discussion.

1. Wages were low and not highly differentiated.
2. Wages were supplemented by universal benefits, including subsidized basic goods and many benefits provided by state enterprises.
3. As a practical matter, work was guaranteed.
4. Resources were mostly allocated centrally, rather than through markets, which were largely suppressed.
5. Government was totalitarian.

The first three facts largely determined the shape of labor market institutions and income transfers. Together they imply that the communist system had

- No unemployment, and hence a system of unemployment benefits that was absent or, at best, rudimentary.
- No poverty, at least officially, and hence little poverty relief. Everyone of working age had a job, with wages supplemented by social benefits, and with basic commodities provided at subsidized prices. Nonworking groups such as pensioners were covered by near-universal social benefits.

BOX 1.1 An Outline of the Communist System

Although the communist countries were not identical, the system in almost all was based largely on central planning and totalitarian government. This brief description illustrates the core elements of an archetypal system.

Resources were publicly owned, and allocation decisions were highly centralized, largely on the basis of a five-year central plan. In consequence, there was little private enterprise and little competition. The planning process applied to labor as well as to material inputs and outputs. Although in most countries work was not guaranteed in a formal sense, there was little chance—provided he or she kept his or her mouth shut—that a worker would lose a job. The roots of job security were partly ideological and partly the result of the labor shortages described below.

The planning process applied not only to quantities, but also to prices. Prices were administratively determined, with wide-ranging subsidies for basic commodities such as food, housing, heating, and transport. These subsidies were topped up by generous, mostly universal benefits: state enterprises provided fringe benefits such as child care, subsidized cafeterias, low-cost housing, and vacation homes; and there were generous social transfers both in cash and kind. Variations occurred across countries, of course; although benefits tended to be generous, some of them, including health care and certain aspects of education, became outmoded.

Wages, too, were largely administratively determined. Given the wide-ranging system of subsidies, wages tended to be low, with less differentiation than is typical in market economies, and distorted relative to an efficient use of labor. "Key features of the prereform labor market [included a] . . . structure of relative wages characterized by compressed differentials bearing little relationship to the market value of workers' skills" (Jackman 1998, p. 123). This picture of equality should not, however, be exaggerated: prices were low but goods were frequently not available at those prices, and access to scarce goods was easier for the *nomenclatura* than for rank and file workers.

Shortfalls in meeting output targets would blight the prospects of the managers concerned; in contrast, financial deficits (losses) were tolerated (in Kornai's [1992] now standard terminology, a "soft budget constraint"). In the face of hard output targets but soft budget constraints, it was rational for managers to hoard inputs and, given low wages, most particularly to hoard labor. With wages held below their market-clearing price, labor shortages became endemic, reinforcing full employment.

Financial institutions supported the central planning process, not least through easy credit to firms. The combined effect of these soft

(continued)

> ### BOX 1.1 An Outline of the Communist System (*Continued*)
>
> budget constraints for state-owned enterprises and endemic shortages of goods, leading to forced saving, created a "monetary overhang," that is, individuals and firms with large holdings of cash. This monetary overhang fed into the extraordinary inflation rates of the early transition, notwithstanding the severe output crash.
>
> Along with these economic characteristics, government was totalitarian—a much more pervasive concept than authoritarian government. The primary distinction is that totalitarian government is typified by an all-embracing ideology that aspires to transform the entire society. Totalitarian regimes
>
> > are characterized by: a single party, usually led by one man; a pervasive and powerful secret police; a highly developed ideology setting forth the ideal society, which the totalitarian movement is committed to realizing; and government penetration and control of mass communications and all or most social and economic organizations. A traditional authoritarian system, on the other hand, is characterized by a single leader or small group of leaders, no party or a weak party, no mass mobilization, possibly a "mentality" but no ideology, limited government, "limited, not responsible, political pluralism," and no effort to remake society and human nature. (Huntington 1991, p. 12) (See also Friedrich and Brzezinski 1956; and Linz 1975.)
>
> Thus, all decision making and enforcement were politically motivated, and such political motivations superseded the rule of law.

- No sophisticated targeting of benefits to certain groups. The relatively flat income distribution had important implications. Benefits were mostly universal: if everyone has similar earnings, there is no need for selectivity by income level. Separately, government capacity to administer benefits was weak, partly because no sophisticated targeting was needed and partly because most benefits were delivered by the enterprise rather than by the state.

The last two stylized facts shaped the health and education systems.

- Health care was publicly funded and publicly organized. More subtly, an implicit goal of totalitarian government was to encourage passive citizens; thus, health was seen as something government "gave" people, not something for which individuals should take some responsibility.

- Education was publicly funded and publicly organized for the same reasons as health care. The skills that were taught tended to be narrow and specific to meet the needs of the central plan; and the system discouraged questioning attitudes, as befitting totalitarian government.

These arguments are taken up in greater detail in the relevant chapters.

The effects of transition and the resulting policy directions

Not all Central and Eastern European countries adhered rigidly to central planning. Some countries introduced significant reform during the 1980s. Transition, too, was a continuum, proceeding at different speeds and, at a detailed level, in different directions in the various countries. Nevertheless, 1989 marked a historical discontinuity: the move to markets became explicit policy and proceeded rapidly; the move to more democratic forms of government was also rapid; and Soviet hegemony dissolved. These three elements defined transition.

A World Bank (2002) study, reflecting on 10 years of reform, offered conclusions about the determinants of successful transition. Initial conditions were significant explanations during the early transition (1990–94), but reform policies had a significant, and over time increasing, impact. In particular, market forces, supported by legal and regulatory institutions, speeded up economic recovery, thus mitigating the extent of transitional recession and promoting growth in the medium term. The main sources of growth were new private enterprises. A key conclusion was that the debate about "big bang" versus gradualism is largely irrelevant—what matters is whether the reform policies are *sustained.*

The effects of transition are discussed in more detail in chapter 2. For present purposes, however, three outcomes stand out, and are shaping forces throughout the book.

- Output fell, leading to a major fiscal crisis. The scale of the decline is disputed, but it is true that welfare fell by less than output.[2] Nevertheless, as discussed in more detail in chapter 2, the fall in output was larger than anything seen in the West since the Great Depression of the 1930s. In Poland and Hungary, the countries least affected, measured output fell by about 18 percent over the first three years of transition, and in the Baltic countries by up to 50 percent.[3] By 2003, output in the accession countries had recovered, being by then 19 percent above the 1989 level. In contrast, across the Commonwealth of Independent States (CIS),[4] output averaged 75 percent of its pretransition level.[5] The output loss and accompanying fiscal crisis were unambiguously adverse outcomes.

- The distribution of income and earnings widened. As discussed in more detail in box 2.2, this outcome is harmful where it derives from monopoly rents or criminal activity—both, it is hoped, becoming less important as the rule of law takes hold. However, widening income disparity may be beneficial, for example, by increasing efficiency in labor markets if rewards are higher for skills that are in demand. This disparity properly remains a permanent part of the post-transition landscape.
- Job security ended, creating particular problems for women with family responsibilities, older workers, unskilled workers, and ethnic minorities.

In addition to these effects, two further sets of changes were the result of deliberate choice by the reforming countries:

- Competition increased in both the public and the newly emerging private sectors.
- Democratic pluralism emerged, in most countries with active encouragement.

These trends, which applied in all the transition countries, define a common set of problems and therefore, at a strategic level, a common set of reform directions.

Falling employment

Falling employment, discussed in chapter 3, arose because of falling participation, as people dropped out of the labor force, and through emerging unemployment. Both problems were new, and both were direct consequences of falling output and the end of job security. In the early transition, unemployment rose sharply, to over 10 percent in most of the reforming countries. The costs of unemployment in terms of forgone output and in personal terms are high. However, it is noteworthy that in countries such as Bulgaria and Romania, where early reform faltered, unemployment was not markedly lower than in Poland, the most aggressive reformer.[6]

A core element in economic and social policy, therefore, was to assist labor market adjustment. Chapter 3 analyzes labor markets and the annex to chapter 3 looks at active labor market policies. Chapter 7 considers the role of education and training in support of an internationally competitive economy and a pluralist society.

Rising poverty

Rising poverty is an inescapable consequence of falling output and a widening distribution of income. As a proposition in pure logic, falling output coupled with a widening income distribution leads to increased poverty.[7] Notwithstanding familiar problems in attempting to quantify poverty (Barr 1999; 2004), empirical evidence overwhelmingly supports that proposition. World Bank estimates (1999, p. 6) suggest that the number of people living on less than US$4 per day in Central and Eastern Europe and the countries of the CIS rose tenfold, from 14 million in 1989 to 147 million in 1996. Radical reformers experienced a substantial increase in poverty rates, from 6 percent of the population to 20 percent in Poland, and from 1 percent to 37 percent in Estonia. For less successful reformers, the increase was even greater: in Romania from 6 percent to 59 percent, in Russia to 50 percent, and in Ukraine to 63 percent.

The story is documented in chapter 2, policy directions in chapter 4, and issues related to particularly vulnerable groups in the annex to chapter 4. It follows that a second core reform policy was to put into place a system capable of relieving poverty that was initially widespread but shallow, but that over time came also to include deep poverty.

Ineffective targeting

Ineffective targeting of benefits follows from a widening distribution of income and, because of continuing fiscal pressures, remains a critical issue. A system designed for a flat earnings distribution, continuous employment, and perpetual labor shortage predictably misallocates benefits in the face of a diversified distribution. There are two sets of problems. Well-targeted benefits aim to avoid gaps in coverage, that is, to assist *all* the poor (known as horizontal efficiency). Immediate failures were inadequate systems of unemployment benefits and poverty relief. A second goal of good targeting—vertical efficiency—is to avoid leaks, that is, to assist *only* (or mainly) the poor. Benefits designed for a flat income distribution will inevitably fail this test in the face of a widening distribution. The most glaring example in the transition countries was relatively high public spending on old age and disability pensions and, for this and other reasons, pension reform (chapter 5) became a central—and politically highly salient—issue.

A third direction for social policy, therefore, was the need to reform the structure of benefits to improve targeting and to strengthen benefit administration to make it fit for that purpose.

Deteriorating nutrition and health

Deteriorating nutrition and health were further consequences of falling output, a widening distribution of income, and the end of job security, although the causal links for health are complex and remain controversial. The connections between unemployment and poverty on the one hand and poor health on the other are increasingly well-documented; and there were significant increases in mortality, at least in the early transition, in a number of countries. Not only was health under stress, so were the systems of health care: falling output, and resulting falling tax revenues, created resource constraints. In addition, health care systems had the same inefficiencies as state-owned enterprises generally, but without the same remedy—privatization—to deal with them. Policies to improve health and, separately, to make the system of health care more effective yet affordable, are thus another core part of reform. Chapter 6 develops these topics.

Inappropriate educational outcomes

The successes of communist education were well known, and the prevailing view in the early transition was that many aspects of educational reform could wait. That view was wrong. Rising unemployment, the result both of economic adjustment and of falling output, exposed increasing divergence between the skills imparted to meet the needs of the central plan and those demanded by the market. Problems included narrow and inflexible skills, missing skills, and unquestioning attitudes. The challenge for education and training—another central reform direction—was not only to put in place a modern, pluralist curriculum, but to impart broader, more flexible skills and to develop more advanced problem-solving skills, as well as to introduce incentives to use resources more efficiently. Chapter 7 covers these topics.

THE PROCESS OF ACCESSION

The nature of the transition process itself thus led directly to a need for policies to assist labor market adjustment by promoting earning opportunities and providing insurance (chapter 3); to relieve poverty and ameliorate social exclusion (chapter 4); to reform pensions (chapter 5), thereby assisting consumption smoothing; to improve health and health care (chapter 6); and to restructure education (chapter 7).

Such reforms could, in principle, have taken a variety of paths. In practice, however, their specific direction was shaped to a significant extent by EU accession. First, the reforming countries voluntarily adopted EU policies in some areas, for example, by looking at Western European systems of health finance and the design of school curricula. Second, given the drive for EU membership for the multiple reasons discussed earlier, aspirant member states were constrained by wide-ranging EU conditionality. The book divides those conditions into four sorts:

- The Copenhagen criteria set out the strategic conditionality for EU accession.
- Specific legislation, notably the *acquis communautaire,* sets out how the economies should operate, including detail that applies to later chapters.
- Other relevant legislation, notably the Stability and Growth Pact and the Convergence Criteria, focus mainly on issues of budgetary balance and exchange rates. While not directly related to social policy, this area of legislation clearly constrains the freedom of policy makers.
- The Lisbon strategy to fight social exclusion, of which the European Employment Strategy was a core element, made social policy an integral EU activity.

Thus, the general reform directions were a consequence of transition but, within that, many of the specifics of reform were a direct consequence of accession.

Two sets of questions arise: what was the influence of EU conditionality on the shape and direction of reform, and was that influence helpful to the overarching objectives of reform?

EU conditionality

Encapsulating a complex history, box 1.2 sets out the major milestones in the development of the EU, highlighting in particular the five treaties that have had the greatest impact on social policy in the EU, set out in more detail in table 1.1.

EU conditionality is wide ranging and continually evolving. The following discussion relates only to the elements most salient for social policy.

The Copenhagen criteria

The Copenhagen criteria, enunciated in 1993, require aspiring member states to ensure

- "stability of institutions guaranteeing democracy, the rule of law, human rights and respect for and protection of minorities"—these are the political criteria;
- "the existence of a functioning market economy as well as the capacity to cope with competitive pressure and market forces within the Union"—the economic criteria;
- "ability to take on the obligations of membership, including adherence to the aims of political, economic and monetary union"—referring to the implementation of the *acquis communautaire* (European Commission 1993).

(*text continues on page 14*)

BOX 1.2   Major Milestones in the Development of the EU

1952	European Coal and Steel Community takes effect
1957	**European Economic Community (EEC) Treaty**
1968	Customs union takes effect
1973	Denmark, Ireland, and the United Kingdom join the European Community (EC)
1981	Greece joins the EC
1986	Portugal and Spain join the EC
1986	**European Single Act**
1989	Madrid Council endorses plan for Economic and Monetary Union (EMU)
1990	The German Democratic Republic enters the EC as part of a united Germany
1991	EC and European Free Trade Association (EFTA) agree to form the European Economic Area (EEA)
1991	Poland, Hungary, and Czechoslovakia sign first Europe Agreements on trade and political cooperation
1992	**Maastricht Social Agreement**
1993	European single market
1993	Copenhagen criteria enunciated
1995	Finland, Sweden, and Austria join the EU
1997	**Amsterdam treaty**
1998	EU opens membership negotiations with Cyprus, the Czech Republic, Estonia, Hungary, Poland, and Slovenia
1998	Eleven EU member states qualify to launch the euro on January 1, 1999
1999	EMU and euro launched in 11 EU countries
1999	European Council meeting in Helsinki decides to open accession negotiations with Bulgaria, Latvia, Lithuania, Malta, Romania, and the Slovak Republic, and to recognize Turkey as a candidate country
2000	Lisbon European Council
2001	**Nice treaty**
2002	The euro becomes legal tender and permanently replaces national currencies in EMU countries
2002	Copenhagen European Council declares that Cyprus, the Czech Republic, Estonia, Hungary, Latvia, Lithuania, Malta, Poland, the Slovak Republic, and Slovenia will become EU members by May 1, 2004
2004	EU enlarges to 25 member states with the accession of Cyprus, the Czech Republic, Estonia, Hungary, Latvia, Lithuania, Malta, Poland, the Slovak Republic, and Slovenia

TABLE 1.1   The attribution of social policy competencies to the European Union in formal treaty reforms

Explicit community competence	EEC treaty, 1957	Single European Act, 1986	Social agreement, 1992	Amsterdam treaty, 1997	Nice treaty, 2001
Measures to improve transnational co-operation under Art. 137	■	■	■	■	▲
Incentive measures to combat discrimination as defined by Art. 13	■	■	■	■	▲
Action against discrimination on grounds of sex, race, ethnic origin, belief, disability, age, or sexual orientation (new Art. 13)	■	■	■	●	●
Measures combating social exclusion	■	■	■	▲	▲
Measures assuring equal opportunities and treatment of both women and men	■	■	■	▲	▲
Employment policy coordination	■	■	■	▲	▲
Funding for employment policy	■	■	●	●	■
Social security and protection of workers	■	■	●	●	●
Protection of workers where employment contract is terminated	■	■	●	●	●
Collective interest representation, co-determination	■	■	●	●	●
Employment of third-country nationals	■	■	●	●	●
Working conditions (general)	■	■	▲	▲	▲
Worker information and consultation	■	■	▲	▲	▲
Gender equality for labor force	■	■	▲	▲	▲
Integration in labor market	■	■	▲	▲	▲
Working environment (health and safety)	■	▲	▲	▲	▲
Social security coordination	●	●	no impact	●	●
Free movement of workers	▲	▲	no impact	▲	▲

Source: Falkner and others 2005, table 3.1.
Note: ■ not mentioned; ● decision by unanimity; ▲ decision by qualified majority.

Along with these requirements on applicants, a further criterion was the capacity of the Union to take on new members while maintaining the momentum of European integration.

The Copenhagen criteria are not mechanistic. They not only allowed, but required, judgments. On what basis, for example, was it possible to decide that guarantees of human rights are "stable?" In addition, the interpretation of the criteria was not static, but continued to evolve over the period of accession.

The Copenhagen criteria were specific to the enlargement process. Three other sets of conditions apply to all member states, and thus had to be adopted by the applicant countries: the *acquis communautaire* discusses the microeconomic structure of economic organization and regulation; the Stability and Growth Pact and the Convergence Criteria for monetary union are mainly macroeconomic; and the Lisbon strategy brings social policy into the EU mainstream.

Specific legislation: the acquis communautaire

The *acquis communautaire,* comprising 31 chapters and 81,000 pages, is the "rule book" of the EU, to which countries joining the Union have to adhere or be close to doing so.[8] The *acquis* is wide ranging in scale and scope, with chapters, among other things, on the free movement of goods, persons, and capital; company law; competition policy; the conduct of agriculture, fisheries, transport, energy, telecommunications, and information technology; consumer protection; regional policy; the environment; external relations; and financial control.[9] In principle, all the accession countries are subject to the entire *acquis,* although in practice there can be some flexibility over timing—for example, Latvia, Poland, and Slovenia were given a transitional period with respect to the health and safety requirements.

The elements of the *acquis* most relevant to labor markets and social policy are Chapter 13 Employment and Social Policy (known as the Social Chapter) and Chapter 18 Education and Training. Although not as comprehensive in these areas as, for example, on the free movement of goods and persons or on taxation, the *acquis* nevertheless has considerable influence on the reform specifics, as table 1.1 makes clear, and recurs throughout subsequent chapters.

Labor market institutions are covered by the Social Chapter. "[L]egislation is . . . used to achieve equality, especially to prohibit discrimination on the grounds of sex. Most of the current legislation relates to employment in the following fields: equal treatment in employment and occupation, social security, occupational social security schemes [and] parental leave . . ." (European Commission 2003a, p. 44). The chapter also gives considerable attention to health and safety and to addressing ethnic discrimination.

The *acquis* treats the funding and organization of social protection as the responsibility of member states. Nevertheless, the EU requires that "the systems of the candidate countries must . . . be capable of co-ordinating with those systems currently operating in the EU . . ." (European Commission 2003a, p. 45). Pension arrangements, for example, should ensure that pension entitlement is portable within the EU.

Although poverty relief is not specifically the subject of the *acquis,* it comes under the same guidelines as pensions. In addition, other elements of accession conditionality, ultimately stemming from the Copenhagen criteria and the Lisbon strategy, emphasize policies to assist socially excluded groups. The treatment of the Roma, for example, was a public and explicit issue in the applications of several countries.

The *acquis* is relevant to the health sector in various ways. The Social Chapter has a section on public health, emphasizing the importance of "a high level of human health protection in the definition and implementation of all Community policies. To protect public health the EU also issued several Directives in the area of tobacco products and advertising" (European Commission 2003a, p. 45).

Chapter 18 of the *acquis* deals with education and training, although specifying that "[e]ducation, training and youth is primarily the competence of the Member States" (European Commission 2003a, p. 58). Thus, countries are allowed to specify the domain of compulsory school attendance. However, they have to meet specific requirements for children within that domain, for example, concerning equality of opportunity, literacy, facilities for minorities, and the education of the children of migrant workers. Related policies on training are included in the chapter of the acquis on employment.

Other relevant legislation: the stability and growth pact and the convergence criteria

The Stability and Growth Pact and the Convergence Criteria are discussed in more detail in chapter 2 of this book. The Stability and Growth Pact is concerned with budgetary balance, specifically with ensuring that short-term deficits do not exceed 3 percent of gross domestic product (GDP) and that in the medium term the budgetary balance is broadly zero. One element of the pact is an early warning system to identify potential problems, another a set of rules to discourage excessive deficits and to correct them.

The Convergence Criteria establish the conditions for entry into the monetary union through a more wide-ranging set of rules about macroeconomic variables, including an inflation target and an interest rate target that keep each country close to the rates in the three countries with the lowest rates of inflation;

targets for the budget deficit and national debt that do not exceed 3 percent and 60 percent of GDP, respectively; and an exchange rate target.[10]

The Lisbon strategy

An ambitious 10-year strategy to make the EU the most competitive, knowledge-based economy in the world with full employment and higher social cohesion was agreed on at the Lisbon European Council in March 2000 and elaborated upon at subsequent summits. The strategy established the goal of social inclusion as an integral component of an EU growth strategy.

> The modernisation of social protection systems is a crucial aspect of the reform of the European social model. The long-term sustainability and quality of social protection systems, particularly in the face of an ageing population, is a crucial aspect determining the success of the reform agenda. (European Commission 2003b, p. 8)

Social policy thus became a mainstream EU activity. Although its time frame was mainly post-accession, the Lisbon strategy was mandatory for old and new member states alike. While not yet fully fleshed out, early elements included the aim of an EU-wide health insurance card and pensions designed to be fully portable throughout the EU.

Political pre-conditions

Despite the enormous range of technical detail in the *acquis,* the Stability and Growth Pact, and the Convergence Criteria, the central issue in accession was at least as much political as technical. Specifically, it was necessary to find a meeting ground between two sets of political imperatives.

* Were the accession arrangements sufficiently parsimonious for EU politicians to sell them to their electorates? A settlement too generous to the transition countries risked rejection by the existing EU members.
* Were the proposed arrangements sufficiently generous that politicians in the accession countries could sell them to their electorates?

The debate over the agricultural arrangements illustrates the dilemma clearly, the size of the quotas for the accession countries remaining the subject of political haggling until the very end. In the social policy area, as discussed in chapter 3, the free movement of workers (that is, labor mobility) was disputed until the last moment, when an interim agreement was reached under which restrictions on freedom of movement would not be entirely removed for seven years.[11]

EU conditionality: Helpful to transition?

This section sets out four arguments: that there are potential conflicts between the objectives of transition and those of accession; that the *acquis* may have imposed some costs on the accession countries that could otherwise have been avoided; that adopting the macroeconomic conditionality might have brought immediate gains; and that some particularly painful conditions were deliberately ignored, that is, that in some areas the conditionality was not wholly binding. As noted at the start of the chapter, the intention is limited to sketching out the issues that experts debate.

Compatible objectives?

Policy makers in the accession countries and scholars have asked whether the various layers of conditionality helped transition. Were the conditions designed to assist transition or in part to protect existing members from competition? Was the sequencing the most helpful to transition? Were the conditions mutually compatible?

The following questions illustrate some of the potential conflicts:[12]

- Did the macroeconomic constraints conflict with the expensive requirements of the *acquis?* Potentially an issue in all countries, it can be argued that, particularly in countries such as Romania and Bulgaria, some of the requirements of the *acquis* were a substantial diversion of resources away from more pressing elements of transition—poverty relief, or building an effective system of tax collection.
- Was the fiscal constraint demanded by the accession process compatible with high welfare state spending directly connected with transition, for example, unemployment benefits and poverty relief?
- Did high Western European standards reduce the competitiveness of the accession countries? (The example of worker protection is discussed in chapter 3.)
- Are global economic pressures compatible with the wide-ranging social policy agenda of the Lisbon strategy? It can be argued that the accession countries are particularly vulnerable to these pressures, given housing market rigidities and the potential for highly educated workers to emigrate to the older member states.

The answers to these questions will differ significantly across countries: EU conditionality was not applicable to the countries of the former Soviet Union apart from Estonia, Latvia, and Lithuania; the conditions became relevant for some countries only later in the decade; and for some countries (Poland, for example), some of the constraints were not binding, in the sense that they referred to things that the Poles would have done anyway.

The core problem is that, at least in principle, EU conditionality is one-size-fits-all. But one size does not fit all. If the resulting conflict between transition and accession was substantial, it may be that the ideal conditions from the viewpoint of transition would have provided for a longer time frame and greater flexibility than actually occurred.

Restrictions imposed by the acquis

In the areas covered by this book, the question of conflict between the needs of transition and those of accession is perhaps most relevant to labor markets. The Social Chapter of the *acquis* mandates considerable worker protection along a range of dimensions. The potential benefits are twofold: workers in the accession countries are given more security during times of continuing rapid change; and the existence of such security can make it easier for workers to take risks (adequate unemployment benefits being the most obvious example). However, there are also costs. First, if the balance between worker rights and employer freedom of action tilts too far to the former, the effect is to impede the creation of new jobs: just as rent control can create a housing shortage, excessive worker protection, if it is ultimately paid for by the employer, can create a shortage of jobs. Second, a requirement to offer generous worker protection can reduce the competitiveness of firms in the accession countries relative to those in the longer-established EU members. At heart, the point is simple: firms in the older member states were competitive because workers were productive; in Central and Eastern Europe, particularly in the early transition, firms were competitive because labor was cheap; making labor more expensive at the margin reduced competitiveness and hence growth.

The *acquis* has less to say about pensions and poverty relief, although more to say about social exclusion, minority rights in particular. The restrictions relevant to the health sector are concerned mainly with public health issues, particularly environmental ones. While the environmental record of communism was appalling, it does not follow that the massive environmental effort mandated by EU accession was necessarily the correct priority in terms of the sequencing of transition. Given scarcity both of resources and of institutional capacity, action on the environment was inescapably at the expense of other activities—basic health care, improving school teachers' pay, and resources to address social exclusion, for example.

Macroeconomic conditionality: Unnecessary? Or were there immediate gains?

The argument that high social spending can harm growth should not be over-stated. In considering the relationship, at least three questions are relevant: How high is too high? By what mechanism might social spending reduce growth? What are the benefits of social spending? The issues remain in dispute.

- Social spending varies widely around the Organisation for Economic Co-operation and Development (OECD) average, with no evidence that growth has been slower in high-spending countries or higher in low-spending countries. Poland, with one of the highest levels of public pension spending of the accession countries, has the strongest growth performance over the period since 1989; Slovenia, with the highest pension spending, is the next best growth performer.
- If the charge is that the *level* of welfare-state spending is too high, then, as Atkinson (1995, p. 123) points out, "the Welfare State is no more than a co-defendant with other elements of the state budget."
- Determining the direction of causation can be difficult. Do countries with higher spending reduce their growth rate, or do countries with lower growth and more poverty need to spend a larger fraction of GDP alleviating poverty?
- Looking at aggregates can obscure other influences on growth, notably the detailed structure—and thus the incentive effects—of benefits. Benefits awarded without an income test, for example, may cost more but have less powerful adverse incentives.
- Finally, public social spending has benefits as well as costs—in terms of security, in addressing market failures, and in potential distributional gains (Atkinson 1999; Barr 2001). Economists should need no reminder of the need to consider benefits and costs together.

For these and other reasons, Solow, in an assessment of cross-country comparative analysis (1994, p. 51, quoted by Atkinson 1995, p. 124), concluded "I do not find this a confidence-inspiring project. It seems altogether too vulnerable to bias from omitted variables, to reverse causation, and above all to the recurrent suspicion that the experiences of very different national economies cannot be explained as if they represented different 'points' on some well-defined surface."

Parallel questions arise about the helpfulness of the Stability and Growth Pact and the Convergence Criteria. The early transition was characterized in all the reforming countries by an output collapse and fiscal crisis. Yet, within a few years, budgets had to be compatible with the considerable constraints designed to put the EMU into effect, requirements that have proved difficult even for some of the older member states, for example, France and Germany in 2003 and 2004. Whether adherence to such stringent policies helped reform by minimizing the costs of transition, or unnecessarily aggravated the costs of transition, or distorted priorities, is the subject of fierce and continuing debate, both on the general topic and in the explicit context of transition.[13] It may be, for example, that the tight deficit requirements of the macroeconomic conditions do not fit the needs of the faster-growing countries of Central and Eastern Europe. Thus, there may be a trade-off between economic cohesion and the growth prospects of the accession countries.

An interesting argument by Bronk is that it is precisely the inflexibility of the accession criteria that make them useful to the accession countries as a commitment device.

> [B]y committing themselves to the goal of EU accession, and thereby submitting themselves to benchmarking and sanctioning in Commission reports and to loss of face if their application is turned down, CEEC governments make themselves less prone to postponing difficult decisions on transition policy for short-term political gain. At the same time, the *de facto* delegation of the policy mix (now dictated by EU conditionality) simplifies the decision-tree for CEECs, and strengthens governments' resolve to resist the demands of rent-seeking special interest groups. (Bronk 2002, p. 3)

Not only are there political gains from adopting such a commitment device, but also immediate economic gains, particularly through increased foreign direct investment and a lower risk premium when borrowing on international capital markets.

The essence of the argument is that a credibility device strengthens the incentives to adhere to a policy path with longer-term gains by building in *short-term* costs of reneging. Such an argument does not, of course, mean that EU conditionality is necessarily efficient, but does point to a gain that may at least partially offset the costs of accession.

Economic optimality or political-economy optimality?

Vanhuysse (2003) poses the question of why radical economic reform with considerable short-run costs was possible in the accession countries with so little political protest. The core of his argument is that governments adopted a policy of "divide and pacify": specifically, they marginalized political opposition to the reforms by keeping high levels of employment (the Czech Republic); or by financing unemployment benefits on relatively generous terms or allowing a tidal wave of early retirement (Poland, Hungary)—or both. One interpretation of these conclusions is that a policy that is clearly suboptimal from an economic perspective (work in the grey economy, fiscally expensive early retirement) may be optimal (or at least roughly so) when considering economics and politics simultaneously. A further interpretation is that any harmful effects of EU conditionality may have been reduced because countries were in practice given sufficient freedom of movement to sidestep any conditions that put at risk the overall success of the reforms.[14]

Two points can be made in conclusion. First, there is widespread acceptance that the fit between EU conditionality and the needs of transition was far from perfect, although with continuing debate about the extent of divergence. Second, whatever those costs in economic terms, the accession countries were content to bear them as the price of returning to Europe, one of the three overarching objectives discussed at the start of the chapter. Membership in the EU, it was argued, would bring long-term economic and political benefits; perhaps most important of all, by embedding the new member states firmly within Western security arrangements, it guaranteed their escape from the communist system and from Soviet domination.

BEYOND ACCESSION

On May 1, 2004, eight former communist countries joined the EU. While there are endless academic debates about how to define transition and by what criteria we can judge when transition ends, this book adopts EU accession as a good working definition of successful transition.[15] The countries were judged to be in compliance with the Copenhagen criteria and with at least a critical mass of the *acquis*. They had strong and persistent growth rates, so that the countries of Central Europe (though not yet the Baltic countries), having more than made up the output loss of early transition (see table 2.1), were absolutely better off than at the end of the communist era. In terms of the level of income, however, the accession countries were still significantly less well off than Western Europe. Income per capita in Slovenia, the richest accession country, in 2001 was approaching three-quarters of the EU average. In the Czech Republic and Hungary, the next two richest, the comparable figures were 60 percent and just over 50 percent. Such differences are no wider than those of earlier accession countries such as Greece, Portugal, and Spain. However, the accession countries as a whole are considerably poorer than the older member states, so that earlier enlargements are not always directly comparable.

For the latter reason, among others, the fact of EU enlargement does not mean that the book on social policy can be closed. EU accession is a wonderful achievement. However, it is only a way station on a continuing journey addressing social policy challenges common to the old and new EU countries—a policy agenda that far outlasts EU accession. The roots of the problems lie in changes in economic and social structures over the past 50 years.

Social policy and social change after the second World War

The postwar welfare state was based on a series of assumptions:

- The world was made up of independent nation states, so that constraints on economic policy were largely domestic.
- Employment was a binary phenomenon: people were either employed or unemployed, or were out of the labor force.
- International labor mobility was low.
- The nuclear family with male breadwinner and female caregiver was the typical arrangement, with divorce rare.
- Skills acquired when young would last throughout a working career.
- The age structure of the population would remain broadly constant.

These assumptions were not wholly true even in the immediate postwar years, but they were true enough. Over the second half of the twentieth century, a series of changes made them increasingly untrue in ways that have major implications for policy.

International competition increased (globalization), partly because of policy developments, particularly increased international capital mobility, and partly because of technological advances, notably the growth of digital commerce, making international boundaries more porous for certain purposes. For both reasons the international economy is more open. Governments can still have independent economic policies, but not to the same extent as before.

Labor markets became more fluid, with more entry and exit by choice (longer education) and by constraint (higher unemployment); and there was more part-time work, again both by choice and by constraint. Thus, it is now necessary to have labor market institutions and social policy arrangements that do not distort choices between part-time and full-time work or between employment and self-employment, that are portable between jobs, and that cumulate easily across different patterns of labor market activity. Major implications result for labor market institutions (chapter 3) and the design of pensions (chapter 5).

Additionally, international labor mobility increased, requiring institutions compatible with and, ideally, supportive of temporary or permanent migration, again with implications that are touched on in chapters 3 and 5.

Family structures became more complex and, for this and other reasons, reform should make it easier for women to combine family and career to avoid a "fertility strike" (Esping-Andersen 1999). The issue is important both for its own sake and because declining fertility aggravates population aging. With changing family structures and more flexible labor market arrangements, entitlement should be based more on the individual rather than the family. For example, husband and wife should each have a pension, rather than the pension arrangement of one being deemed to cover both.

The life of job skills declined. Technological advances have brought about the information age, resulting in a need for more education and training, greater diversity of that education and training, and repeated education and training. These issues are explored in chapter 7. Major issues about the financing and organization of tertiary education also arise, and are discussed in some detail in the annex to chapter 7.

Population aging has clear and major implications for pensions and health care. The projected age-dependency ratio in Europe is higher than in any other part of the world, highlighting the particular importance to the wider Europe of raising employment rates and increasing occupational and geographical labor mobility (discussed in chapter 3), and of adjusting pensions to longer life expectancy (discussed in chapter 5).

It is, therefore, not surprising that the European Commission, in a review of the social policy agenda in 2003, concluded that

> the established challenges underlying the social agenda—including the pervasive structural weaknesses in labour markets, demographic trends, the persistent gender inequalities, the changing nature of families, technological change and the requirements for the knowledge-based economy, disparities and poverty, the internationalisation of the economy—should remain a firm basis for future EU action in the field of employment and social policy. (European Commission 2003b, p. 3)

On enlargement, the review continued:

> In May 2004 the European Union will welcome ten new Member States, bringing a definitive end to the division of Europe following the second World War.
>
> The 2004 enlargement will distinguish itself from previous enlargements in terms of growing diversity across the board. A new challenge in the social field will concern the discrimination face by ethnic minorities and in particular the Roma. . . .

The increased diversity also concerns particularly economic divergence. The average income level of the ten accession countries will be less than half of the average GDP per head of the current Member States. (European Commission 2003b, p. 4)

The resulting reform directions

The resulting reform directions follow from the European Commission's recognition of these various trends. Policy includes a more complex mix of public and private arrangements. What is needed are labor market and social policy institutions that

- assist labor mobility;
- strengthen social inclusion;
- are compatible across countries, professions, and jobs (that is, transparent with respect to family structure, labor mobility, type of employment, and retirement decisions) but do not require harmonization;
- accommodate the pressures of population aging;
- improve health and safety at work;
- facilitate lifelong learning.

The simplest approach is the "open method of coordination" (box 1.3), which is directly relevant to assisting labor mobility within and across countries, to developing sustainable pension systems, and, in a more limited way, to

---

BOX 1.3 The Open Method of Coordination

The open method of coordination was defined by the European Council in Lisbon in March 2000. Its purpose is to spread best practice, to achieve greater convergence toward EU goals, and to help member states develop their own policies in accordance with those goals. The underlying idea is that countries need not fully harmonize their institutions, for example, by adopting a common EU-wide system of unemployment benefits or pensions, but instead can adjust their domestic institutions to make them as compatible as possible with the domestic institutions of other countries. The process is assisted and reinforced by periodic monitoring on the basis of commonly agreed on and defined indicators and by a process of peer review in which countries share information on progress and reform strategy in selected areas.

improving the portability of social benefits such as pensions and health care across countries. Major tasks remain, however. One is to strengthen the support that social benefits give to diverse family arrangements—the importance of the task was a recent focus of literature on the welfare state (Esping-Andersen and others 2002). Action to adjust pensions in the face of rising life expectancy has been minimal, despite much lip service, but is essential. Action on education and training has started but major gaps remain, notably in adjusting the content and structure of education, and in the financing of vocational training and retraining, and the financing of higher education.

A central debate: What vision of social policy?

From the viewpoint of the individual, the welfare state has two functions:

- *Consumption smoothing*, that is, redistribution over the life cycle, notably old-age pensions;
- *Insurance* against events that may happen, but may not, for example, unemployment or ill health

Public policy has additional objectives:

- *Poverty relief* seeks to ensure that nobody falls below some minimum level of income or consumption.
- Governments may also have broader *distributional objectives*. They may wish to reduce inequality; they might want to favor particular activities, for example, protecting the pension rights of people with caregiving responsibilities; and they may wish to subsidize the consumption smoothing of people whose earnings are somewhat above the poverty line.

At its core, the long-standing debate about social policy is about the relative importance people attach to growth and to distributional objectives, which in turn determines the weights accorded to these various objectives. For the state to ignore poverty relief completely (to give poverty relief a zero weight) is both inefficient (Barr 2004) and, for most people, morally repugnant. The other extreme—the pursuit of complete equality (giving equality a weight of 100 percent)—is equally untenable, a fact of which citizens of the former communist countries need no reminder. Between the two extremes, however, is a serious and continuing debate, which can be encapsulated by two competing views.[16]

A parsimonious welfare state (often referred to as a residual welfare state [Wilensky and Lebeaux 1965]) gives greater weight to growth and less to social cohesion generally and to redistribution in particular. Thus, the approach emphasizes basic poverty relief but with minimal distributional objectives beyond that, leaving insurance and consumption smoothing mainly to private institutions and individual choice. Income transfers are generally parsimonious, with a low state pension and heavy reliance on targeted (usually income-tested) poverty relief.

A more fully articulated welfare state (referred to by Wilensky and Lebeaux as an institutional welfare state) has a less austere poverty line and a greater emphasis on redistribution and social cohesion. This vision is characterized by a relatively generous state earnings-related pension, often incorporating redistribution, and by benefits—family benefits, for example—awarded without an income test.

The debate between these competing visions recurs throughout the book. It emerges in chapter 3 as a debate between labor market flexibility and worker protection; in chapter 4 as a debate about the merits, or otherwise, of universal family benefits; in chapter 5 as a debate between the potential incentive and growth effects of individual pension accounts and the greater security that redistributive state pensions might offer; in chapter 6 on the role of private finance in health care; and in chapter 7 as a debate about whether education should be designed for the elite or to foster social inclusion.

The book's core argument is that the proper aim of public policy generally, and social policy in particular, is to maximize people's well-being, which in turn depends both on economic growth (which determines material living standards) and on security (which affects people's well-being directly). Thus, a policy to maximize growth with little security is almost certainly suboptimal, as is a policy that maximizes security to the point that growth stagnates or turns negative. Put another way, an overemphasis either on growth or on security ends up being counterproductive. Social policy needs to assist the optimal balance between the two—a balance that will differ across countries. "Catching up" is a major thrust of policy in the former communist countries, suggesting greater emphasis on growth; electorates in the richer countries of Western Europe might choose a somewhat different balance.

In short, this book gives automatic primacy neither to growth nor to security. Both are important, but with relative weights that are likely to differ over time and across countries.

NOTES

1. We do not discuss East Germany. Its experience of being absorbed into Germany is unlike those of the other countries. The World Bank works only in poorer countries; East Germany, as part of Germany was above the cutoff, so none of the authors worked there; hence, none of us is knowledgeable about East Germany.

2. For analysis of the output collapse, see World Bank (2002) and the interchanges in Stiglitz (1999); Dabrowski, Gomulka, and Rostowski (2000a); Stiglitz and Ellerman (2000); and Dabrowski, Gomulka, and Rostowski (2000b). Welfare fell by less than output not least because much of the previous output was of low quality.

3. During the first four years of the Great Depression (1929–33) output in the United States fell by 35 percent.

4. The countries of the former Soviet Union excluding Estonia, Latvia, and Lithuania.

5. European Bank for Reconstruction and Development (2004, Annex 2.1).

6. The fact that even in radical reformers such as Poland unemployment initially remained relatively low despite the sharp fall in output suggests that during the early transition, firms, whether by choice or in response to political pressures, maintained employment to compensate for deficiencies in the social safety net, thus to some extent delaying restructuring. In political economy terms, it can be speculated, this might have been optimal (see Vanhuysse 2003).

7. Suppose that the distribution of income widens at both lower and upper incomes but average income remains constant. It must then be the case that there are more people with lower incomes, that is, poverty increases. If economic growth is positive, the effects of rising income might outweigh the effects of rising inequality—the entire income distribution might shift to the right sufficiently so that poverty falls. In contrast, if inequality widens and growth is negative, it must be the case that there are more people with lower incomes. Because the early transition was characterized by negative growth and widening disparity of income, we know that poverty increased almost without looking at the data.

8. "The European Commission has committed itself to ensure that the legislative acquis is fully complied with" (European Commission 2003b, p. 11).

9. For a more detailed summary, see European Commission 2003a.

10. Although the original motivation for the Stability and Growth Pact and the Convergence Criteria was to underpin the European Monetary Union, the two sets of conditions apply also to the accession process because all EU members have to devise their economic policies as "a matter of common concern." Thus, all members of the EU, whether or not part of the monetary union, are subject to policy coordination under the Broad Economic Policy Guidelines. The only difference is that countries that violate any of the conditions, and are not members of the monetary union, are not subject to the Excessive Deficit Procedure; they might get a reprimand but will not be fined.

11. Many of the longer-standing member states pledged not to apply any of the restrictions.

12. For fuller discussion, see Mayhew 1998 and Grabbe 2002; and on competition policy (perhaps the area where potential conflict is greatest), Estrin and Holmes 1998; and Fingleton, Neven, and Seabright 1996.

13. For robust contributions to the latter debate, see Balcerowicz (1995), Stiglitz (1999), and the debate between Stiglitz and Ellerman (2000) and Dabrowski, Gomulka, and Rostowski (2000a, b). For an overview reflecting on 10 years of transition, see World Bank (2002).

14. Berger, Kopits, and Székely (2004) take a similar line.

15. For a survey of debates about defining transition, see Kopecý and Mudde 2000. On "transition ends when certain tasks have been accomplished," see Roland 2000. On "transition ends with accession"—the approach taken here—see Carlin, Estrin, and Schaeffer 2000.

16. Each of these comes in many varieties; see, for example, Esping-Andersen 1990.

REFERENCES

Atkinson, A. B. 1995. *Incomes and the Welfare State: Essays on Britain and Europe.* Cambridge: Cambridge University Press.

Atkinson, A. B. 1999. *The Economic Consequences of Rolling Back the Welfare State.* London and Cambridge, MA: MIT Press.

Balcerowicz, Leszek. 1995. *Socialism, Capitalism, Transformation.* Budapest: Central European University Press.

Barr, Nicholas, ed. 1994. *Labor Markets and Social Policy in Central and Eastern Europe: The Transition and Beyond.* New York and London: Oxford University Press.

———. 1999. "Comments on 'Economic Policy and Equity: An Overview' by Amartya Sen." In *Economic Policy and Equity,* ed. Vito Tanzi, Ke-young Chu, and Sanjeev Gupta, 44–48. Washington, DC: International Monetary Fund.

———. 2001. *The Welfare State as Piggy Bank: Information, Risk, Uncertainty and the Role of the State.* Oxford and New York: Oxford University Press.

———. 2004. *The Economics of the Welfare State,* Oxford: Oxford University Press, and Stanford CA: Stanford University Press.

Barr, Nicholas, and Ralph W. Harbison. 1994. "Overview: Hopes, Tears and Transformation." In *Labor Markets and Social Policy in Central and Eastern Europe: The Transition and Beyond,* ed. Nicholas Barr, 1–28. New York and London: Oxford University Press.

Berger, Helge, George Kopits, and István Székely. 2004. "Fiscal Indulgence in Central Europe: Loss of the External Anchor?" Working Paper 04/62, International Monetary Fund, Washington, DC.

Bronk, Richard. 2002. "Commitment and Credibility: EU Conditionality and Interim Gains." European Institute Working Paper 2002-02, London: London School of Economics. http://www.lse.ac.uk/collections/europeanInstitute/pdfs/EIworkingpaper2002-02.pdf.

Carlin, Wendy, Saul Estrin, and Mark Schaeffer. 2000. "Measuring Progress in Transition and Towards Accession: A Comparison of Manufacturing Firms in Poland, Romania and Spain." *Journal of Common Market Studies* 38 (5): 699–728.

Dabrowski, Marek, Stanislaw Gomulka, and Jacek Rostowski. 2000a. "Whence Reform? A Critique of the Stiglitz Perspective." *Journal of Policy Reform* 4(4): 291–334.

———. 2000b. "The Stiglitz-Ellerman Rejoinder: Our Main Criticisms Remain Unanswered." *Journal of Policy Reform* 4(4): 339–348.

Davies, Norman. 1997. *Europe: A History.* London: Pimlico.

Esping-Andersen, Gøsta. 1990. *The Three Worlds of Welfare Capitalism.* Cambridge: Polity Press.

———. 1999. *Social Foundations of Post-Industrial Economies.* Oxford and New York: Oxford University Press.

Esping-Andersen, Gøsta, Duncan Gallie, Anton Hemerijck, and John Myles. 2002. *Why We Need a New Welfare State.* Oxford and New York: Oxford University Press.

Estrin, Saul, and Peter Holmes, eds. 1998. *Competition and Economic Integration in Europe.* Cheltenham, Glos., and Northampton, MA: Edward Elgar.

European Bank for Reconstruction and Development. 2004. *Transition Report 2004.* London: EBRD.

European Commission. 1993. *EU Enlargement–A Historic Opportunity.* Brussels: European Commission. http://europa.eu.int/comm/enlargement/intro/criteria.htm.

———. 2003a. "Enlargement of the European Union: Guide to the Negotiations Chapter by Chapter." Brussels: European Commission. June. http://europa.eu.int/comm/enlargement/negotiations/chapters/negotiationsguide.pdf.

————. 2003b. "Mid-Term Review of the Social Policy Agenda, Communication from the Commission to the Council, the European Parliament, the European Economic and Social Committee and the Committee of the Regions." COM(2003) 312 final. Brussels: European Commission. http://europa.eu.int/comm/employment_social/news/2003/jun/com2003312_en.pdf.

Falkner, Gerda. 2005. "EU Social Policy over Time." In *Complying with Europe? The Impact of EU Minimum Harmonisation and Soft Law in the Member States,* eds. Gerda Falkner, Oliver Treib, Miriam Hartlapp, and Simone Leiber. Cambridge: Cambridge University Press.

Fingleton, John, Damien J. Neven, and Paul Seabright. 1996. *Competition Policy and the Transformation of Central Europe.* London: Centre for Economic Policy Research.

Friedrich, C., and Z. Brzezinski. 1956. *Totalitarian Dictatorship and Autocracy.* Cambridge, MA: Harvard University Press.

Grabbe, Heather. 2002. "EU Conditionality and the *Acquis Communautaire.*" *International Political Science Review* 23(3): 249–68.

Huntington, Samuel P. 1991. *The Third Wave: Democratization in the Late Twentieth Century.* Norman, OK, and London: University of Oklahoma Press.

Jackman, Richard. 1998. "Unemployment and Restructuring." In *Emerging from Communism: Lessons from Russia, China, and Eastern Europe.* Peter Boone, Stanislaw Gomulka, and Richard Layard, 123–152. London and Cambridge: MIT Press.

Kopecý, P., and C. Mudde. 2000. "What Has Eastern Europe Taught Us about the Democratisation Literature (and Vice Versa)?" *European Journal of Political Research* 37(4): 517–39.

Kornai, János. 1992. *The Socialist System: The Political Economy of Communism.* Princeton, NJ: Princeton University Press.

Linz, J. J. 1975. "Totalitarian and Authoritarian Regimes." In *Handbook of Political Science,* volume 3, eds. F. I. Greenstein and N. W. Polsby. Reading, MA: Addison-Wesley.

Mayhew, A. 1998. *Recreating Europe. The European Union's Policy towards Central and Eastern Europe.* Cambridge: Cambridge University Press.

Roland, G. 2000. *Transition and Economics.* Cambridge, MA: MIT Press.

Solow, Robert M. 1994. "Perspectives on Growth Theory." *Journal of Economic Perspectives* 8(1): 45–54.

Stiglitz, Joseph E. 1999. "Whither Reform? Ten Years of the Transition." Keynote Address. World Bank Annual Conference on Development Economics. Washington, DC, April 28–30. http://www.worldbank.org/research/abcde/pdfs/stiglitz.pdf.

Stiglitz, Joseph E., and David Ellerman. 2000. "Not Poles Apart: 'Whither Reform?' and 'Whence Reform?' " *Journal of Policy Reform* 4(4): 325–38.

Vanhuysse, Pieter. 2003. "Divide and Pacify: The Political Economy of the Welfare State in Hungary and Poland, 1989–1996." PhD diss., London School of Economics.

Wilensky, Harold L., and Charles N. Lebeaux. 1965. *Industrial Society and Social Welfare.* New York: Free Press; London: Collier-Macmillan.

World Bank. 1999. *World Development Indicators.* Washington, DC: The World Bank.

————. 2002. *Transition: The First Ten Years: Analysis and Lessons for Eastern Europe and the Former Soviet Union.* Washington, DC: The World Bank.

2

THE COURSE OF
TRANSITION
Growth, Inequality, and Poverty

Dena Ringold

T he EU accession countries[1] traveled quickly from the severe output collapse
of the early 1990s to resumed growth and economic recovery. These developments had direct and rapid effects on people's lives. While opportunities
expanded and incomes increased for some, others experienced greater vulnerability, poverty, and unemployment. By the time of accession, the countries of
Central and Eastern Europe shared many challenges and woes with the older
member states—most critically the need to reduce chronic poverty and long-term
unemployment. The countries also faced common economic policy trade-offs.

This chapter sets the stage for the policy discussions in subsequent chapters
by describing the economic and institutional backdrop of transition and its
human impact. The first section maps the path of economic reforms in the
accession countries from output collapse to recovery and examines the
impact of the accession process on reforms and countries' preparations for
membership in the European Union (EU) and European Monetary Union. The
second section discusses two dimensions of institutional change—decentralization and governance—that have important implications for the design and
implementation of social policy. Finally, the chapter looks at the impact of the
output collapse on income distribution and poverty. In the end, despite
remaining differentials in income levels, the accession countries came to look
very much like the older member states, with regard to both future policy challenges and the profile and characteristics of poverty.

FROM OUTPUT COLLAPSE TO RECOVERY

By the mid-1990s, most accession countries were well on their way to recovery. The growth rates of all of the accession countries were positive for the first time in 1995, and their average growth exceeded that of the EU (table 2.1). Despite this turnaround, the accession countries were significantly poorer than their EU counterparts. Gross domestic product (GDP) per capita (adjusted for price differences) in half of the countries remained below 40 percent of the EU average in 2001.[2] By contrast, the four poorer countries that joined the EU in the 1970s and 1980s—Ireland, Greece, Spain, and Portugal—had GDP levels between 51 and 71 percent of the EU average when they became member states (figure 2.1).

Central and Eastern Europe's recovery was clear based on all economic indicators, including public spending. After an initial decline, the share of government expenditures in GDP stabilized. By 2001, spending ranged between 36 and 50 percent (table 2.2). In all countries, except Hungary, the share of government expenditures in GDP was below the EU average of 47 percent. Inflation also stabilized, following some dramatic peaks in the early transition years. Between 1990 and 1997, all of the accession countries experienced bouts of high inflation (table 2.3). In Lithuania in 1992, Estonia in 1992, and in Bulgaria in 1997, inflation exceeded 1,000 percent per year. Annual inflation averaged across countries exceeded 30 percent, and in most countries it topped 100 percent at least once. At the outset of the accession negotiations in 1998, however, no country, with the exception of Romania, had an inflation rate above 20 percent (table 2.4).

Three paths of transition

Across the region, the trajectories of collapse differed, based on patterns of reform and responses to transition. The accession countries fall into three categories, based on their transition paths[3] (figure 2.2):

- The Czech Republic, Estonia, Hungary, Poland, the Slovak Republic, and Slovenia all experienced a relatively small collapse in output, followed by rapid recovery. By 2001, their GDP per capita exceeded 1990 levels.
- Latvia and Lithuania suffered a larger collapse of output (GDP per capita fell to below 60 percent of 1990 levels) but then experienced a gradual yet continuous recovery.
- The less fortunate—Bulgaria and Romania—experienced a relatively small fall in output, followed by recovery and then recession when restructuring lagged. In 2001, GDP per capita in these countries was about 90 percent of 1990 levels.

TABLE 2.1 Growth rates of accession countries

	Average growth rate												
	1991	*1992*	*1993*	*1994*	*1995*	*1996*	*1997*	*1998*	*1999*	*2000*	*2001*	*1991–2001*	*1995–2001*
Bulgaria	-7.5	-6.3	-0.7	2.3	3.3	-9.7	-6.5	4.2	3.0	6.3	5.1	-0.6	0.8
Czech Republic	-11.1	-0.6	-0.1	2.2	6.0	4.5	-0.7	-1.1	-0.2	3.0	3.6	0.5	2.1
Estonia	-7.7	-20.1	-6.7	-0.8	6.0	5.7	12.4	6.3	0.3	7.8	5.3	0.8	6.2
Hungary	-11.8	-2.9	-0.4	3.1	1.6	1.5	4.7	5.0	4.3	5.3	4.0	1.3	3.8
Latvia	-10.1	-34.1	-13.4	2.1	0.5	4.4	9.6	4.7	2.7	8.5	9.0	-1.5	5.6
Lithuania	-5.8	-21.2	-15.8	-9.2	4.1	5.5	8.0	5.8	-3.2	4.6	4.3	-2.1	4.2
Poland	-7.3	2.3	3.5	5.0	6.9	5.9	6.7	4.8	4.1	4.0	1.2	3.4	4.8
Romania	-12.8	-7.2	1.7	4.1	7.4	4.3	-5.8	-3.9	-1.0	1.9	5.5	-0.5	1.2
Slovak Republic	-14.6	-7.1	-4.0	4.5	6.4	6.0	6.0	4.0	1.8	2.1	3.2	0.7	4.2
Slovenia	-9.1	-5.2	4.4	4.1	4.0	3.4	4.9	4.0	5.0	4.5	2.9	2.1	4.1
Accession average	-9.8	-10.2	-3.1	1.7	4.6	3.1	3.9	3.4	1.7	4.8	4.4	0.4	3.7
EU average[a]	1.4	1.2	0.2	3.3	3.1	2.6	3.9	3.7	3.7	4.4	2.2	2.7	3.4
EU economy	1.3	1.1	-0.4	2.8	2.4	1.7	2.7	2.9	2.6	3.4	1.7	2.0	2.5

Source: World Development Indicators (World Bank 2002c).
Note: Weights are proportional to GDP.
a. Based on the weighted average of the growth rates of EU member countries.

FIGURE 2.1 (**Top**) GDP per capita of countries that joined the European
Union earlier (at the year of accession). (**Bottom**) GDP per
capita of the accession countries as percentage of GDP per
capita in the European Union, 1991–2001.

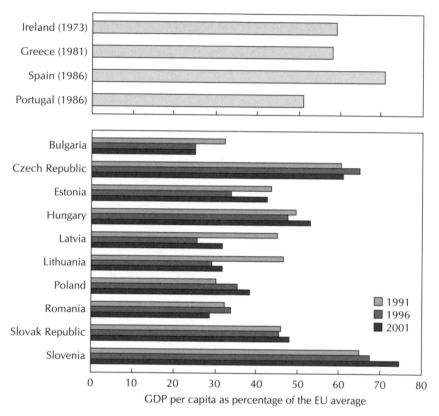

Source: World Bank 2002c; European Commission 1994.
Note: Numbers adjusted for purchasing power parity, which accounts for price differentials across
countries.

These different transition paths were shaped by three related forces: initial
conditions; the timing and phasing of key reforms; and the influence of the
accession process itself.[4] Initial conditions encompass geographic factors and
pre-communist and communist-period experience with market mechanisms.
Countries such as the Czech Republic, which had more developed market institutions before the communist period, were better positioned to make the transition. Similarly, countries where the transition began before 1989 were also
more favorably positioned, including Poland and Hungary, which both exper-

TABLE 2.2 Government expenditure as a percentage
of GDP, 2001

	Percentage of GDP
Bulgaria	40.3
Czech Republic	47.1
Estonia	38.4
Hungary	50.2
Latvia	43.0
Lithuania	36.1
Poland	45.3
Romania	40.1
Slovak Republic	46.6
Slovenia	45.6
Accession average	43.3
EU average	47.2

Source: EU 2002.

imented with market-based reforms in the 1980s (World Bank 2002b). Countries
that stopped and started reforms lagged behind. In Bulgaria and Romania,
reforms stagnated until the late 1990s, when their resumption put recovery
back on track.

The timing of landmark reforms also shaped the ability of countries to
recover from the transition shock (table 2.5). Although economists generally
agree on the main ingredients of reform—stabilization, price and trade liber-

TABLE 2.3 Inflation in the accession countries, consumer price index,
1991–97

	Consumer price index							
	1990	*1991*	*1992*	*1993*	*1994*	*1995*	*1996*	*1997*
Bulgaria	26	334	82	73	96	62	123	1,058
Czech Republic	10	57	11	21	10	9	9	9
Estonia	23	211	1,076	90	48	29	23	11
Hungary	29	35	23	23	19	28	24	18
Latvia	11	172	951	108	36	25	18	8
Lithuania	8	225	1,021	410	72	40	25	9
Poland	586	70	43	35	32	28	20	15
Romania	5	161	210	256	137	32	39	155
Slovak Republic	11	61	10	23	13	10	6	6
Slovenia	550	118	207	33	21	13	10	9

Source: EBRD *Transition Report,* various years.

TABLE 2.4 Inflation in the accession countries and the European Union, as measured by the CPI, 1998–2001

	Inflation (percentage increase in CPI)			
	1998	1999	2000	2001
Bulgaria	18.7	2.6	10.3	7.4
Czech Republic	10.6	2.1	3.9	4.7
Estonia	8.2	3.3	4.0	5.7
Hungary	14.2	10.0	9.8	9.1
Latvia	4.7	2.4	2.7	2.5
Lithuania	5.1	0.8	1.0	1.2
Poland	11.7	7.3	10.1	5.5
Romania	59.1	45.8	45.7	34.5
Slovak Republic	6.7	10.6	12.0	7.3
Slovenia	8.6	6.6	10.8	9.4
Euro area "3 lowest average"	0.8	0.6	2.0	2.2
Maastricht target	**2.3**	**2.1**	**3.5**	**3.7**
Euro area average	1.5	1.4	2.9	3.2
Euro area maximum	2.8	2.3	5.6	4.9

Source: World Bank 2002c.

alization, privatization and enterprise reform, and legal and judicial reform—they still debate the right way to implement and phase these reforms (World Bank 2002b). While countries such as Poland adopted a "big bang" approach and implemented reforms as a package, others, like Hungary, took a more gradual approach, opting to phase in liberalization and privatization.

Proponents of rapid reforms argued that countries should take advantage of the window of opportunity presented by transition and pass difficult reforms that the public might not support at a later stage, as well as limit the opportunities for former regime elites to sabotage reforms—through asset stripping by enterprise managers, for example. Gradualists, however, argued that reforms should not get ahead of institution-building. Regardless of the pace of specific reforms, the ability of countries to sustain and fully implement reforms was a critical element (World Bank 1996). The ability to sustain and implement reform has three key components: adoption of the main elements of reform mentioned above; political sustainability to ensure the reforms can take hold; and sufficient implementation capacity to make them work. In countries such as Bulgaria and Romania, where reforms stalled and restarted, recovery took far longer.

Moreover, the EU accession process itself was important. Beginning in 1991, the EU offered membership to the front-running transition countries.

FIGURE 2.2 Accession countries' classification by economic performance
during transition

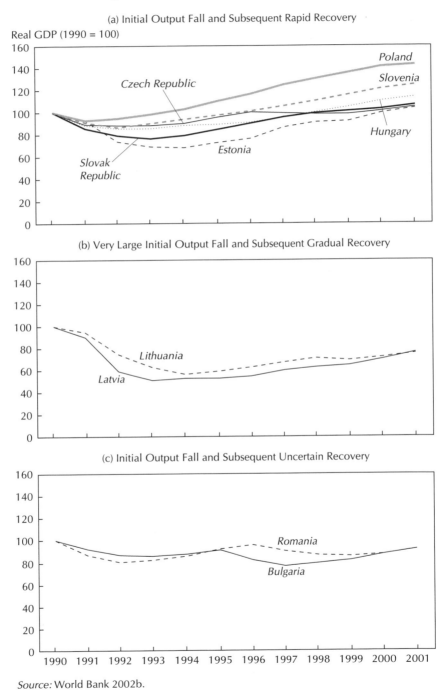

(a) Initial Output Fall and Subsequent Rapid Recovery

Real GDP (1990 = 100)

(b) Very Large Initial Output Fall and Subsequent Gradual Recovery

(c) Initial Output Fall and Subsequent Uncertain Recovery

Source: World Bank 2002b.

TABLE 2.5 Reform strategies in the accession countries

					Reform strategies				
	Political reform	Liberalization	Stabilization	Tax reform	SME entry	Privatization	Enterprise restructuring	Bankruptcy reform	Banking reform
Bulgaria	1989	1991 (big bang)	1991	1994	1993	1994 (gradual)	1991	1994	1997
Czech Republic	1989	1991 (big bang)	Not relevant	1993	1991	1992 (mass)	1993 (gradual)	1993	1991
Estonia	1991	1992 (big bang)	1994	1994	1991	1991 (mass)	1993 (gradual)	1992	1993
Hungary	1989	1968 (gradual)	1995	1988	1982	1990 (gradual)	1992 (gradual)	1992	1991
Latvia	1991	1992	1994	1992	1991	1991 (gradual)	1993 (gradual)	1996	1995
Lithuania	1990	1992 (big bang)	1995	1994	1992	1991 (mass)	1993 (gradual)	1992–97	1992–96
Poland	1989	1990 (big bang)	1990	1992	1990	1990 (gradual)	1993 (gradual)	1992	1993
Romania	1989	1990 (big bang)	1994	1993	1991	1991 (gradual)	1993 (gradual)	1995	–
Slovak Republic	1989	1991 (big bang)	Not relevant	1993	1991	1992 (gradual)	1993 (gradual)	1993	1991
Slovenia	1989	1965 (gradual)	1990	1990	1965	1993 (gradual)	1989 (gradual)	1989	1993

Source: Roland 2000; EBRD Transition Report 2001 (Baltic countries).
Note: Big bang = Rapid reform simultaneously across broad parts of the economy. Gradual = Reforms phased in. Mass privatization = Rapid large-scale privatization, for example, by distributing vouchers representing share ownership. – Incomplete in 2000.

The subsequent influence of the transition process in these countries presents a chicken and egg dilemma—were the high performers rewarded with accelerated accession timetables, or did the prospect of accession itself accelerate reforms? As illustrated in figure 2.2, the consistent frontrunners for accession were those where recovery resumed more quickly. In contrast, in Bulgaria and Romania, which were among the second wave of accession countries, reforms lagged and growth came later. In other words, the countries most likely to become EU member states from the beginning of the 1990s experienced less profound output declines and earlier growth recovery.

Regardless of the direction of causality, the accession process was clearly an influential carrot for reform. The lure of joining the western club gave the countries of Central and Eastern Europe more incentives to stomach the costs of reforms and provided governments a timeframe. However, the window of opportunity was open longer in some countries than in others. The prospect of accession also increased the credibility of political and economic transition by making the costs of policy reversal apparent, especially the risk of being left out of the EU altogether (Roland 2000).

Accession criteria and Maastricht targets— where do the countries need to go?

The EU's influence over economic policies in Central and Eastern Europe came through the main instruments of accession described in chapter 1, including adherence to the Copenhagen criteria and the *acquis communautaire*. The EU also directly influences macroeconomic policies in the member states through two main instruments: the Stability and Growth Pact, adopted by the European Council at the Amsterdam European Council in 1997, and the Convergence Criteria included in the 1992 Maastricht treaty.

Adoption of the *acquis* is a wide-ranging and costly affair. For the accession countries, the costs of complying with EU policies in environment, transport, nuclear safety, and steel would require an estimated total investment of about 225 billion euro (about US$ 225 billion)—equivalent to 120 percent of Polish GDP (Wallden 1998). The costs of compliance will, however, bring substantial benefits in medium- and long-term productivity and growth.

The Stability and Growth Pact focuses on the general macroeconomic environment by setting targets to limit budget deficits to 3 percent of GDP and maintain budgetary balance. The pact has two key aspects: a preventive, early-warning system for identifying and correcting budgetary slips, and regulations to encourage member states to avoid deficits and to take measures to correct them quickly if they occur. The pact also requires that the general government balance be close to zero or in surplus over the medium term. As of January 2002, most accession countries had not satisfied the budget deficit target. In contrast, Slovenia had satisfied the budget constraint for five consecutive years, Bulgaria for three years, Estonia and Lithuania for two, and Latvia for one year.

In November 2002, the European Commission introduced several changes in the interpretation of the Stability and Growth Pact. These did not change its legal standing but made it easier for countries to comply with the pact while undertaking structural reforms. Among other things, the commission proposed that budgetary dynamics be reviewed over a longer period of time and that business cycle effects be removed from budget reports. Member states close to their budgetary target and with low debt ratios would be allowed to diverge temporarily from the budgetary target. Longer divergences may be permitted to countries with sustainable finances, including debt ratios considerably below the target. However, the 3 percent deficit limit was maintained, even for planned deficits.

The Maastricht treaty—or the Treaty on European Union—formally established the EU in 1992, by granting the populations of the then 12 member states European citizenship, adding justice and home affairs and foreign and security policy to its areas of competence, and mapping out a plan for economic and monetary union. Along with the Stability and Growth Pact, the Maastricht treaty set the Convergence Criteria for membership in the European Monetary Union (EMU) including adoption of the euro currency. Older member states could opt out of the EMU, but accession countries were required to comply with the criteria. The five Convergence Criteria are

- inflation no more than 1.5 percent above the average inflation rate of the three lowest-inflation countries in the EU;
- long-term inflation rates no more than 2 percent above the average of the three countries with the lowest inflation rates;
- budget deficit no more than 3 percent of GDP;
- national debt no more than 60 percent of GDP;
- exchange rates that keep the currency within the normal bands of the European Exchange Rate Mechanism (ERM), with no realignments for at least two years.

When will accession countries adopt the euro? In their 2002 pre-accession economic programs, Poland and Hungary said they planned to meet the convergence criteria by 2005, and the Slovak Republic and Slovenia said they would follow as soon as possible after accession. Other countries did not state target dates, although Bulgaria, Estonia, and Lithuania already had currency board arrangements pegging their currencies to the euro.

All accession countries except Romania had single-digit inflation in 2001, but only Latvia and Lithuania would have satisfied the convergence criterion on inflation in 2001 (table 2.4). By 2001, all accession countries except Bulgaria had satisfied the Maastricht national-debt target. On average, the accession countries were much less indebted in 2001 than the older member states, the mean debt-to-GDP ratios for the two groups being 30 percent and 63 percent, respectively.

A short-term macroeconomic policy challenge for the accession countries is to strike a balance between meeting the Maastricht budget deficit target and the fiscal demands of complying with EU policies without compromising social expenditure. This balancing act is one shared with the older member states and is a recurrent theme throughout the book.

Some accession countries satisfied the convergence criteria before membership, while existing member states had not. In 2001, both Germany and France had budget deficits exceeding 3 percent, and three countries—Ireland, the Netherlands, and Spain—did not satisfy the inflation target.

INSTITUTIONAL DEVELOPMENTS

Along with economic transformation came dramatic changes in the role and size of the state. Lower public expenditures cut state involvement in the economy, including its role in providing jobs and delivering public services. Privatization and restructuring also recast the role of government. These changes affected the overall quality of institutions and governance in the accession countries. Two related issues are particularly relevant for the equity, efficiency, and quality of social policy: decentralization and governance.

Decentralization

Decentralization to lower levels of government has been an ongoing process in the accession countries. Local governments, which lacked real decision-making power under communism, became involved in financing social assistance services and education. They became direct providers of cash benefits, managers of health facilities, operators of institutions for the elderly, employers of participants in public works programs, and contractors of social assistance services. Implicit in these roles was local responsibility for social service delivery, including setting policy priorities through the allocation of resources, defining the types of services offered, and determining the eligibility of beneficiaries.

Decentralization was one natural outcome of the dismantling of central planning. Other forces fueled the process. First among these forces was an increased demand for decentralization at the local level. Many countries had strong traditions of local government before the communist period. The geographic and ethnic differences within countries led localities to press for increased autonomy—in, for example, the largely Hungarian regions of Romania and the Slovak Republic, or Turkish communities in Bulgaria.

Second, economic collapse provided incentives for central governments to diversify funding sources and shift responsibility for financing and delivering services and benefits to lower levels of government. Pressure to reduce budget deficits also led countries to transfer expenditure responsibility downward. Some countries reformed their systems of intergovernmental finance, which grant local governments authority to raise local revenues, collect taxes, and borrow. However, the transfer of expenditure authority to local governments was often not matched by adequate local resources and led to gaps or lapses in service delivery. In many cases, local governments lacked the mandate or capacity to raise revenues through taxation. Even where local governments did have authority to tax, high levels of informal sector activity and tax avoidance limited actual revenues (World Bank 2002b).

Third, the accession process also played a role. The European Charter of Local Self-Government, adopted in September 1988, emphasized the role of local governments in public policy and introduced the principle of "subsidiarity," by which public responsibilities were to be carried out by those officials closest to the people. The charter also called for local governments to have access to adequate financial resources to carry out their responsibilities and provided for fiscal equalization across local government entities. Outside of the charter, EU policy on decentralization and regional development was driven by aspects of the *acquis communautaire* that addressed local issues in different sectors.

Decentralization poses both opportunities and risks for social policy. The key trade-off is between equity and efficiency. On the one hand, local governments have better information to respond to local needs; on the other, localities may be too small to deliver services efficiently. Locally elected and autonomous governments theoretically have more accurate information about the preferences of their constituents and are more responsive to local needs and preferences. Targeting of benefits and services should improve and services should be better tailored to the local context. Moreover, as a result of local competition between local governments and the ability of citizens to "vote with their feet," decentralization is expected to decrease the cost of public services (Tiebout 1956).

However, decentralization can be inefficient if economies of scale are lost. Municipalities may simply be too small to deliver services efficiently. This issue has been particularly relevant for services such as education and health, where not every small locality can afford its own school or clinic. Decentralization may also undermine equity as the provision of public services becomes more dependent on local resources. In the mid-1990s, for instance, financing of social assistance benefits was transferred to local governments in Bulgaria and Romania. As a result, many municipalities—most frequently the poorest with the greatest need—could not pay benefits. Similar instances of regional inequality have been documented in education. Another potential pitfall is the risk of corruption if resources are hijacked by local elites.

The appropriate level of decentralization, therefore, depends on the country as well as the sector. This issue will be explored further in the cases of social assistance (chapter 4) and education (chapter 7). Lessons from the transition period include the importance of well-defined roles and responsibilities for financing and service delivery across levels of government, as well as effective incentive mechanisms and accountability mechanisms to keep public officials in check.

Governance

The development of new political and economic institutions simultaneously with a massive redistribution of state assets limited the quality of governance and created fertile ground for corruption in the transition countries.[5] Corruption undermines both the competitiveness and quality of public institutions and adversely affects equity and quality of social services, through informal, under-the-table payments to health and education (Lewis 2000). In the accession countries, average payments for administrative corruption constituted 2.2 percent of firm revenues in the late 1990s. The incidence of informal payments for health care range from 78 percent in Poland in 1998 to 60 percent in the Slovak Republic in 1999 and 21 percent in Bulgaria in 1997 (Lewis 2000).

While corruption is a problem for all transition countries, its extent varies. Pre-communist legacies explain much of these differences. Countries with more experience of democracy before the communist takeover and closer links to European traditions of civil service and judicial administration entered the transition with more highly developed systems of public administration and better-trained officials. Such conditions increased government effectiveness, enhanced regulatory quality, and strengthened the rule of law. These countries were also more likely to have adopted variants of market socialism during the communist period. As a result, the state already played a smaller role in the economy, and some rudimentary market institutions were in place when the transition began.

Furthermore, these countries tended to develop more active civil society and social networks, which generated reform movements like Solidarity in Poland in the late 1980s. Consequently, the collapse of communism in these countries was accompanied by a break with the old oppressive elites. That led to greater political competition, new elites, and more accountability to the public.

The worst excesses of corruption were lessened in countries that broke with the old political system, had greater state capacity, and had a civil society strong enough to promote change and accountability. (In countries such as Bulgaria and Romania, elites from the previous regimes transformed themselves into the new owners of capital and property. In such cases insider privatization was more common and corruption more serious.) State capture has been limited by stronger political competition and civil society, while administrative corruption has been limited by higher levels of accountability, as well as by higher levels of government effectiveness and regulatory quality associated with a happier historical legacy.[6]

LIVING STANDARDS AND POVERTY

This section discusses post-1989 income distribution, living standards, and poverty. By the time of accession, the countries of Central and Eastern Europe shared features of the older member states.

Widening income distribution

The transition from central planning to the market predictably widened income distribution as wage compression lifted, employment-related benefits were lost, and education and experience began to influence earnings levels. However, the range of distributional outcomes that emerged was unanticipated. Although disparities between the upper and lower income levels increased in all transition economies during the late 1980s and 1990s, the extent of this increase varied greatly.

In the Czech Republic, Poland, and Latvia, although inequality rose substantially, the distribution remained more equal than the EU average. In Estonia and Bulgaria, inequality rose more sharply. In most accession countries, Gini coefficients for income—a standard measure of inequality—rose to between 0.25 and 0.35 in the late 1990s (table 2.6), in comparison to the EU average of 0.3.[7] There are also outliers among current EU members. In 1995, Gini coefficients in Portugal and the United Kingdom were 0.36 and 0.37, respectively. These measures may underestimate the extent of inequality because of the high level of informal activity and the difficulty of measuring incomes (box 2.1).

TABLE 2.6 Income inequality in the accession countries and the
        European Union

	Year	Gini coefficient
Bulgaria	1995	0.41
Czech Republic	1996	0.25
Estonia	1998	0.37
Hungary	1997	0.25
Latvia	1998	0.32
Lithuania	1999	0.34
Poland	1998	0.33
Romania	1998	0.30
Slovenia	1997/98	0.25
Accession average		0.31
Austria	1995	0.31
Belgium	1996	0.29
Denmark	1992	0.25
Finland	1991	0.26
France	1995	0.33
Germany	1994	0.30
Greece	1993	0.33
Italy	1995	0.27
Luxembourg	1994	0.27
Netherlands	1994	0.33
Portugal	1995	0.36
Spain	1990	0.33
Sweden	1992	0.25
United Kingdom	1995	0.37
EU average		0.30

Source: World Bank 2002b, 2002c.
Note: Figures refer to different years for reasons of data availability.

The increase in income inequality across transition economies was driven
by common forces, although to different extents across countries. Most important, increased inequality of labor earnings, resulting from wage dispersion and
the growth of nonwage incomes associated with entrepreneurial activities influenced the distribution. (See box 2.2.) Earnings from wages and self-employment
are estimated to account for between 60 and 80 percent of all observed income
inequality (World Bank 2000b).

In many countries, government transfers and taxes played an important
equalizing role, dampening the effect of rising wage inequality. Milanovic
(1998) found that countries including Poland, Hungary, and Slovenia, where
wages and social transfers increased as a share of GDP during the early years
of transition, experienced a much smaller increase in inequality than other

BOX 2.1 The Measurement Challenge

Quantitative data on economic and social issues under communism were scarce and flawed. While data quality and availability have improved substantially since 1989, a lack of timely and accurate information still impedes policy making and limits the evaluation of reforms.

Why the data constraint? The availability and usefulness of data are limited by two main complications: definitions that frequently differed from western standards or were inconsistent across countries, and problems with data collection. Comparison of indicators across countries was impossible due to the lack of comparable definitions. Even within a single country, data with the same label may have meant very different things in different regions. In the early years of transition, this problem was aggravated by poor data documentation in the national statistical agencies. During the transition period, leading firms of transition countries accepted western accounting standards, but many still ran dual books to comply with local tax rules and other regulations. Datasets may therefore still mix figures with western and local meanings.

Early in transition, the only widely available employment and output figures were calculated by national statistical offices based on the reports of enterprises. While the statistical offices were able to collect information from large communist enterprises, they were not able to capture the thousands of emerging small firms in the informal sector. Unemployment data were especially difficult to collect. Registered unemployment rates most frequently capture individuals who are registered with labor offices as unemployed and exclude those who have exhausted their benefits and dropped out of the labor force. Data from labor force surveys, which ask households about both formal and informal labor market activities, are thought to be more reliable (chapter 3). Administrative data on education have similar problems. Enrollment rates tend to be misleading, as children who are enrolled in schools may not actually attend classes (chapter 7).

Methodological problems. Even where data are available and reliable, significant challenges limit their comparability and usefulness. Poverty and inequality are particularly hard to measure. In the highly volatile transition period, sharp changes in relative prices made it difficult to estimate inflation and its real impact on household welfare.

Estimating household welfare is further complicated by problems in measuring incomes and consumption. Consumption is generally considered a better measure of welfare than income because of the difficulties of measuring informal sector incomes and in-kind income (benefits and services, for example). As a result, poverty analysis is commonly based on consumption data from household surveys.

(*continued*)

BOX 2.1 The Measurement Challenge *(Continued)*

Improvements over the decade. Household surveys existed by the early 1990s in virtually all countries of Central and Eastern Europe; however, their quality was often questionable. Citizens remembered the recent past when governments were enemies and the less they knew about you, the better you felt. Survey response rates are usually much lower than in advanced capitalist countries, and the reliability of results remain dubious.

Sources: World Bank 2000b; Filer and Hanousek 2001.

countries. The average increase in the Gini coefficient for these countries was 0.2 points. In contrast, in countries where social transfers did not compensate for declining wages, or where only wages or social transfers increased as a share of income, the Gini coefficient grew an average of 0.1 to 0.12 points.

Wage inequality increased mainly because returns to education rose rapidly. Interindustry and occupational wage differentials also increased, and a large increase in inequality within industry occupation groups occurred. In Central and Eastern Europe, the increase in education premiums happened quickly. The difference in earnings between university-educated workers and workers with primary education in some of the leading accession countries more than doubled between 1989 and 1993 (Rutkowski 1996; 1999). Poland is a good example. Before the transition, a university-educated worker earned about 35 percent more than a worker with a primary education. By 1993, this difference had increased to 75 percent. Wage inequality will be discussed further in the next chapter.

Interestingly, the increase in returns to education happened at the very beginning of the transition. Differences in wages across education levels in Poland in 1998 were roughly the same as in 1993. As a result of this quick adjustment, returns to education in the accession countries soon reached the range observed for Organisation for Economic Co-operation and Development countries. Between 1992 and 1994, differences between education groups alone explained between 12 percent and 16 percent of all income inequality in Poland, Hungary, and the Czech and Slovak Republics (Bailey 1997).

Trends in inequality were also influenced by differences in privatization strategies. Countries that privatized more and relied less on insider privatization experienced smaller declines in formal incomes and a smaller increase in the share of the unofficial economy—both of which were associated with

BOX 2.2 Income Disparities

A wider distribution of income and earnings—one of the strategic outcomes of transition—was both good and bad.

Rising disparity was, in part, a sign of successful transition. Earnings bearing at least some relationship to individual productivity encourage workers to improve the quality of their work, move into jobs in which they are most productive, and acquire new skills. Though labor is often motivated by nonfinancial factors such as job satisfaction, the issue during the early transition was to rectify an inheritance in which wages bore more or less *no* relation to individual performance. (As the pre-1989 truism went, "work was somewhere we went, not something we did.")

A key outcome of liberalization was that workers with skills valued by the market could command a market wage. This was precisely the result the reforms were meant to bring about: performance-related pay is important in improving incentives, contributing to labor-market efficiency, and boosting economic growth. In addition, the liberalization of property ownership, by extending the scope of private wealth, increased the incomes of wealth holders. Where wealth is acquired legitimately, this outcome, among other things, contributes to the growth of new enterprises and output.

That does not mean that all disparities are beneficial. Along with higher incomes were lower incomes. In part, again, this was intended. People with few skills or low motivation faced incentives to acquire skills and work harder. As discussed in this chapter, among the major costs of the reforms were rising unemployment and increasing poverty. Given the importance of full employment and the extent of security under the old system, unemployment, poverty, and insecurity can be argued to have been even more costly in relation to well-being in the transition countries than in western economies where unemployment had a longer history.

Disparity emanated from other malign sources. Not all monopolies are bad: monopoly profits can encourage new entrants to an industry. However, monopolists can prevent rivals from establishing themselves, for example, through a monopoly of information. This could arise because the reform of ownership took longer than price and wage liberalization. Similarly, some individuals, often officials from the communist regime, were able to expropriate former state assets through dubiously legal methods. Even more malign, criminal behavior, often backed by violence, increased during the early transition and remained a problem through the accession period.

smaller increases in income inequality (World Bank 2000a). Corruption and other forms of criminality also contributed to inequality, with increased rent-seeking.

The landscape of poverty and vulnerability

Poverty rose substantially in all the accession countries, in some cases well beyond the incidence of poverty in the older member states (discussed later in this section).

Poverty in the accession countries

The widening income distribution and erosion of full employment caused increasing poverty in the accession countries. Over the course of the 1990s, this entailed a shift from transient poverty, resulting from the output collapse, to chronic long-term poverty and the emergence of vulnerable groups, such as large families and some ethnic minorities.

Workers were initially protected from the output collapse by unsustainably low wages. However, with restructuring, mass layoffs, and the eventual closure of enterprises, many eventually became unemployed, resulting in a large and sudden upswing in transient poverty and the number of families living just above the poverty line. Poverty was closely linked to labor market status. Workers moved in and out of poverty as they were laid off and found new jobs.[8]

As discussed in chapter 4, in the early 1990s, social protection focused on managing transient poverty by introducing unemployment benefits, employment services, and social assistance. Sick pay, disability, and old age pensions through early retirement were also widely used and abused to shift workers off the payrolls of state-owned enterprises. In most countries, inflation reduced the real value of social benefits, including universal child benefits, further increasing the vulnerability of families. More radical reformers, such as Poland and Hungary, which maintained the value of social benefits fared better over the long term than countries that cut these benefits more radically.

From transient to long-term "pockets of poverty." As recovery began, consumption levels for most households stabilized, and the pool of transient poverty started to decrease. Still, a large pool of at-risk families remained just above the poverty line. In the meantime, as household income differentials widened and income status became increasingly correlated with educational achievements, workers with low skills, limited experience, and poor education became increasingly left behind. A group of chronic long-term unemployed emerged, and an unusually large portion of the working age population withdrew from the labor force. The employability of these long-term unemployed and discouraged workers was limited, and some of these workers slipped into long-term, chronic poverty.

Following families over time through panel surveys illustrates this shift from transient to chronic poverty. Two countries, Poland and Hungary, have panel data for the 1993–96 period that can be used for this purpose. Panel surveys show that household incomes and expenditures varied significantly, but the shocks were largely transitory in nature. Interestingly, fluctuations in the expenditures of poor households were only slightly less than changes in their incomes, suggesting that families may find it difficult to smooth their consumption. The large fluctuations in household expenditure meant that households moved in and out of poverty. For example, 37 percent of households in Poland experienced at least one bout of poverty during the four-year period; 9 percent of the population in Poland and 8 percent of the population in Hungary moved in and out of poverty between 1994 and 1995.[9]

The transient poor are vulnerable to economic shocks but can escape poverty, at least some of the time. In contrast, the persistently poor are an underclass that is ill-prepared to take advantage of new economic opportunities.[10] Given the large fluctuations in measured expenditures that move households in and out of poverty in Central and Eastern Europe, the number of individuals who were persistently poor according to their observed poverty status was small. Only 6 percent of Poles and 9 percent of Hungarians were poor during all four years of the survey.

As transient poverty gave way to persistent poverty, a distinct profile of poverty emerged in the accession countries, similar to that of the older member states. The unemployed and those with low education and skill levels were disproportionately represented among the chronically poor. Ethnic minorities, especially Roma, were at high risk, due to a combination of social exclusion and outright discrimination. Poverty was also regionally concentrated in many countries. There were distinct "pockets of poverty" where poverty was multidimensional—encompassing disparities in access, coverage, and quality of public services. Other distinguishing features of the profile include the following:

- The unemployed are at a high risk of poverty in the accession countries. On average, poverty risk among households headed by an unemployed person was 4.7 times higher than for the population as a whole (World Bank 2000b).
- Households with fewer income earners have higher rates of poverty, as do households headed by people with lower education and skill levels.

- In most of the accession countries (the Czech Republic being the only notable exception), the risk of poverty among the rural population is one-and-a-half to two times higher than among the population as a whole.
- Households with three or more children are at a higher risk of poverty in all accession countries. On average, poverty risk for households with three or more children is 2.9 times higher than for the population as a whole (figure 2.3).
- While pensioners are generally not poor in the countries of Central and Eastern Europe, some groups of pensioners are—especially elderly women who live alone.

Poverty is multidimensional and linked to factors other than low income. As explored in chapters 6 and 7, poverty has serious implications for health and education. Increased morbidity and mortality were associated with stress and unhealthy behaviors, such as alcoholism, which increased during the transition period. Poverty is also associated with communicable diseases, including tuberculosis and hepatitis.

Declining living conditions have also influenced the ability of households to send their children to school. Poverty limits access by increasing the opportunity cost of education for families in which children must work. The increasing

FIGURE 2.3 Poverty risks for households with different numbers of children

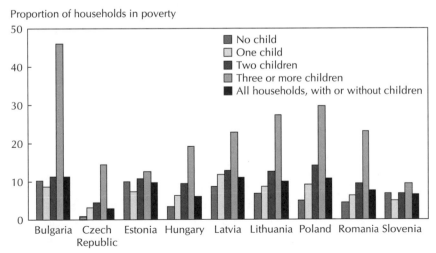

Proportion of households in poverty

Source: World Bank 2000b.
Note: Source contains no data for the Slovak Republic.

economic costs of education, including school fees and payments for clothing and books can also become prohibitive (Vandycke 2001). There was growing evidence of drop-outs and declining enrollments among poor households, and particularly among vulnerable groups, such as rural residents and Roma.

Insecurity. Along with the emergence of poverty came an across-the-board increase in vulnerability and insecurity. The collapse of communism meant a loss of certainty for the people of Central and Eastern Europe. Under central planning jobs and housing were guaranteed, and welfare supposedly provided from cradle to grave. The erosion of the paternalistic state left many households vulnerable, and many more feeling vulnerable. Uncertainty affects choices, including how many children to have, whether to participate in the labor force, and whether to retire early. These choices have implications for the design of social policies that are discussed in subsequent chapters.

Increased insecurity was reflected in opinion surveys that showed a large disconnect between subjective and quantitative poverty measures. Many Central and Eastern Europeans felt poor. In Bulgaria in 2001, nearly three-fourths of the population felt that they lived in poverty (World Bank 2002a). The trends are also striking; while the survey data indicated that poverty in Bulgaria declined substantially between 1997 and 2001, the share of the population who called themselves poor increased from 63 percent to 73 percent during the same time period. Moreover, 63 percent of Bulgarians surveyed in 2001 noted that their living standards were worse than in November 1989, when only 26 percent considered themselves poor.

There are several possible explanations for this disconnect. Subjective assessments reflect a broader concept of welfare than income alone. Perceptions are also shaped by higher expectations and more available goods that households may not be able to afford. More goods on shop shelves creates the impression that others can afford them. While prices and wages were artificially supported during the communist period and employment was guaranteed regardless of productivity concerns, restructuring eroded this false sense of security. Since then, widespread unemployment and poverty have emerged.

Poverty in the EU

EU countries report poverty based on relative measures that allow for both national and cross-country comparisons (table 2.7). Relative poverty is defined by establishing a poverty line that is some fraction of either mean or median income.[11] In 1999, around 15 percent of EU citizens fell below the poverty line in their country, set at 60 percent of the median income (Dennis and Guio 2003).

TABLE 2.7 Poverty in the European Union

		Poverty definition			
	Income poverty rate (%)	Poor people who have great difficulty making ends meet (%)	Poor people who cannot afford a week's holiday (%)	Poor people who have bad or very bad health (%)	Poor people who meet friends or relatives less than once a month (%)
Denmark	12	10	24	10	7
Netherlands	12	14	38	6	4
Luxembourg	12	14	44	16	14
Austria	13	15	49	14	12
Germany	16	8	29	10	8
France	16	18	67	11	13
Belgium	17	12	47	10	9
Ireland	18	29	68	4	1
Spain	18	36	80	14	3
United Kingdom	19	17	64	13	6
Italy	19	15	70	15	n.a.
Greece	21	43	85	15	3
Portugal	22	31	86	40	13
EU Average	17	18	59	15	8

Source: Eurostat 2000.
Note: Poverty rates are calculated based on the official definition of the poverty line (see the text). n.a. Not applicable.

Poverty in the older member states varies widely. The proportion of people living in low-income households was relatively high (over 20 percent) in Greece and Portugal, and lowest in Denmark, and the Netherlands (12 percent). The incidence of long-term poverty followed the same country patterns.[12] The proportion of people living in households with persistently low income was highest in Portugal at 14 percent, and lowest in Denmark, the Netherlands, and Finland (3 to 5 percent) (Dennis and Guio 2003).

Subjective measures further illustrate the cross-country differences. In 1996, 7 percent of EU citizens stated that they were a member of a household that reported great difficulties in "making ends meet." This varied from less than 4 percent in Germany and Luxembourg to more than 20 percent in Greece. Differences across age groups also varied. In the EU in 1996, 9 percent of children reported difficulties in making ends meet. An even higher proportion of under-18-year-olds lived in a household in arrears with utility bills or housing costs. With age, the likelihood of facing one of these financial problems decreased sharply. Only 5 percent of those 65 and older had great difficulties in making ends meet, and just 3 percent were behind in paying utility bills or housing costs (Dennis and Guio 2003).

Poverty rates in the accession countries (table 2.8) are mostly higher, sometimes considerably higher, than in the older member states. In addition, disparities in per capita income among the older member states were small compared to disparities between members and applicants and among applicants. Slovenia, the richest accession country, falls just behind Greece, the poorest of the current member states. Living standards in Bulgaria, the poorest among the candidates, are nearly one-third of those in Slovenia.

There are also significant disparities among the older member states. If welfare was measured relative to a single European norm in the 13 member states included in the European Community Household Panel, the poverty rate would range from one in every 20 persons in Denmark and Austria (and even fewer in Luxembourg) to almost one in two in Portugal and one in three in Greece and Spain.[13]

If a single EU poverty line was used common to all members, old and new, most people in most of the new member countries would have been poor. Five states that started accession negotiations in 1998—the Czech Republic, Hungary, Estonia, Poland, and Slovenia—would have an average poverty rate of almost 60 percent if poverty were defined as living on less than 50 percent of median consumption in the expanded EU. In other accession countries, poverty rates could be even higher, reaching as high as 80 percent in Latvia (Micklewright and Stewart 2001, based on Eurostat 2000 and Piachaud 2001).

TABLE 2.8 Poverty rates in the accession countries according to different definitions

	Year	Poverty rate, $2.15/day	Poverty rate, $4.30/day	50% of the median Theta=0.75
Bulgaria	1995	3.1	18.2	11.4
Czech Republic	1996	0	0.8	2.8
Estonia	1998	2.1	19.3	9.7
Hungary	1997	1.3	15.4	6.1
Latvia	1998	6.6	34.8	11.1
Lithuania	1999	3.1	22.5	10.0
Poland	1998	1.2	18.4	10.8
Romania	1998	6.8	44.5	7.6
Slovak Republic	1997	2.6	8.6	—
Slovenia	1997/98	0	0.7	6.5

Source: World Bank 2000b.
Note: — Not available. Dollars are U.S. dollars

Poverty and accession

"Europe is heartless if there is no poverty target beside the Maastricht targets. What was possible for the euro—clear objectives—must be possible for the fight against poverty" (Frank Vandenbroucke, Belgian Minister of Social Security, 1999, "The Active Welfare State: A European Ambition," Den Uyl Lecture, Amsterdam).

The EU does not have an explicit policy on poverty, and poverty reduction was not among the accession criteria. As discussed in chapter 4, the EU sees poverty and welfare through the lens of social inclusion. Policy priorities for achieving social inclusion include increasing employment and access to social services.

Regardless of the focus of the accession criteria and EU policy, poverty and welfare are of concern for Europe, for reasons of equity and social justice—as well as for the overall health and competitiveness of the union.

CONCLUSIONS

Over a short period of time, accession countries came to share characteristics, challenges, and opportunities with the older member states. While transition has been painful—with the collapse of output and the subsequent rise in unemployment and poverty—the good news is that the countries of Central and Eastern Europe recovered by the mid-1990s and face bright prospects for further growth within the expanded EU.

The bad news is that difficult economic conditions are not over. Poverty and unemployment are a reality. While the output shock led to a burst of transient poverty early in the transition period, a group of long-term chronically poor now share many characteristics of the poor in the older member states.

Addressing this poverty problem through efficient and equitable social policies poses real trade-offs. The constraints of the Stability and Growth Pact and the Convergence Criteria mean that countries must manage expenditures while maximizing welfare. This leaves important choices for the reforms of social assistance, social insurance, health, and education, which are discussed in the following chapters.

NOTES

1. The eight former-communist countries that joined the EU in 2004 are the Czech Republic, Estonia, Hungary, Latvia, Lithuania, Poland, the Slovak Republic, and Slovenia.
2. Adjusted for purchasing power parity (ppp), which accounts for price differentials across countries.

3. This typology draws from Roland (2000).

4. For more indepth and nuanced discussion of the forces driving differences in transition paths, see Cornia and Popov 2001.

5. "State capture" refers to the actions of individuals or firms to influence the formation of laws and government policies to their own advantage through illicit and nontransparent payment of private benefits to public officials. "Administrative corruption" refers to the intentional distortion of laws, rules, and regulations to provide advantages to state or nonstate actors, through illicit and nontransparent provision of private gains to public officials.

6. The level of state capture is also influenced by endowments of natural resources. It is higher in countries with greater endowments and in those countries that are well placed to serve as transit routes for the distribution of resources.

7. The Gini coefficient ranges from 0, which means that everybody earns the same income, to 1, which means that all income is earned by one person. In practice the coefficient varies from about 0.2 to 0.6.

8. Unless otherwise indicated, poverty is defined as the share of the population living under a set poverty line.

9. This and the next paragraph summarize an analysis by Luttmer (2000), which uses a relative measure of poverty: the line is set so that in each year 20 percent of the population is poor.

10. In the analysis, "persistently poor" refers to those households who appear as poor in every period of observation.

11. EU poverty rates use equivalence scales that take account of differences in household size and composition. The household's total income is divided by its "equivalent size," computed using the weights of the modified OECD equivalence scale (1.0 for the first adult, 0.5 for the second and each subsequent adult, 0.3 for children under age 14 living in the household).

12. Measured as the share of the population below the poverty line for three consecutive years.

13. The poverty rate is defined as 60 percent of median household equivalent income.

REFERENCES

Bailey, D. 1997. "Separate but Equal? Comparing and Decomposing Income Inequality in Central and Eastern Europe." Center for Policy Research, Syracuse University, Syracuse, NY.

Cornia, G., and V. Popov. 2001. "Structural and Institutional Factors in the Transition to the Market Economy: An Overview." In *Transition and Institutions—The Experience of Gradual and Late Reformers,* eds. G. Cornia and V. Popov. London: Oxford University Press: WIDER Series in Development Economics.

Dennis, I., and A. Guio. 2003. "Poverty and Social Exclusion in the EU after Laeken-part 1." Luxembourg: European Communities. http://europa.eu.int/comm/eurostat/.

EBRD (European Bank for Reconstruction and Development). 2001. Transition Report. London, UK.

EBRD (European Bank for Reconstruction and Development). 2002. Transition Report. London, UK.

European Commission. 1994. *Annual Report.* Brussels.

European Union. 2002. "Evaluation of the 2002 Pre-Accession Economic Programmes of Candidate Countries." Enlargement paper no. 14. Brussels, Belgium.

Eurostat. 2000. "European Social Statistics: Income, Poverty and Social Exclusion." Eurostat, Luxembourg.

Filer, R. K., and J. Hanousek. 2001. "Data Watch: Research Data from Transition Economies." Working Paper 416, William Davidson Institute, Ann Arbor, MI.

Lewis, M. 2000. "Who Pays for Health Care in Europe and Central Asia?" World Bank Technical Paper, Washington, DC.

Luttmer, E. 2000. "Inequality and Poverty Dynamics in Transition Economies: Disentangling Real Effects from Data." Background Papers for *Making Transition Work for Everyone: Poverty and Inequality in Europe and Central Asia.* World Bank. Washington, DC.

Micklewright, J., and K. Stewart. 2001. "Poverty and Social Exclusion in Europe: European Comparisons and the Impact of Enlargement." *New Economy* 8(2): 104–9.

Milanovic, M. 1998. *Income, Inequality, and Poverty During the Transition from Planned to Market Economy.* World Bank Regional and Sectoral Studies, Washington, DC.

Piachaud, D. 2001. "Poverty and Enlargement of the European Union." Centre for the Analysis of Social Exclusion paper, London School of Economics.

Roland, G. 2000. *Transition and Economics: Politics, Markets, and Firms.* Cambridge, MA: MIT Press.

Rutkowski, J. 1996. "High Skills Pay Off: The Changing Age Structure During Economic Transition in Poland." *Economics of Transition* 4 (1): 89–112.

Rutkowski, J. 1999. "Wage Inequality in the Transition Economies of Central Europe: Trends and Patterns in the Late 1990s." World Bank, Social Protection Discussion Paper No. SP 0117, Washington, DC.

Tiebout, C. 1956. "A Pure Theory of Local Expenditures." *The Journal of Political Economy* 64(5): 416–24.

Vandycke, N. 2001. "Access to Education for the Poor in Europe and Central Asia: Preliminary Evidence and Policy Implications." World Bank Technical Paper No. 511, Washington, DC.

Wallden, A. S. 1998. "EU Enlargement: How Much it Will Cost and Who Will Pay." EU Working Paper E5-1-8 FB. Brussels, Belgium.

World Bank. 1996. *From Plan to Market: World Development Report 1996.* Washington, DC: World Bank.

World Bank. 2000a. *Balancing Protection and Opportunity: A Strategy for Social Protection in Transition Economies.* Washington, DC.

World Bank. 2000b. *Making Transition Work for Everyone: Poverty and Inequality in Europe and Central Asia.* Washington, DC.

World Bank. 2002a. "Bulgaria: Poverty Assessment." Washington, DC.

World Bank. 2002b. *Transition: The First Ten Years, Analysis and Lessons for Eastern Europe and the Former Soviet Union.* Washington, DC.

World Bank. 2002c. World Development Indicators Database. Washington, DC.

3

LABOR MARKETS

Mansoora Rashid, Jan Rutkowski, and David Fretwell

Low employment is the main adverse labor market outcome of the transition (manifesting itself in either high unemployment or low participation), and is a major problem confronting all European Union (EU) members. The focus of the European Employment Strategy on generating employment is appropriate, given an aging population and increasing social inclusion. While three main methods of implementing the European Employment Strategy—promoting job growth, investing in human capital, and reducing employment disparities (across regions, gender, and age)—are not controversial, the fourth element—balancing flexibility and security—engenders greater debate. Full security is not an option—it contributed to the collapse of communist economies—and neither is full flexibility, given its large adverse effect on welfare. The choice lies somewhere between the two. To reach the employment targets set by their strategy, EU countries may need to err on the side of greater flexibility and lower security. This may be the case for newer EU members[1] in particular, because they have much poorer business environments, lower employment rates, and far greater disparities in employment.

THE LOGIC OF TRANSITION: LABOR MARKETS

This section first describes labor policy under central planning and why it was consistent with the communist system, then examines the impact of the transition on labor market outcomes (mainly employment and wages), and finally describes the main policy choices that led to these changes.

The inherited system

Under the communist system, central planners had two main employment objectives: to provide jobs for all their citizens for all their working lives, and to remunerate them with roughly equal wages. Not surprisingly, labor force participation rates were very high; there was virtually no open unemployment; and measured wage inequality was low. Full state protection of workers meant that, at least in principle, no programs for protection against unemployment or poverty were needed or in place (see chapter 6) and that labor institutions (legislation, unions) naturally favored worker security over labor market flexibility.

The socialist system was, in part, a response to early 19th century capitalism, characterized by rampant business cycles (which Marx regarded as inefficient), and by low wages and wide disparities in income and wealth (regarded by Marx as inequitable). As a result, two main principles guided the production and distribution decisions under socialism: all labor should be utilized, and every unit of labor should be equally rewarded.

At least in part because of intractable information processing problems, communist central planners made poor production decisions, leading to acute shortages or excess supplies of goods. This mismatch of demand and supply in the product market contributed to frequent revisions in production targets. The resulting uncertainty about production goals led to the hoarding of inputs, including labor, and to high labor mobility across firms. To attract labor and avoid taxes, employers often had to offer nonwage benefits to workers.

The determinants of worker wages were therefore strikingly different than in market economies. Instead of being explained largely by differences in human capital and other productivity-reflecting attributes of workers, differences in wages across workers were attributable to noneconomic and unobserved differences. This lack of association between education or skills and wages dampened incentives to increase productivity, lowered labor effort and innovation, and reduced worker morale. Both sets of factors—reinforced by much more wide-ranging incentive problems—contributed to a loss of productivity and output, which ultimately led to the abandonment of the communist system.

In sum, the communist objectives—jobs for life and egalitarian wages— although in many ways laudable, were economically unsustainable (and in the case of wages, not achievable), and ultimately contributed to the collapse of communist systems.

The impact of transition

The large decline in output in the years after 1990 (see chapter 2) changed two main labor market outcomes: the level and structure of employment, and the level and distribution of wages.

Impact on employment

The fall in employment was an expected labor market response to the output declines encountered at the onset of the transition. What was puzzling was the limited response of employment to economic recovery. While most transition economies started to recover in the mid-1990s, and the recovery continued until accession, employment did not rebound. As a result, in virtually all Central and Eastern European countries around the time of accession, employment levels were well below the levels observed before the transition, and (with the exception of the Czech Republic) much lower than those prevailing in EU countries (Eurostat 2005).

Poland provides one example of this process. After a short transitional recession, output grew rapidly, so that output at accession was well above 1990 levels. Despite strong economic growth, however, unemployment in Poland was very high by European standards (around 18 percent). Furthermore, after the initial deep fall, employment stabilized at a low level, with only 55 percent of the working age population employed, compared with the EU-15 average of close to 65 percent.

The weak response of employment to output growth observed in Central and Eastern European economies is explained by what may be termed a "productivity catch-up." The increased demand for goods and services was largely met by increased productivity and minimally by increases in the labor input. In short, firms in Central and Eastern European made a conscientious effort to catch up with their international competitors by rationalizing their workforce, improving management and organizational structure, investing in new technology, and adopting innovations. The resulting productivity gains allowed them to increase production without the need to increase employment. Obviously, the intensity of this process differed across firms, industries, and countries.[2]

Nonetheless, the big picture is clear: economic transition in Central and Eastern Europe was associated with a strong employment-productivity trade-off that has been unambiguously resolved in favor of productivity. One reason is that in all Central and Eastern European countries productivity gains were translated into wage growth, implying that the productivity gains contributed little to the reduction in unit labor costs. Accordingly, higher productivity did little to foster labor demand and employment growth.

This long-term decline in employment had two direct impacts: substantially higher unemployment, or substantially lower labor force participation rates, or both. For example, while employment rates were virtually the same (and low) in Hungary and Poland, unemployment was relatively low (around 8 percent) and nonparticipation was high in Hungary, while in Poland, nonparticipation was low while unemployment was much higher (18 percent) (Eurostat 2005).

NONPARTICIPATION. During the transition, labor force participation rates declined because fewer persons of working age were working or were looking for work. The decline in labor force participation rates reflected layoffs of workers near retirement age. Male and, particularly, female participation rates, kept artificially high during communism, also declined over time because many workers opted for nonparticipation in the labor force. Labor force participation rates also fell because many workers became discouraged by the futility of their job searches and ceased believing they could find work.

HIGH AND PERSISTENT UNEMPLOYMENT. Unemployment rates were high (usually exceeding 10 percent and in some cases approaching 20 percent) and persistent in transition countries—particularly in Poland, Bulgaria, the Slovak Republic, and Lithuania.[3] Unemployment was concentrated among low-skilled workers, workers with only vocational education, younger individuals, and in economically less developed regions:

- The risk of unemployment declined with an increase in educational attainment. This disparity in unemployment rates between high- and low-skilled workers was much higher in transition countries than in the EU.
- Workers with obsolete and narrow skills, such as vocational education graduates, also had difficulty finding jobs in a labor market in which demand shifted to highly skilled, generally trained, and adaptable workers.
- Youth unemployment was also extremely high in transition countries. For example, in Bulgaria and Lithuania the youth unemployment rate was twice as high as that of prime age workers. In Poland the differential was still larger: young people were almost three times more likely to become unemployed as prime age workers. Disproportionately high youth unemployment points to barriers to labor market entry, limited hiring, and low worker turnover.
- The strong association between the level of urbanization, infrastructure, physical capital, and human capital contributed to the pronounced regional variation in labor market conditions, and in particular to huge rural-urban disparities in terms of access to jobs (Scarpetta and Huber 1995; Rutkowski and Przybyla 2001). For example, in Lithuania the most successful regions

created twice as many jobs (relative to employment) as the least successful ones. In Bulgaria, it was only the capital region that created jobs on a net basis, while in all remaining regions job destruction exceeded job creation.

A particularly worrisome and socially costly feature of unemployment in transition economies was its long duration. Inflows into unemployment were high while outflows from unemployment to jobs were very low. Under such conditions, the share of long-term unemployed (that is, workers who are unemployed for over one year) was extremely high, often exceeding 50 percent.

CHANGES IN THE COMPOSITION OF EMPLOYMENT. Falling participation and rising unemployment were both costs; more positively, changes in employment patterns represented a move toward a more efficient allocation of resources. The composition of employment shifted in four ways:

- *Industry and agriculture to services.* The communist countries overemployed workers in heavy industry and agriculture, and employment in these sectors contracted significantly during the transition—although it remained larger than in the EU. In contrast, the service sector increased its share of employment. Some countries, such as Poland and Romania, with traditionally large agricultural sectors, saw the agricultural share of employment increase as individuals migrated from urban to rural areas and from industrial to agricultural jobs.
- *Public to private sector.* The contraction of the public sector led to a shift in employment from public to private sector jobs. While the private sector increased its share of GDP and employment, the private sector share remained smaller than the share found in EU countries. This shift was consistent with higher service sector employment because most private sector jobs emerged in the service sector.
- *Permanent to more flexible contracts.* Workers under communism were given almost complete job security, and employment contracts of indefinite duration were the norm. During the transition more flexible, contingent employment contracts—such as fixed-term or temporary contracts—became increasingly common. This meant more flexibility for employers but less job security for workers.
- *Formal to informal sector.* In most transition economies, the incidence of self-employment and informal employment increased dramatically. Some of this shift reflected the creation of new small firms that avoided tax and other legalities associated with the formal sector, and some reflected increased productivity. However, many jobs in the informal sector were often irregular,

low-productivity jobs that provided only subsistence income while not lifting the workers and their families out of poverty (for example, agricultural jobs). Thus, the informal sector was a mix of productive new firms and low productivity menial jobs, and did not uniformly signal a loss in productivity.

Impact on wages

Along with these adjustments in employment, the transition reduced real wages and increased their dispersion. The influence of the transition on the level of real wages was transitory. Wages fell dramatically at the early stage of the transition but started to recover at the later stage, responding to emerging economic growth. Wage growth mirrored productivity growth, but sometimes even exceeded it because of wage pressures exerted by unions.

The influence of the transition on wage distribution was more profound and permanent. Wage distribution, compressed under central planning, widened considerably during the course of the transition. Most of the increase in wage inequalities happened during the early stage of transition (early 1990s). Wage inequality stabilized thereafter at a level that was relatively high (wage Gini coefficient of 0.3; see chapter 2) but not exorbitant by EU standards (Rutkowski 2001).

The positive effect of growing wage inequality overshadowed its negative effects. The increase in premiums for skill and educational attainment—a positive impact of the transition—was the most important determinant underlying the widening of wage differentials in transition countries (Orazem and Vodopivec 1997; Rutkowski 1996). Growing wage inequality created strong incentives for individuals to invest in education and skills, and contributed to human capital formation and to improvements in productivity. Absent some degree of wage flexibility, which accommodated demand and supply shocks associated with the transition, unemployment might have been even higher.

On the negative side, the increase in wage disparities may have contributed to the rising income inequality and to poverty and social marginalization among some of the low-paid workers. However, low-paid workers are often secondary earners whose earnings complement incomes of other family members. If this is the case, low pay does not necessarily imply poverty. Moreover, an increase in earnings dispersion may *reduce* poverty if the higher number of available low-paid jobs implies lower unemployment than would have been the case otherwise. Which effect of higher wage inequality prevailed—the negative or the positive one—cannot be determined intuitively and remains an empirical question. However, it does appear that the growth in wage inequality in transition economies was on balance a positive feature, with little negative social consequence.

In the early transition, wages and employment became decentralized and started to reflect labor market conditions and worker productivity. The large decline in output at the start of the transition led to a fall in both employment and real wages, and a growth in wage inequality. However, despite economic recovery in the mid-1990s, employment was very low, manifesting itself in high unemployment or low participation (or both) and was the main labor market outcome of the transition. Real wages responded to output growth and the increase in wage inequality was largely positive, reflecting increasing returns to human capital.

Policy directions

While there are many policies that can affect the performance of the labor market, four main policy areas undertaken by transition countries have been selected that are most often cited in the literature, as well as in the European Employment Strategy, as determining labor market outcomes: promotion of economic growth, promotion of labor market flexibility, enhancement of labor market skills, and provision of social protection benefits.

Policies to promote economic growth

Economic growth is the main driver of employment and wage growth. Therefore, in the early 1990s transition countries adopted market-oriented policies to bring about private sector development and sustained economic growth, with the hope of eventually joining the EU. These policies included opening up product markets to international and domestic competition, liberalizing output and input prices (wages, for example), removing state subsidies to firms, and the restructuring and sale of state enterprises. At the first stage of the transition, because labor hoarding and overmanning was common under central planning, liberalization and economic restructuring naturally led redundant labor to be shed, and reduced employment. Moreover, the large reduction in aggregate demand and the decentralization of wages allowed wages to reflect labor market conditions and worker productivity, reduced real wages, and increased wage disparities (World Bank 2002).

About the mid-1990s, the second stage of the transition, economic reforms started to bear fruit and economic growth resumed in transition countries. Economic liberalization, opening of trade, inflows of foreign direct investment, adoption of new technologies, and an increased pace of the diffusion of innovations led to growth in labor productivity and real wages.

The employment response was limited. The increase in labor productivity crowded out a potential increase in employment. However, the slow pace of job creation also reflected a constraint to the growth of the private small and medium enterprise sector: the high cost of doing business, even in the most successful transition economies. While transition countries made considerable efforts to improve the business environment and attract private firms in their bid to develop into market economies, administrative costs for setting up firms remained high, ranging from regulatory constraints (such as permits, licenses, and certificates), to bureaucratic harassment and corruption (frequent and lengthy audits and inspections), to poor infrastructure. As one example, the number of procedures and amount of time necessary to open a business were significantly greater than in more liberal EU economies (Ireland or the United Kingdom, for example).

Another constraint on employment growth in the private sector were the large payroll taxes associated with generous social insurance programs, notably pensions (see chapter 5), but also health care (see chapter 6). Labor taxes were high in formerly communist countries, well above EU levels, and even increased in the early transition, as a result of a low contributor base and the generosity of social insurance programs (relative to the level of income in those countries). High tax rates likely had adverse effects on the level of formal employment and provided incentives to engage in informal transactions in the labor market.

For this reason, in the second phase of the transition, pension reforms in many countries attempted to strongly link contributions to benefits, thereby reducing the tax component of pension levies (see chapter 5); even so, payroll taxes remained quite high in the transition era, limiting formal employment growth.

Policies to promote labor market flexibility

Communist countries inherited labor market institutions that were protective of workers (difficult hiring and firing conditions, and so forth) and contributed to economic stagnation. Making labor market institutions fully flexible, with no security offered to workers, was not a realistic option. Transition countries faced a dilemma of how much flexibility to introduce in labor market institutions. Flexibility was necessary to facilitate the restructuring of enterprises, but the legacy of worker protection, the presence of strong unions, and the geographic proximity of the European employment model made it difficult to introduce this flexibility. The ways in which labor market institutions—labor legislation, minimum wages, and unions and collective bargaining (considered most important in labor market literature)—evolved and influenced labor market development in transition countries are examined in this section (Svejnar 2002).

Labor legislation. Central and Eastern European countries inherited stringent labor legislation that reflected the communist ideology of worker rights and employment protection. Although this legislation was less restrictive by EU standards, dismissals of workers were difficult and costly. Some evidence of a negative relationship between the strictness of job protection legislation and the rate of job creation for Central and Eastern European countries is presented in Haltiwanger, Scarpetta, and Vodopivec (2003). For example, employment protection legislation in Croatia and Slovenia is among the strictest in Europe. This naturally leads to low firing and limited job destruction. A marked contrast is offered by labor legislation in Estonia, which has low firing costs. Estonia traded job security for employment growth and created many more new jobs than Slovenia, where firing costs are much higher (Rutkowski 2003; Haltiwanger and Vodopivec 2002).

Considerations of this kind provided impetus for labor market reforms in some Central and Eastern European countries, with reforms carried out in Poland in 2002 providing one successful example. To be sure, these reforms represented a compromise between the position of trade unions and the demands of employers. Still, they were successful because of two key factors: First, the interest of private business was represented by a strong, vocal, and articulate employer lobby. Second, the government (with the Ministry of Labor acting as an agent of change) was committed to labor market reforms as a means of fostering hiring and employment.

Minimum wages. The excessive growth in wage inequality (experienced, for example, in former Soviet Union countries) was kept in check by Central and Eastern European countries mainly as a result of enforcement of reasonably high minimum wages—typically about 40 percent of the average wage (less than the EU average of 50 to 60 percent of average wage). However, the high unemployment of low-skilled, inexperienced workers (youth, for example) in economically depressed regions indicates that minimum wages may have reduced the hiring of these workers by increasing the wages that employers need to pay them above their productivity. For example, in Poland the minimum wage accounts for as much as 80 to 90 percent of the going wage for low-skilled labor in high unemployment regions of the country, potentially locking out low productivity workers from employment. The relatively high minimum wages reflect the power of trade unions and developed mechanisms of tripartite bargaining on the national level.

Unions and collective bargaining. At the start of the transition, decentralization of wage and employment decisions meant that labor unions took their place as important stakeholders in wage determination in transition countries, mirroring the unions in EU countries. Unions played a valuable role in representing the interests of workers in a market economy. By giving workers a voice in employment and wage determination, and taking a greater role in protecting workers against egregious contract violations, poor safety and health standards, and discrimination, unions most likely contributed to higher worker productivity and welfare.

At the same time, unions in transition countries established their credibility by bidding up wage claims. The pressure on real wage growth originated from large, state-owned or privatized enterprises with strong union presence. Private firms, usually small and with weak or nonexistent unions, were followers, raising wages in reaction to changes in the national average wage. Some categories of workers, largely less skilled, blue collar ones, enjoyed a significant public sector wage premium (along with greater job security). To the extent that this wage pressure translated into wage growth in excess of productivity, the price was paid in lower employment.

Transition countries often had rival unions (for example, post-communist and independent) that competed to maintain and attract new constituents by raising wages. There was also little coordination between unions and employers because of the considerable imbalance of power in favor of unions. Employers' organizations were nonexistent under communism and the fledgling organizations that emerged during the transition were often not worthy opponents to powerful trade unions, and were not able to dampen wage pressures. These conditions made the coordination of bargaining to stem wage growth difficult to attain for accession countries.

Developing labor market skills

Transition countries took two policy actions in response to the emerging skills mismatch in the labor market. First, the countries responded by reforming their education systems. These changes are detailed in chapter 7. Second, most countries created national employment services, often with local offices, that served to improve the skills of the long-term unemployed through Active Labor Market Programs, such as training and retraining, job-insertion training (sometimes through wage subsidy programs), and development of entrepreneurial skills.

By providing services mainly to laid off workers, Active Labor Market Programs also facilitated economic restructuring and layoffs. These programs were found to improve worker skills and help workers reenter the labor force in cases in which services were well targeted to the populations most in need and where financing was adequate. However, successful programs were costly to implement, both administratively and financially.

The impact of Active Labor Market Programs on improving the skill level of the unemployed and facilitating their return to the workforce was marginal, although these programs have helped facilitate the transition. Programs require adequate financing and targeting to be most effective; but even so, are costly.

Providing social protection

As the social costs of layoffs became apparent, transition countries used existing social support programs (such as pensions or severance pay), or introduced new programs modeled after those in Organisation of Economic Co-operation and Development countries (such as unemployment benefits and means-tested social assistance benefits) to cushion the impact of the decline in incomes, to promote social cohesion, and to maintain political support for reforms (Rashid and Rutkowski 2001).

As open unemployment emerged at the start of the transition, unemployment benefits programs were introduced in all transition countries to protect the unemployed against the fall in income associated with job loss. Laid-off workers were eligible for unemployment benefits, and the original programs had generous benefit levels and duration. Laid-off workers were also eligible for severance pay, and those nearing retirement were laid off using early retirement programs financed by the pension system. When unemployment proved of long duration, social assistance programs for the long-term unemployed who had exhausted unemployment benefits were introduced (discussed in chapter 5).

The introduction of generous social protection programs in the early transition facilitated the transition and protected individuals against abject poverty (Boeri and Terrell 2002). However, the large number of beneficiaries increased the fiscal costs and led to the eventual contraction of social support packages, such as unemployment benefits. The level of benefits and their duration were reduced in many countries, and eligibility, earlier open to all unemployed, was restricted to those with previous contributory records.

It has been argued that social protection benefits, including unemployment benefits, made nonparticipation a viable option, and thus reduced labor supply and employment. This may well be the case. However, these benefits were much lower than those provided by the EU (Riboud, Sanchez-Paramo, and Silva-Jauregui 2002), and it is unlikely that they accounted for a significant part of unemployment in transition countries (Vodopivec, Wörgötter, and Raju 2003).

LABOR MARKETS UNDER ACCESSION

Accession to the EU has the potential for significant and positive effects on the labor market in Central and Eastern European countries. Accession should allow member countries access to each others' product and factor markets. It should facilitate physical investment as well as an exchange of skills and technical and managerial know-how—all of which should help promote employment and productivity growth in new members. Whether this potential is realized will depend in large part on the criteria for accession and how these are implemented in the new Europe.

To join the EU, accession countries have to meet two criteria:

- The binding technical criteria that align the common rules, standards, and policies that make up the body of EU law. For labor policy, this has meant an alignment of the standards of worker protection (discrimination, health and safety, contractual provisions, and information in the labor law) in new member states with those of older member states, and agreement on an implementation schedule.
- The Open Method of Coordination—in the labor area this involves the adoption and monitoring of objectives of the European Employment Strategy, which has as its focus an increase in employment in all member states, and an open migration policy for labor.

This section discusses each of these criteria in turn and evaluates their possible impact on the functioning of the labor market.

Binding technical criteria

The main objective of the technical conditions—the harmonization of labor law, the equality of treatment of gender and other groups (ethnic, race, religious, and so on), health and safety conditions, and the inclusion of social partners in the determination of social policy—is to ensure that workers in all member states have the same level of protection of rights, no matter where they work.

Harmonization of labor law

The harmonization of labor law is to be carried out in the following areas: provision of information and consultation to avoid redundancies and to protect workers if redundancies occur; safeguarding of employment rights if the firm is sold to a new owner; provision of information to employees by employers regarding the employment contract; worker guarantees against insolvency; posting of workers (ensuring workers working in particular member states obtain basic contractual rights set out in the law of the member state); specifications on hours of work; protection of youth and children; and protection of workers on part-time and fixed contracts.

Equal treatment of gender and other groups

The Amsterdam treaty and Article 141 of the European Community Treaty support the equal treatment of men and women, explicitly providing that in all its activities the Community must aim to eliminate inequalities, and to promote equality, between men and women. The practical implementation of this gender mainstreaming is spelled out in the Community Framework Strategy on Gender Equality (2001–2005), which involves policy analysis and planning, the collection of statistical data broken down by sex, as well as training and awareness-raising of the key actors involved. As appropriate, legislation is also to be used to achieve equality, especially to prohibit discrimination on the basis of sex.

In addition to gender, accession countries are to reduce other forms of discrimination, such as discrimination by race, religion, or ethnic origin. In most countries, considerable progress has been made in implementing the provisions on equality of treatment.

Health and safety conditions

The Single European Act, which came into force in 1987, gave new impetus to social policy in the areas of health and safety at work. The considerable *acquis* in this field are aimed at harmonizing, through directives, minimum health and safety standards for working conditions in the EU. Common EU rules establish the baseline standards in a wide range of areas, including protection against specific health risks, such as noise or exposure to chemicals, or in specific circumstances, such as pregnancy or where workers are under age 18. Compliance with the health and safety *acquis* is essential to reap the benefits from, for example, fewer work accidents and occupational injuries and diseases. To achieve this goal, timely and complete implementation of EU legislation on health and safety at work must be accompanied by the effective operation of labor inspection institutions.

By and large, the technically binding conditions for accession are not "binding" on the labor markets of accession countries. That is, many new members already had similar provisions in their labor laws, although many were not strictly enforced. Thus, the Employment and Social Policy chapter of the *acquis* was closed, with 10 countries considered to be in compliance in December 2002. The chapter has been provisionally closed with Bulgaria and Romania. Candidate countries were asked to provide detailed timetables for adoption and implementation of all measures (in particular, health and safety directives). This requirement has, in general, been satisfied. Candidate countries were also requested to provide further details on enforcement and practical implementation, particularly with regard to the role of the various inspection bodies and the systems of redress open to aggrieved persons.

The open method of coordination

As a final condition, as part of enhanced coordination under the EU, accession countries (like older members) are also required to adopt and implement the European Employment Strategy. The main objective of the Employment

Strategy articulated in Lisbon (in 2000) is to move the EU toward full employment and make the EU the most competitive and dynamic knowledge-based economy in the world. In a sense, the emphasis on full employment brings accession countries back full circle to the socialist goals that they had earlier abandoned, although the importance placed on a competitive and knowledge-based economy indicates that the EU's emphasis on full employment is based on attaining employment growth based on market principles.

The full employment objective is embodied in specific targets that the EU has set for itself. By 2010, the EU should have an overall employment rate of 70 percent, an employment rate for women of 60 percent, and an employment rate for older workers (age 55 to 64) of 50 percent. Other targets relevant to labor markets (under preventive measures) are that every unemployed person is to be offered support for a new start before reaching 12 months of unemployment, and women are to be provided child care to facilitate their participation in the labor force (see chapter 5).

This overall goal is to be achieved through actions in four broad areas, also known as the four main pillars of the strategy:

- Improving employability through investment in skills
- Developing entrepreneurship (facilitating the start up of businesses, especially small and medium-sized enterprises)
- Encouraging adaptability in businesses
- Strengthening policies for equal opportunities by region, gender, and age

These broad goals are supplemented by specific policies or guidelines on actions that would facilitate their outcome, including increasing entrepreneurship and increasing job quality, enhancing skills, and reducing disparities in employment between regions, genders, and older workers. The inclusion of the social partners in implementing the strategy is also an important EU goal (although it is sometimes argued that the need to involve the social partners in economic policy has created a stranglehold on necessary policy reforms in countries with powerful trade unions). It is important to note that the Employment Guidelines are subject to change and will evolve as labor market conditions and requirements change.[4]

Other criteria

The European Social Charter (ESC) is an agreement between the member states of the Council of Europe aimed at securing for their populations social rights to improve standards of living and social well-being. The rights include those that directly relate to labor markets, such as the right to just conditions of work (Article 2), the right to safe and healthy working conditions (Article 3), the right to fair remuneration (Article 4), the right to protection in cases of termination of employment (Article 24), and the right to be informed and consulted in collective redundancy procedures (Article 29). These rights are deemed an essential part of what constitutes the European socioeconomic model. All Central and Eastern European accession countries are presently members of the Council of Europe and adopted the ESC.

Informal processes

For the Central and Eastern European accession countries, becoming part of the EU involves not only meeting formal conditions associated with EU accession and embedded in the *acquis communautaire,* but also an involvement in an informal process that influences European labor market institutions. This informal process may in some instances be even more important in shaping labor market institutions in the transition economies than the formal process of accession. For example, the conformity of states' law and practice with the ESC is decided upon by the European Committee of Social Rights.[5]

In its assessments, the committee establishes its own criteria to determine if a situation in a given country is in conformity with the ESC. These criteria tend to be extremely stringent, implying a high target level of employment and wage protection. For example, the committee threshold for the minimum wage is set at 60 percent of the average wage. This is very high, even by standards of the current EU economies, let alone the transition economies. No wonder, then, that in the committee's judgment no Central and Eastern European economy (except Slovenia) secures the right to fair remuneration (Article 4). Similarly strict criteria are used for the assessment of the other employment protection provisions, such as advance notice of dismissal, compensation for unfair dismissal, or overtime work. Accordingly, the level of employment protection in most Central and Eastern European countries is found to fall below the thresholds established by the ESC.

The criteria established by the committee are arbitrary and not based on any sort of economic considerations. They represent solely the committee's vision of the desired level of social welfare, including employment protection, and thus are not officially agreed on or adopted. Consequently, the conclusions of the European Committee of Social Rights are not binding or enforced. Nonetheless, the committee's conclusions are official documents of the Council of Europe and the ESC. As such, they do have significant influence, even if not formal. They promote a vision of a generous welfare state and highly protected labor market as essential for European identity, an ideal toward which European countries are expected to strive. This pressure tends to tilt the balance toward more protection and less labor market flexibility and adaptability. As has been argued, such pressure may have negative consequences for job creation and growth prospects in the Central and Eastern European countries.

———————•———————

In sum, the goals of the European Employment Strategy are consistent with increasing labor supply among aged and other minority groups (social cohesion), and the technical conditions of the *acquis* are not binding for accession members—and thus not an additional restraint on employment creation. However, the interpretation of the European Employment Strategy and the ESC may cause countries to err on the side of instituting greater protection than labor market flexibility, and therefore run counter to the main objectives of the European Employment Strategy—to increase employment and promote social inclusion. This issue is taken up in the next section.

BEYOND ACCESSION: BALANCING FLEXIBILITY AND SECURITY

Increasing employment consistent with the goals of the European Employment Strategy is one of the main objectives of the EU beyond accession. The EU has recently made considerable progress in increasing employment. A mid-term review of member states' progress in the Luxembourg Process conducted at the level of the Employment Committee concluded that the Employment Title of the treaty has had some success in reducing unemployment. The average EU employment rate rose from 63.2 percent in 2000 to 64 percent in 2002, with further increases expected. While integration of the accession countries into the EU may have reduced the employment rate (because employment rates in accession countries are lower than in older member states), this decline is likely to be moderate given the small share of the population of the accession countries in total EU population (Eurostat 2005).

Although output and employment growth slowed down in the EU in the run up to accession as a result of the economic contraction in the United States, the effect on employment and participation rates was not significant. Employment increased over time, became more responsive to economic growth in the 1990s, and was accompanied by a long-term decline in unemployment, from a high of 10 percent to below 8 percent in 2002. However, despite recent growth, the EU faces a significant challenge: employment rates in the EU remain lower than those prevailing in the United States and Japan and unemployment rates are much higher.

Sustaining these increases in employment while fostering declines in unemployment is one of the main objectives of the EU beyond accession. Most of the policy choices to be pursued in reaching this objective, noted in the Employment Strategy and Employment Guidelines cited above, are not contentious, including fostering entrepreneurship and job creation, enhancing skills, and reducing regional, gender, and age disparities. However, as alluded to in the previous section, a fourth objective, not explicitly discussed in the Employment Strategy and left to the discretion of member states, is to seek an appropriate balance between worker protection and labor market flexibility. This policy choice may be more contentious. Full security and no flexibility is not an option, as former communist countries well know; full flexibility and no security is not an option either. Between these extremes, the flexibility and protection combination chosen by EU member states will require trade-offs. If greater protection is chosen, higher employment objectives could be compromised. Similarly, minimal protection might generate greater employment, but would compromise worker welfare.

Less contentious reform directions

This section and the next discuss in turn less contentious reform directions, and those that are controversial.

Fostering output growth

Competitive product markets and enabling business environments that ensure growth of firms and output are the main drivers of job creation and employment. Clearly, business climate improvements, deregulation of business activity, and removal of barriers to firm creation would bring about faster job creation and employment growth. The EU employment policy supports promotion of formal employment and small and medium enterprises (SMEs) through the creation of a sound business environment, the formalization of employment, and the reduction of taxes.

These goals will be a particular challenge for new members, some of which have considerable administrative barriers to entry for SMEs and substantially higher payroll taxes. Reducing administrative requirements for new business and reducing corruption and vested interests (which dampen firm entry) should be a priority for new members. Continued restructuring of enterprises in accession countries will also be essential for fostering SME growth, particularly in the private service sector, and for promoting sustained increases in employment over the medium to long term. Although creating an enabling business environment and competitive product markets is a noncontentious reform direction, vested interests and the political economy of product market reforms may make these goals difficult to achieve.

Skill enhancement

Employment prospects in the EU are brighter for highly skilled workers. Globalization and technological progress are changing both the structure of markets and the nature of work relationships. Between 1995 and 2001, employment in the high-tech sector and knowledge-intensive services of the older EU members accounted for slightly more than half of total employment. A significant share of all those in the EU high-tech sector are high skilled (having completed tertiary education), while the share is much larger, about one-half, in the knowledge-intensive services sector. Improvement in the quality of education and skill levels and adaptability of skills of the workforce are critical to long-term employment performance in the EU (see chapter 7).

Given the low level of skills among the unemployed, active policy measures, such as training and retraining, may help specific workers reenter the workforce. These programs have been emphasized by the European Employment Strategy as important for increasing employment. However, given the emerging evidence on Active Labor Market Programs, the expansion of employment services should be implemented with care. Policy makers need to recognize that while well-designed and targeted programs may have a positive net impact, poorly designed and targeted programs probably will not have any economic impact. Finally, it is economic growth, not labor redeployment programs, that creates jobs. (See annex 3A on Active Labor Market Programs.)

Reducing employment disparities across gender, age groups, and regions

GENDER. The EU objective is to reduce the gender gap in employment rates and in pay by 2010. Some progress has been made toward this goal. Nevertheless, gender differences in employment and pay in the EU remain significant. There are also major differences in the unemployment rate. The unemployment rates for women, including long-term unemployment rates, are much higher than those for men. In addition, differences in pay between men and women persist in the EU (Eurostat 2005). It should be noted that gender gaps not only represent discrimination, but also signify less intensive job search by women (who are often secondary earners), and greater volatility in labor force participation—as a result of decisions to leave the labor force (temporarily or permanently) for marriage or child care.

Greater investment in the education of women to increase their participation in occupations that pay a higher wage should help reduce gender differences in employment and wages. Reducing the strictness of employment legislation (such as reducing the costs of hiring workers, and lowering excessive benefits for women) would also help increase employment prospects for marginalized and low-skill groups. Access to affordable child care would also facilitate labor force participation for adult family members with children. Given its multiple sources, however, the gender wage gap is not likely to be eliminated quickly.

OLDER WORKERS. The aging of the population is a major challenge for the European labor market. While changes in the age structure of the EU have not had a significant effect on employment so far, they will have an important impact in the future. Increasing the participation of older individuals will become important for increasing overall employment. However, the employment rate for older workers remains far below the 50 percent Stockholm target, and is much lower in new accession countries because of more generous early retirement policies.

Creating a policy framework that encourages older workers to remain employed longer will contribute to increasing their employment rates (see chapter 5). This policy framework could include reforms in several areas, including inter alia the tax and pension systems and in employers' recruitment and training practices: Efforts should focus on making lifelong learning a reality for people of all ages and (as called for by the Barcelona council) on measures to encourage older workers to remain in the labor market through flexible retirement formulas.

REGIONAL DISPARITIES. The EU is likely to confront large regional disparities in income, employment, and unemployment. Interestingly, regions with low employment rates are invariably those that have a lower skilled working age population and low rates of female labor force participation. The difference in female labor force participation between the best and worst performing regions in terms of employment is substantial (Eurostat 2005).

Promoting favorable physical, financial, and human capital investment in lagging regions, being considered in the EU to reduce regional disparities, should contribute to reducing regional employment differences. A critical policy for reducing regional disparities includes easing restrictions to labor mobility. Lifting direct controls on migration is already an EU goal. However, easing housing market constraints, which also adversely affect mobility, particularly in Central and Eastern European countries, is also likely to have a positive impact on reducing regional employment differences.

Debates about strategic choices: Balancing labor market flexibility and worker security

At accession, there were significant variations between new and older EU members with regard to the protection they provided workers. Older member states had more protective labor market institutions relative to new member states (Riboud, Sanchez-Paramo, and Silva-Jauregui 2002). Going forward, new and older EU countries will have to decide how much protection they will provide labor force participants.

In the industrial world, there is also considerable variation in the protection offered to regular workers by labor market institutions, which include labor law, unions and collective bargaining, minimum wages, and unemployment benefits. According to OECD rankings, Southern European countries generally have stricter employment protection arrangements and provide greater protection to the unemployed (unemployment benefits and so forth) than Northern European countries. However, the United Kingdom, the United States, and Japan have lower protection than almost all continental European countries.

These variations in protection (and therefore flexibility) across countries are determined in part by history (Balkan countries have high worker protection as a result of the worker management system instituted in the communist era), political pressures (strength of unions, or lack thereof), and the envisioned role of the state (large or small) in providing protection against income uncertainty.

Which model will the integrated Europe adopt—the more protectionist model of older Europe or the more flexible model of the United States, the United Kingdom, and Japan, or some model in between? There is considerable debate about how much protection should be provided to labor market participants. It is important to note that the debate is not about whether protection should be provided. Proponents of less protection (or greater flexibility) argue that protecting workers or insiders through restrictive employment protection legislation that makes it difficult to fire workers compromises the employment prospects of new entrants or outsiders. These high firing costs reduce employers' incentive to hire new workers. Employment protection also reduces the flexibility of employers to adjust their labor input to competing economic conditions, reduces economic competitiveness, and compromises economic growth. Lower economic growth results in lower hiring and ultimately has a further effect on lowering labor demand.

Advocates of lower protection also argue for a lower minimum wage because this provides modest protection to workers; does not significantly raise the cost of labor to employers, thus not dampening their competitiveness; and does not discourage employers from hiring low-skilled workers. Proponents of less protection also discourage the provision of generous unemployment benefits. Unemployment benefits should protect workers against abject poverty, but should not be so generous as to reduce the incentives of workers to search for jobs and impose a fiscal burden. To sum up, proponents of flexibility argue that protection should be provided to labor market participants, but it should not be so high as to discourage competitiveness, impose a fiscal burden, compromise incentives, or discourage employment of less skilled workers.

In contrast, proponents of restrictive employment protection legislation believe that workers should have significant protection against being fired without due notice or process because this imposes great hardship on workers and their families. Protectionists believe that strong unions are needed to give workers voice against the strong bargaining power of employers. Without strong worker voice in decision making, most employers would violate the basic rights of workers; provide them low wages; and break contractual provisions on pensions, and health and other benefits; and invest little in worker training or improving health and safety conditions in the workplace. According to this view, worker protection improves the quality of the job, allows greater investment in workers, and therefore contributes to higher worker productivity and economic growth. Advocates of strong protection believe that a high minimum wage protects low wage workers against poverty, and reduces wage inequality among workers. Proponents of higher protection also believe that the unemployed should be entitled to generous benefits to reduce poverty among the jobless. Moreover, considerable efforts should be made by the state (provision of training, job counseling, and so forth) to help these individuals reenter the labor force. Stemming the depletion of skills and helping the unemployed reenter the labor force reduces the loss of human capital for society and reduces social costs associated with nonemployment. Thus, more protection may be costly, but also raises worker productivity and worker welfare.

The choice made by European countries will have an impact on the labor market. Growing evidence in economic literature demonstrates that countries with less protective labor market institutions, such as the United Kingdom, the United States, and Japan, generally tend to enjoy higher employment and greater responsiveness of employment to output. In contrast, countries with greater worker protection, such as many European countries, are subject to lower employment rates and less responsiveness of employment to economic growth. Therefore, in making the choice regarding how much protection to provide, old and new EU countries will have to carefully weigh the benefits and costs of their decisions.

Annex 3A. Active Labor Market Programs

David Fretwell

Three unemployed people illustrate the challenge of finding employment in a tight and changing labor market, and the role of Active Labor Market Programs (ALMPs) in assisting the process.

- Leszek Madejski, a 40-year-old coal miner in Silesia, Poland, received a two-year lump salary payment when his mine was closed. There was little opportunity for reemployment in mines, because others were also closing. Leszek's family owned a rural home in the next region. Leszek had 18 years of work experience but was not eligible for social security benefits for 12 months. He had two years of secondary vocational training, and wanted to start a small transport business but was unsure how to proceed.
- Maria Kovacs from Miskolc, Hungary, a 28-year-old single woman, was laid off from the local steel mill. She had worked as an accountant for three years, and had a secondary education in economics, and a degree in accounting. She had heard that a number of new medium-size electronics companies, including those started by international investors, were opening up in the Lake Balaton area near Budapest, but she did not know how to look for work.
- Silviu Sandi, a 20-year-old Romanian, had recently completed secondary education, and had a one-year technician's certificate in repairing farm equipment. He lived in northern Romania, where state farms were being privatized and broken into small units, and the existing workforce displaced. He had worked as a clerk in a store for 12 months, but had been laid off because of the recession in the region, and could not find further work in the area. He was willing to move, wanted to find employment related to his training, but did not know where to start.

Their governments assisted the three individuals in different ways:

- Leszek wanted to start a new business, but was unsure how to proceed even though he had funds from his severance payment. Several types of assistance were offered, including micro loans, access to a small business incubator, and a voucher for consulting services. Leszek bought a vehicle with his severance package, used the voucher program to help him start the business, and felt that this assistance helped him overcome several start-up problems. The type of assistance he received tends to be more expensive than other services because of the cost of the consulting services, but the services can have a positive impact both on start-up and sustainability of new businesses (Fretwell, Benus, and O'Leary 1999).

- Maria received intensive assessment and job placement services, together with support for remote job search and relocation in the Miskolc provincial labor office. It turned out that an international computer manufacturing company had contracted with the labor office to screen applicants for a new plant in Szeged. She applied, was given a travel grant to visit the factory site, and was hired as a bookkeeper and relocated to Szeged. The assistance did not cost much as it was short-term. Job placement services often have a substantial positive impact on reemployment for people who are frictionally unemployed, but are not useful in addressing structural unemployment.

- Silviu's situation was different, because his limited mechanical skills were not in demand. Though he received on-the-job and institutional training, he could not find permanent work. At some point he was close to being hired as an assembly line worker, but in the end, the company reduced its demand for workers. Training has a significant positive impact only if carefully linked to the labor market and targeted at clients with the appropriate interests and aptitudes. The record, however—as in Silviu's case—is quite poor.

General features of ALMPs

ALMPs are common in the European Union (EU), and have been implemented fairly extensively in the transition economies. Their use is directly encouraged in the European Employment Strategy and Guidelines for Member and Accession Countries, which state:

> Member States will develop and implement active and preventative measures for the unemployed and the inactive designed to prevent inflow into long-term unemployment, and to promote the sustainable integration into employment and inactive people. (Official Journal of the European Union 2003)

Objectives. ALMPs should be viewed in the context of a comprehensive social support program, including transitional income support. From an economic standpoint, the objectives of ALMPs are to facilitate the rapid return of workers to productive employment and thus reduce the duration of publicly financed income support payments. From a social standpoint, transitional income support programs help to prevent unemployed workers and their families from slipping into poverty. From a political standpoint, ALMPs and transitional income support programs provide a safety net during times of economic restructuring and signal to citizens, communities, and labor representatives that government is attuned to the needs of affected workers.

Administration, financing, and delivery of ALMPs vary by country. In general, the National Employment Service, normally linked to a Ministry of Labor, administers the programs through its provincial and local labor offices. Financing may be from the state budget (Turkey, Australia, United States), payroll taxes (Czech Republic and Hungary), or a combination (Poland). In many middle-income countries, revenue from payroll taxes finances both ALMPs and unemployment benefits, with the aim of providing reliable finance for programs. In practice, however, during times of high unemployment, the majority of resources are often allocated to unemployment benefits, crowding out ALMPs. Some countries are therefore establishing minimum budget set-asides for ALMPs, or providing some budgetary finance for general employment services and ALMPs. Delivery of ALMPs is generally through local service providers through contracts with local labor offices, often integrating performance contracting (that is, agreed job placement rates or small business start up rates). However, performance standards need to be sensitive to rates of unemployment in different regions. Finally, ALMPs need to be coordinated with temporary income support payments, in particular unemployment benefits, to stimulate job search and to ensure that recipients of temporary income support are provided with services to help them rejoin the labor force quickly.

Costs. Services are normally used by about one-third of unemployed workers. Unit costs per participant, when compared to long-term income support, can be relatively low (averaging US$50 to US$1,000 per client served) in middle-income countries. However, the cost per job placement may be much higher, particularly if job placement is very low, as in temporary community service programs. See table 3A.1.

The impact of ALMPs is a subject of continuing debate. One side argues that the most cost-effective way to generate employment is to create a positive investment climate and to reduce government intervention. The counterargument is that if the unemployed do not have the appropriate human capital or are otherwise impeded from competing in the labor market, the government needs to intervene. OECD reviews (Fay 1996) show that ALMPs differ widely in their objectives and their impacts, both across and within countries. Recent World Bank reviews indicate that there is evidence that labor redeployment programs can have a significant positive impact if appropriately targeted and well run (Fretwell, Benus, and O'Leary 1999).

To help the unemployed and to address market failure, individual countries, the EU through the European Social Fund (ESF), and the World Bank have financed ALMPs. The Bank has financed performance-monitoring and net-

TABLE 3A.1 ALMPs by country and approximate unit costs per participant
1999 US dollars

Program	Czech Republic	Hungary	Poland	Turkey
Employment services	12	25	30	17
Training	265	500	300	200
Public service employment	625	1,200	800	n.a.
Wage subsidy	885	950	560	n.a.
Self employment[a]	885	1,000	2,830	n.a.

Source: Fretwell, Benus, and O'Leary 1999, table 2.1.
Note: n.a. = Not applicable.
a. Figure represents the gross costs of a micro-credit program, net will be reduced because
50 percent of credits were repaid (with interest) by the recipients.

impact evaluations in a number of accession countries. Such evaluation prompts the following general observations. ALMPs are more likely to achieve their objectives if policy makers

- ensure sufficient finance so programs do not have to be terminated early;
- use performance-based contracting (that is, negotiate job placement or business start-up rates) with service providers;
- implement ongoing evaluations;
- assess and screen unemployed applicants before entry to programs;
- limit the use of temporary community employment programs, because their medium-term impact on employment may be negligible, and the programs are very expensive—use other types of income support;
- are careful in generalizing from research on impact of programs from other countries—instead evaluate ongoing programs and adjust as necessary;
- realize that well-designed and targeted programs may have a positive net impact, but poorly designed and targeted programs probably will not have any economic impact.

A key conclusion is the need to offer a menu of services that recognizes different types of unemployment: frictional unemployment (general employment services); structural unemployment (different types of retraining); and a lack of demand for labor (micro-enterprise support, local economic development planning). Finally, it should be emphasized that ALMPs do not create jobs. They help to create human capital and improve the mobility of labor. In the end, it is investment and economic development that create employment.

Poland: Transition to accession—
active labor market programs

In Poland in 1990, the labor marked switched in a matter of months from excess demand to excess supply. Registered unemployment jumped from 55,000 people (0.2 percent) to 1,125,000 (6.1 percent) in 12 months and continued to climb to about 3 million or 16.4 percent in 1994, as the labor market reacted to structural changes. In 1990 labor force participation was almost 90 percent; there had been large rural to urban migration; about 30 percent of the workforce had only an eighth grade education; there was no system of unemployment benefits or means-tested social assistance; and, while there was a network of regional labor offices, their primary role had been to act as a local labor exchange and to deal with specialized labor programs (for disabled people, for example). The offices were understaffed and underequipped to deal with rapidly increasing numbers of unemployed.

In response to the developing crisis, the government enacted an Employment Law in January 1990, which established policies for unemployment benefits, employment services, and limited active labor programs (that is, small business loans, loans to employers for creating jobs, training, public service employment, and wage subsidy programs). Seventy-four percent of funding was from the State budget, and 24 percent from a 2 percent payroll tax. Sixty-four percent of expenditures went to unemployment benefits, and the remainder to ALMPs, including an apprenticeship system. Parallel actions were taken to strengthen the institutional structure of the national and local employment services, including additional staffing, training, and automation of services. (Considerable external bilateral and World Bank resources were obtained.)

By 1997, refinements had been made in the design and implementation of both income support and ALMPs. Unemployment abated to 10.8 percent in 1998. Labor office staffing was increased, 500 local labor offices existed, automation of services was well advanced, and a National Labor Office with a tripartite governing structure was established to implement labor programs based on policies established by the Ministry of Labor and Social Policy. However, while revenues allocated to the Labor Fund grew considerably, to 2.2 percent of GDP, only 14 percent of these funds (or 0.3 percent of GDP) were used for active labor programs. In comparison, in OECD countries, about 0.75 percent of GDP is spent on such programs. ALMPs included up to 12 months of retraining, public works paying salaries of up to 75 percent of average income, intervention works paying six months of wages and social charges for workers hired by firms, micro loans for small business start-up, and general employment services. A significant event during this period was implementation of performance monitoring of ALMP outcomes, and implementation of a net impact study by MOLSP to inform policy makers and Parliament about the net impact of ALMPs.

By 2002, several policy and organizational changes had emerged. A National Employment Strategy, adopted in 2002, was linked to EU accession requirements and the National Development Plan. It focused on employment improvement, equality of opportunity, enterprise development, and improving adaptability of the labor market. This plan recognized that, despite significant investments in labor programs, unemployment had again increased, remained stubbornly high (17 percent in 2003, while labor force participation dropped to 56 percent), and that additional measures had to be enacted. Meanwhile, the National Labor Office was disbanded and operations decentralized to local authorities as part of the overall decentralization of government. The Labor Fund declined to 1.4 percent of GDP in 2002. ALMPs continued, but in a reduced fashion, supplemented with World Bank financing in rural areas. As Poland moved to accession, the EU Joint Assessment of Employment Priorities for 2002 identified these priority areas:

- Completion of education reform (including increasing the level of general education of adults) and expansion of continuing adult education
- Refining wage, tax, and benefit systems to provide incentives for employment
- Increasing the role of the social partners
- Addressing high regional unemployment
- Addressing gender gaps
- Strengthening employment services and promoting a shift from passive (income support) to active labor measures for the unemployed.

Poland clearly made significant advances in developing and implementing employment policies, including ALMPs, to respond to the market economy. In spite of these advances, Poland found that there was more to do: in some cases employment conditions had regressed and labor force participation rates dropped significantly, the commitment of resources to and refinement of ALMPs was still a "work in progress," and senior management in government continued to ask questions about the effectiveness of ALMPs as expansion was being planned through the use of the European Social Fund.

NOTES

1. The eight former communist countries that joined the EU in 2004 are the Czech Republic, Estonia, Hungary, Latvia, Lithuania, Poland, the Slovak Republic, and Slovenia.

2. The idea that output growth was achieved through productivity rather than employment growth assumes that output is demand constrained. If output growth is supply constrained, then there is not necessarily a trade-off between productivity and employment. The extent to which output growth in transition economies has been demand constrained, and to which it has been supply constrained is a matter of discussion.

3. We do not know exactly what factors accounted for the variation in employment outcomes across transition economies. For example, there is no satisfactory answer to the question of why unemployment in the Czech Republic was so much lower than in Poland.

4. To meet the objectives of the Employment Strategy prior to accession, in accordance with the provisions of the Accession Partnership, the governments of each accession country prepared with the European Commission a Joint Assessment of Employment Priorities (JAP) of short-term employment and labor market policy priorities. In parallel, the consistency of member states' employment policies, beyond accession, will be examined through a yearly Joint Employment Report established by the commission and the council. Furthermore, the European Council has adopted yearly Employment Guidelines for the member states (broadly in a similar manner as in the field of economic and monetary policy), on the basis of which member states developed National Action Plans for Employment. The commission may propose and the council adopt recommendations to individual member states.

5. The committee was established by Article 25 of the ESC.

REFERENCES

Boeri, Tito, and Katherine Terrell. 2002. "Institutional Determinants of Labor Reallocation in Transition." *Journal of Economic Perspectives* 16(1): 51–76.

Eurostat. 2005. http://europa.eu.int/comm/eurostat.

Fay, Robert G. 1996. "Enhancing the Effectiveness of Active Labor Market Policies: Evidence from Program Evaluations." Labor Market and Social Policy Occasional Papers No. 18, OECD, Paris.

Fretwell, David, Jake Benus, and Chris O'Leary. 1999. "Evaluating the Impact of Active Labor Programs; Results of Cross Country Studies in Europe and Central Asia." Social Protection Discussion Paper No. 9915, World Bank, Washington, DC.

Haltiwanger, J., and M. Vodopivec. 2002. "Gross Worker and Job Flows in a Transition Economy: An Analysis of Estonia." *Labour Economics* 9(5): 601–30.

Haltiwanger, John, Stefano Scarpetta, and Milan Vodopivec. 2003. "How Institutions Affect Labor Market Outcomes: Evidence From Transition Countries." Social Protection Working Paper, World Bank, Washington, DC.

Official Journal of the European Union. 2003. Council Decision of July 22, 2003, on Guidelines for the Employment Policies of the Member States, Brussels. August 5, 2003.

Orazem, Peter, and Milan Vodopivec. 1997. "Value of Human Capital in Transition to Market: Evidence from Slovenia." *European Economic Review* 41(3–5): 893–903.

Rashid, Mansoora, and Jan Rutkowski. 2001. "Labor Markets in Transition Economies: Recent Developments and Future Challenges." Social Protection Discussion Paper No. 0111, World Bank, Washington, DC.

Riboud, Michelle, Carolina Sanchez-Paramo, and Carlos Silva-Jauregui. 2002. "Does Eurosclerosis Matter? Institutional Reform and Labor Market Performance in Central and Eastern European Countries in the 1990s." Policy Research Working Paper No. 591, World Bank, Washington, DC.

Rutkowski, Jan. 1996. "High Skills Pay-Off: the Changing Wage Structure During Economic Transition in Poland." *Economics of Transition* 4(1): 89–112.

———. 2001. "Earnings Inequality of Transition Economies of Central Europe. Trends and Patterns During the 1990s." Social Protection Discussion Paper No. 0117, World Bank, Washington, DC.

———. 2003. "Does Strict Employment Protection Discourage Job Creation? Evidence from Croatia." Policy Research Working Paper No. 3104, World Bank, Washington, DC.

Rutkowski, Jan, and Marcin Przybyla. 2001. "Poland: Regional Dimensions of Unemployment." *In Labor, Employment, and Social Policies in the EU Enlargement Process,* eds. B. Funck and L. Pizzati. Washington, DC: World Bank.

Scarpetta, Stefano, and Peter Huber. 1995. "Regional Economic Structures and Unemployment in Central and Eastern Europe: An Attempt to Identify Common Patterns." In *The Regional Dimension of Unemployment in Transition Economies,* eds. Stefano Scarpetta and Andreas Wörgötter. Paris: OECD.

Svejnar, Jan. 2002. "Labor Market Flexibility in Central and Eastern Europe." William Davidson Institute Working Paper No. 496, William Davidson Institute at the University of Michigan, Ann Arbor, MI.

Vodopivec, Milan, Andreas Wörgötter, and Dhushyanth Raju. 2003. "Unemployment Benefit Systems in Central and Eastern Europe: A Review of the 1990s." Social Protection Discussion Paper No. 0310, World Bank, Washington, DC.

World Bank. 2002. *Transition: The First Ten Years. Analysis and Lessons from Eastern Europe and the Former Soviet Union.* Washington, DC.

4

SOCIAL SAFETY NETS
Evolution from Inclusion and Control to Inclusion and Participation

Sándor Sipos and Dena Ringold

This chapter argues that social safety nets in the new European Union (EU) member states[1] have moved from social integration and inclusion in an egalitarian and totalitarian society with a planned economy toward social integration and inclusion in a democratic pluralist society with a market economy by way of an intermediate period of transition confined more narrowly to poverty relief. Accession to the EU facilitates restoration of broader and more active instruments of social inclusion.

THE LOGIC OF TRANSITION: SOCIAL SAFETY NETS

This section discusses in turn the inherited social safety net, the impacts of transition, and the directions for reform that those impacts implied.

The inherited system

The inherited system was, by and large, well-adapted to the old order, and therefore systematically ill-suited to the needs of a market economy.

Social inclusion and control

The roots of pre-accession social safety nets, including family support and the little social assistance that existed were presented in chapter 1. These safety nets were characterized by the following features:

- A functioning social assistance system for fighting poverty was lacking because, at least in principle, there was no poverty. Instead, a number of institutions took occasional remedial action to guide at-risk people to employment and to benefits that were largely linked to employment. People living with disabilities were entitled to special, noncontributory social pensions, and, for a few select cases, limited social assistance benefits and services were provided to families or individuals at risk of social exclusion because they were not able to participate in society. These latter benefits were provided in a highly discretionary way by a patronizing state apparatus.

- Family benefits were generous and nearly universally available to assist families in all main life events.[2] Family benefits played a much more important role than poverty-oriented social assistance benefits.

- The system relied heavily on special institutions that were set up to handle people with special circumstances. Once it was determined that such people could not function productively in the world of work, they were largely removed from the working mainstream population and spent long spells of their life in secluded institutions that were part of the state apparatus.

- Only the state and state-owned enterprises provided family support, social assistance, and social services, because very few nongovernmental organizations (NGOs) were tolerated and civil society was cornered by the Communist Party and discouraged from engaging in charity and provision of social services.

In sum, the inherited social safety net was characterized by a disproportionate focus on preemptive interventions to ensure social inclusion and control over individual and family life, a proliferation of small and uncoordinated benefits, weak administration, and an overreliance on institutionalized care.

Fit with the old order

These features were fully consistent with the old economic and social order.[3] Because income distribution was kept relatively flat, and incomes together with free access to health care and education provided for a fully functional life style at a relatively low level of consumption and choice, there was no need for the design of benefits to take account of income differences. Benefits were designed to support the two central objectives of communist social policy: to ensure that a two-earner, nuclear family was functional and able to work or study; and to maintain a sense of purpose, security, and equality in society. Interventions were designed to address specific contingencies that threatened these objectives. The focus on full employment derived from Marxist ideology and the realities of the shortage economy. According to Marx, only labor can create value;

therefore, policies maximized the creation of value by removing "capitalist obstacles to full employment." The soft budget constraint with which socialist enterprises operated to fulfill central plans and create employment led to hoarding and an insatiable demand for labor (see chapter 3 for more details). Given the combination of low and fairly equal wages and generous transfers in-kind and price subsidies, the average individual or family needed no additional interventions, and virtually all families lived under average conditions. The contingencies that threatened the workers' capability to work emerged from deviations from social norms.

Social assistance and certain family benefits were perceived as necessary instruments for making corrections, either due to accidental malfunctioning of the communist welfare system or, more commonly, due to individual failure, delinquency, or pathological behavior. The able-bodied were forced by law to be employed, and people with disabilities were separated out into special jobs or granted various categories of disability pensions.

Wages were fairly evenly distributed and the elderly were taken care of by a generous pension system; thus, the number of children made the biggest difference in determining the consumption potential of a family. Demand for labor was ever increasing, so the state was interested in maintaining high fertility. In contrast, families responded to incentives to maximize their consumption and to be available to work by having fewer children. Hence the social policies of the old order became heavily reliant on family benefits to counterbalance these incentives for having fewer children. Family benefits grew even more important after the state abandoned failed coercive efforts to force more births that led to dangerous illegal abortions and a surge in the number of institutionalized children, but could not reverse the rapid decline in fertility.[4] Typically, every country had a relatively large child allowance[5] accompanied by a plethora of smaller benefits. The purpose of the large child allowance was to equalize the consumption potential of families (ensuring both horizontal and vertical equity). The smaller "cradle-to-grave" benefits targeted life events that could threaten the functioning of the communist family in the world of work and inclusion in society. In many countries, these included birth and funeral grants, layette, parental leave arrangements, school grants, school and work uniforms, maternal and child health services, subsidized housing and consumer goods, school meals, meals at work, travel allowances, holiday referrals to sanatoria and summer camps, and child care at all ages (crèche, kindergarten, and before- and after-school supervision with meals harmonized with the parents' work schedule).

The communist system was characterized by an overreliance on institutionalized care for similarly logical reasons (see Tobis 2000). With both husband and wife in full-time employment, and no help available due to chronic labor shortages, institutions were needed to care for the elderly, disabled, and orphans. Neither wages nor pensions were high enough to pay for home care if a family's working capacity was endangered, for example, by the need to take care of an elderly person or a disabled child. In addition, small housing units were not suitable for extended families.[6] These constraints were binding—families could not save enough from their low wages, and it was difficult to find better housing or construction materials in a shortage economy. If not impossible, it was often irrational to make large private efforts to improve housing to accommodate an extended family because housing was, for the most part, state- or company-owned. These factors caused many children, disabled, elderly, mentally ill, and other vulnerable groups throughout the region to be placed into overcrowded, poorly run facilities, isolated from the rest of society.

Children were particularly subject to institutionalization. Foster families were in short supply as families reduced their fertility[7] to live a better life and, with full employment and near universal social insurance coverage, children played no foreseeable role in the old age income security of active workers. Also, the state generally encouraged institutionalization in the hope of breeding a new generation of "socialist man" raised on community-oriented educational principles and free from the individualistic, "petty bourgeois baggage" of many families.[8] Institutionalization was particularly encouraged in cases where the state saw the need to "correct the deviations" that the children suffered due to the lack of a well-functioning "socialist family." In addition to the stigma associated with asking for special social assistance benefits, families, especially Roma and other minorities, were reluctant to apply for these benefits for fear of the scrutiny involved that often led to forced institutionalization of their children.

Private charity and independent community initiatives were extremely limited and discouraged by the socialist state, which regarded NGOs as potential challenges to the Party-state.[9] NGOs were also discouraged for ideological reasons, particularly because the society of workers, peasants, and the "working intelligentsia" was supposed to march toward less rather than more stratification, and during this march all social problems would be solved, partly by infinitely increased productivity after the removal of the capitalist cycles of production, partly by the very amalgamation of all social strata into a liberated working class. Because of these factors, civil society was underdeveloped, or lacking, in most countries. Nonstate associations were limited to groups of families and friends and a few highly controlled religious, ethnic (for example, folk dance groups), or occupational organizations. These organizations had limited capacity to exercise charity, and if it happened it was more as part of their tolerated ritual than out of an acknowledged social role. No private initiative could play a role in addressing social problems, as unattended need was either seen as a malfunction of the state or an individual deviation from social norms. Malfunction of the state had to be addressed immediately by the state itself. Individual deviation called for professional intermediation (medical, legal, political, or criminal), for which non-state actors were not seen as qualified.

Despite the large number of in-kind and cash benefits provided through the workplace and special institutions, the administration of family support and social assistance was weak (Sipos 1994; Milanovic 1998). This weakness was due to the fragmentation of benefits and division of responsibilities for financing and administering these benefits between numerous government ministries and agencies, which had little contact with each other, leading to gross inefficiencies and a significant administrative burden. Although determining how best a family in need could be helped would have required an individualized approach, the profession of social work to provide this individual attention essentially did not exist. This shortcoming, too, was logical in the old order. Most benefits were paid at the workplace, so the main task of the social assistance administration was to determine whose fault it was that corrective intervention was needed. Once this was determined, social assistance administrators referred the emerging cases back to employers and medical and custodian committees responsible for determining disability or institutionalization. In cases in which social assistance administrators suspected willful work avoidance, they turned to law enforcement institutions, because avoiding employment was regarded as a criminal action threatening public order and could be sanctioned by imprisonment—another factor that discouraged people from asking for social assistance.

Because of the fragmentation of responsibilities, a strong statistical system would have been needed to monitor welfare outcomes. However, statistics in the old communist order were built to document the planned economy by counting inputs and outputs to build national plans and monitor their implementation. Administrators had little motivation to conduct household budget surveys on consumption and social welfare because average conditions were determined by highly predictable wages and benefits. Also, as the Party was above the law and external political scrutiny, monitoring of welfare outcomes was pointless. In this spirit and to prevent any dissent, objective monitoring of these outcomes and impacts and independent scholarship and research were not encouraged. Because of this, even the little data produced on living conditions or social stratification was often regarded as confidential and access to it was restricted.

Path dependency

While highly characteristic of the old communist order, the social safety nets of these countries still showed some similarities with then-contemporary models of Western welfare states,[10] indicating social preferences that went beyond the pure logic of the old communist order. These revealed preferences might also predict variations in how the welfare systems of these countries would try to comply with the requirements of the market economy, both during the transition and beyond.[11] The welfare system of the old communist order in the accession countries strove to ensure universal access, like the Scandinavian social democratic systems, by addressing all citizens according to their perceived needs so they could function in the mainstream of an egalitarian society. In both models, the state replaced a wide array of market and family responsibilities. State welfare was also meritocratic in the old communist order, somewhat similar to the continental European conservative welfare states, in aiming at preserving or reproducing (on retirement) the socioeconomic status of workers and their families. For example, in many communist countries, retired miners received in-kind coal allocations from their companies until the end of their lives, in addition to their pensions, just as they did during their active years; also, housing arrangements varied across various categories of workers and remained unchanged after retirement or even after the death of one's spouse. This meritocratic feature was intended to nurture loyalty to the social order and a sense of reciprocity rather than to reinforce social rights.

The welfare system of the old order differed significantly from the parsimonious model of the liberal welfare states discussed at the end of chapter 1, in which the intention of the state is to provide relative equality of welfare at the level of the poverty line for recipients of public assistance after all private efforts, including charity, are exhausted, and which differentiates welfare among the majority on the basis of market incomes with a minimum of state redistribution. The old communist order aimed at assuring adequate consumption levels to all to allow average functionality in the restrained socialist society through flat wages and wide-ranging benefits. It was also different from the family-based systems of Southern Europe because it expected much less private provision of welfare and security from the broader family network. The system was fragmented in both the family-based Southern European model and in the old communist order, but the welfare system of the communist order was more robust with a much more egalitarian welfare outcome.

Without exception, the accession countries inherited complex safety nets that were intricately interwoven with the economic planning framework, and suited both the economic and sociopolitical needs of the old communist system well. Precisely for these reasons, and predictably, these inherited safety nets badly suited the needs of the market economy, especially during the early stage of the transition when subsidies were cut, unemployment surged, and poverty became an open challenge. However, the legacy of communist institutions, policies, and processes put a strong mark on the making of social policy in the transition period, and some argue that they will continue to affect the shape of the welfare state in these countries well beyond the transition.[12] The extensive web of benefits and subsidies that were provided to households helped to maintain the standards of living in many countries. However, the wide range of benefits forestalled cost-containment efforts and proved to be fiscally unsustainable, even prior to the transition period. At the enterprise level, untargeted social benefits and services were a financial burden to unproductive firms that wanted to shed them. However, the inheritance of a paternalistic welfare state of pervasive benefits and services created high expectations that benefits and privileges would be maintained. As a result, streamlining and scaling back entitlements was politically difficult in the transition period. Despite severe fiscal constraints, the state often stepped in to replace firms in social policy roles they had abandoned. Similarly, the stigma attached to poverty engendered little popular and political support for targeted safety net benefits initially, despite growing needs.

The impact of transition

The transition from a totalitarian planned economy to a democratic market economy refocused family support and social assistance to targeted poverty relief, because of sharply increasing poverty and equally sharply decreasing public resources, especially during the early stage of the transition. Rising poverty, unemployment, and income differentiation exposed the weaknesses of old social policies and institutions in targeting assistance to the needy. The old social safety net was well-suited to the old economic and social order but was unable to respond to the initial transition shocks and meet the needs of a market economy. In addition, the capacity of social insurance was reduced by the increase in informal activity and patchy tax compliance among failing old enterprises and emerging small companies (see chapter 5). Because of this, the old communist welfare system failed to provide protection through income support.

Economic shock

The economic shock of the early transition, as described in the previous chapters, rapidly undermined the foundations of family support and social assistance, and the rationale behind the communist social policies quickly evaporated. There was no longer a labor shortage, and income disparities were accepted as a natural outcome of the move to the market (Kornai 1995). Poverty surged and was accompanied by the highly visible affluence of the winners of the transition, which aggravated the subjective perception of poverty among the losers and even among the average. Rapid differentiation of wages would have required a large increase in transfers for family support to keep the consumption of families more equal in a period when the fiscal base of the state contracted due to falling output and tax revenues. These transfers did not happen. It was clear that maintaining horizontal equity objectives was not sustainable because of fiscal constraints. Also, there was a heavy trade-off between this old objective and the urgent need to fight rapidly emerging poverty. In addition, focusing on horizontal equity was in stark contrast with the needs of the emerging market economy, which required motivated workers. As a result, high inflation quickly eroded the real value of family benefits. In Hungary, where family benefits grew from 2.8 percent of gross domestic product (GDP) in 1980 to more than 5 percent in 1991, they fell back to 1.7 percent by 1997, in a period when successive governments kept social expenditures high to cushion the adverse impacts of the transition (Sipos and Tóth 1998).

Not only did wages differentiate quickly while real wages dropped and family benefits lost part of their real value, but a large part of consumer and producer subsidies were withdrawn with no or inadequate compensation, making key consumer goods more expensive and less available for lower-income families. Social services formerly provided by state-owned enterprises were gradually shed because they were no longer affordable or appropriate for a private company subjected to cost-cutting market competition. As companies closed or shed labor in the quest to survive, open unemployment surged, and the old social protection system had no instruments to combat it. Neither insurance-based nor social assistance–based unemployment benefits were in place at the start of the transition, and most modern labor market services and institutions were lacking (see chapter 3).

Rising number of beneficiaries

As a result of open unemployment, increasing poverty, and the deterioration of family benefits, the number of social assistance claimants increased sharply. In most countries, social assistance was ill-equipped to deal with such a rise in poverty. The situation was exacerbated by the fact that decision makers often did not understand that in times of need allocations for social assistance should be increased rather than cut. Because of this ignorance, uniform budget cuts were, far too often, applied to all budget items, including social assistance (Sipos and Tóth 1998). Improving targeting became a central issue, but the information base was poor and the institutional setup inadequate for the surging case load. Bureaucratic approaches prevailed when sound discretionary judgment was needed.

A particularly sad aspect of the transition was that institutionalization of children increased significantly in a period when conditions in these institutions deteriorated.[13] This was logical as there were many more newly poor families that could not cope with their poverty. Increased family strife and break up of families landed many more children in such institutions. Even families that did not eventually break up, cooperated more willingly with social assistance administrators in making decisions on the institutionalization of their children when there was no wage earner to support them.

Although civil society and churches organized quickly, they lacked the experience, resources, and often the legal standing to prevent institutionalization or to provide alternative social services. Nonetheless, they contributed significantly to fighting absolute poverty in the most difficult times. In the meantime, these organizations developed their capacities to assume a greater role as people's needs became more manageable with the rising tide of resumed economic growth (Palubinskas 2003).

From transient to chronic poverty

As described in detail in chapter 2, sound economic policies in the successful reformers led to a relatively quick turnaround of economic fortune. Changes in the poverty status of families frequently followed changes in the employment status of the head of the household, even before overall poverty rates started to decline toward the end of the 1990s with the return of economic growth. During the most difficult years of the transition, many families experienced repeated periods of poverty driven by the employment status of wage earners in the family. However, the poverty of these families was usually shallow with but one prospect of a way out: regaining employment (Milanovic 1998). This prospect was important to motivate people to seek employment, even if, especially in the early years of the transition, a large number of employed workers remained just above the poverty line in occupations whose relative importance decreased. These families just above the poverty line felt poor and insecure, but at least remained integrated in society.

At the same time, however, pockets of deep and chronic poverty emerged among the long-term unemployed and discouraged workers, as well as among disadvantaged ethnic minorities, most typically Roma. While social policies of the early transition were characterized by fighting a large and shallow transient poverty, the rising tide of economic growth left some boats behind and exposed social exclusion and deep and chronic poverty as new challenges for social policy (Sipos 2004). Increased need, reduced fiscal capacity to maintain the value of benefits, and the frustration associated with increasing absolute, relative, and subjective poverty called for realignment of the system with the emerging market economy and new democracy. This realignment required different measures in the early transition, when fighting transient income poverty dominated the agenda, and toward the end of the transition, when societies realized the perils of social exclusion in the pockets of deep chronic poverty. This is why the first volume on transition also focused on fighting transient income poverty (see Sipos 1994).

Resulting reform directions: Targeting poverty relief to the poor

The old communist welfare system not only failed to keep people at an acceptable average living standard during early shocks of the transition, it also failed to provide even a basic safety net to the new unemployed and poor. The direction of reform, therefore, was to transform interventions that previously ensured average consumption for families in specific situations and life events into a targeted safety net of last resort. This new safety net had to be able to provide a socially acceptable minimum level of consumption to all families. The distance between the average and a socially acceptable minimum started to widen, as an increasing segment of the population benefited from higher market wages and large segments lost access to market wages altogether. There was an increasingly widening income distribution behind the average, which became less of a norm, at least in the early stages of the transition. Improving targeting required major changes in the design, and in the financing and administration of benefits. The development of social safety nets during the transition varied widely by country, in part due to divergent pretransition starting points, differing socioeconomic conditions, and political and cultural factors. Despite these differences, similar benefits emerged to respond to unemployment and poverty. The differences were much larger in the way these benefits were financed and administered. European integration influenced social policy choices through instruments like the European Social Charter of the Council of Europe, which declared the right to family support and social assistance (see Council of Europe 1992).

As open unemployment emerged, real incomes declined, and inequality approached EU levels, the first response was to create unemployment benefits for workers who lost their jobs due to restructuring (see chapter 3). Such benefits were insufficient in duration and amount to deal with the problems of the newly unemployed who exhausted their benefits, especially in countries in which unemployment rates reached double digits. Existing benefits, including those cash benefit programs that did exist, were scaled back because of fiscal constraints. New social assistance schemes were needed that could respond to short and long-term unemployment, that were adequately financed, and that could be implemented easily with relatively low cost. A more active involvement of NGOs and civil society was needed to provide alternatives to institutionalized care.

Unemployment benefits

The design, financing, and delivery of the new unemployment benefits presented several major challenges.

The first challenge was the design of the unemployment benefit package: decisions regarding level and duration were critical. Design options varied between flat rate systems based on a proportion of the average wage or some other constant such as minimum wage, to more complex systems based on past earnings. The flat rate system often appeared as an initial priority, but it quickly lost its appeal as issues emerged surrounding the definition and maintenance of baseline data, erosion of baseline standards (for example, the average wage was often close to the minimum wage), and the reaction of the unemployed to such an approach. The wage-related alternative was, however, more complex to define and administer and could easily lead to benefits that would have provided disincentives to search for work until the benefits ran out. In many cases a compromise was developed in which prior wage experience was used for initial calculations with a cap on payments. Initial durations varied from six months to two years in the region, with longer durations for individuals with a longer work history and in countries that did not have a social assistance scheme already operating. Durations were reduced as social assistance benefits were introduced, and when it was realized that long durations often encouraged longer spells of unemployment. Often the new social assistance benefits continued to be called "income replacement benefits for the unemployed" but they were means-tested and usually lower than social insurance–based initial unemployment benefits. An alternative and somewhat simplistic scheme was a severance payment approach in which workers received a lump sum based on years worked (for example, one month's wages per year worked, up to a limit of 10 years). While simple, this approach had built-in problems with portability between employers or when an enterprise was liquidated and not able or willing to pay displaced workers. As a result, this option was used mainly to facilitate mass layoffs during the downsizing of specific sectors.

New social assistance benefits

The second response to the disintegration of the planned economy was a hodgepodge of subsidies and benefits intended to reduce the shocks of inflation and of lower standards of living. These subsidies were eventually removed or scaled back in the majority of cases (in part due to fiscal constraints and in part due to the efforts of international institutions; see Deacon, Hulse, and Stubbs 1997). The end result of this uncoordinated approach generally was a complex mix of benefits that were ineffective in protecting the population from the economic shock of transition.

As poverty increased in the early 1990s, countries began to introduce or strengthen existing social assistance cash benefit programs and focus them more systematically on the poor. The transition countries adopted diverse approaches to targeting, setting of benefit levels, and administration. Poland, Hungary, and the Czech and Slovak Republics passed new legislation on social assistance in the early 1990s that built upon existing programs. Social assistance schemes in these countries adopted many different approaches to targeting benefits to vulnerable groups, most of which involved an income test combined with other criteria on household assets, employment status, household size and composition, and health. A notable and logical trend was the emergence of guaranteed minimum income schemes, such as the one in Bulgaria introduced in 1995 (see World Bank 2002). These guaranteed minimum income schemes had the potential of replacing the existing hodgepodge of schemes and focusing public assistance on a clear-cut definition of income poverty. This clear-cut definition was driven by a poverty line and the concept of topping up family income to this poverty line after adjusting for family size, because consumption needs do not increase linearly with the number of family members. Age differentials also affect consumption needs, but most guaranteed income schemes decided to leave this effect to smaller secondary benefits, a plethora of which were inherited from the past.

Means-tested social assistance benefits coexisted with traditional family benefits throughout the transition. In most countries, these family benefits were maintained, albeit at a lower real level, as a first guard against poverty. Research showed that, particularly during the early transition, in most countries, the number of children was one of the most important factors leading to poverty (Milanovic 1998). Therefore, family benefits, especially the ones in which the level was differentiated by the number of children, were exceptionally effective in reaching the poor. This categorical targeting was easy and cheap to administer because it did not require costly, tedious, and stigmatizing means testing. These benefits, logically, erred more on the side of inclusion rather than exclusion, from the point of view of poverty targeting. Some countries attempted to subject these family allowances to a full means test but found it neither administratively nor politically attractive. Society still had a strong sense that the state should share in the cost of rearing children (horizontal equity). Instead of full means testing, most countries introduced high income thresholds to exclude richer families. Because subjective poverty was much higher than reasonable absolute or relative poverty measures indicated, the adopted income thresholds usually ended up higher following the political process than intended in the original proposals (see Fox 2003; World Bank 2002; Ravallion and Lokshin 1999). In Hungary, for example, the much criticized Bokros package ended up excluding only the richest 10 percent of families instead of the originally intended 20 percent (Sipos and Tóth 1998). While wasteful from the objective of income poverty targeting, high eligibility thresholds for means-tested family allowances were useful in maintaining political support for a benefit that had a good record in reaching the poor.

In addition to their good benefit take-up records, family allowances also helped maintain sound labor market incentives in social assistance benefits.[14] The ideal logic for labor market incentives is that means-tested social assistance benefits should be lower than the combination of social insurance benefits and the minimum wage, thus encouraging return to paid employment and consequent contribution to social insurance. At the same time, social assistance benefits should provide an acceptable minimum standard of living. This was impossible during the early transition when minimum wages were low. There was no family with any number of children that could have lived only on social assistance benefits calibrated to the minimum wage. Family allowances solved this problem by remaining practically universal for low-wage earners (only the highest income brackets were excluded) and not work-tested at all, because they included no or low disincentives to work. Social assistance benefits only had to close the gap between whatever remained uncovered between the wage and family benefit income of the family and the threshold of the top-up benefit.

Providing tax allowances and credits for children also became common practice in countries that introduced personal income taxes (Hungary, for example, had already introduced personal income taxes in 1987, prior to the transition). This measure obviously played a limited role in fighting poverty because most of the poor remained below income thresholds set for personal income taxes or had no taxable income at all. Another practical limit of using tax measures to alleviate poverty was that poor families needed monthly benefit flow while tax allowances and credits were reconciled and paid only once a year.

Financing poverty relief

Governments could not always ensure that the budget allocation for financing family support and social assistance increased when other transfers decreased during economic crises and other budgetary adjustments (see chapter 2). Linear budget cuts in times when increased allocations were needed for social assistance placed a high degree of pressure on the new system.

How to finance unemployment benefits was one of the first questions. State budget financing was the main alternative, because no insurance scheme was in place when transition began. This approach remained, at least partially, in a number of countries (Poland, for example) where a small payroll tax or training levy provided partial income for unemployment benefits and active labor market policies, as well as training. Over time, most countries moved toward an insurance system based on contributions from employers, employees, and, at times, the government. This approach, while common in most industrial countries, encountered several problems:

- Which agency would collect and invest the revenue needed to be determined. (Ministries of Labor were often reluctant to have this done by Social Insurance Agencies because they feared the funds would be used for other purposes);
- In times of high levels of unemployment, revenue would fall while state budget financing was still needed.
- The addition of a new payroll tax for unemployment benefits increased the cost of labor, which discouraged investment and encouraged fraud and misreporting of payroll, and as a result some countries (Poland, for example) did not institute tax regimes that fully funded unemployment benefits.

However, with the stabilization of inflation and unemployment, most accession countries have moved to financially viable schemes funded by some combination of payroll, worker tax, and government contributions.

Social assistance was frequently the first public program to be decentralized (see chapter 2). Decentralization was driven by multiple factors, including the dismantling of central planning, demands for increased local autonomy, a strong sense that applying the principle of subsidiarity[15] could help target benefits to the neediest, and pressure to off-load budgetary responsibilities onto lower levels of government. Results were mixed for social benefit programs. While there is evidence that local government involvement in social assistance can contribute to better targeting (for example, by having better information about who is poor), it also appeared to pose risks when local governments lacked resources and incentives to pay benefits. In Bulgaria and Romania, many local governments were unable to pay out social assistance benefits that were otherwise well targeted, having reached mainly poor beneficiaries and reducing their pre-transfer poverty significantly, because they did not have adequate budgets or real opportunities to raise local taxes. Because of this, benefit financing in both countries was eventually recentralized.

An important aspect of decentralization is the mobilization of local communities to design and carry out programs that reduce poverty at the local level. This can be particularly important in countries such as Bulgaria where municipalities are relatively large (over 50,000 on average) and where the poor tend to concentrate in communities of minorities (pockets of poverty) that may not be adequately represented in the municipal governments, typically dominated by the majority ethnic group. The Bulgarian government launched an ambitious social investment fund[16] project to reach these small pockets of poverty and to empower them to start small projects to improve their own socio-economic conditions. (See box 4.1.) In countries such as Hungary, Romania, or the Slovak Republic, where local governments are smaller, there is a greater likelihood that communities of the poor and local governments overlap. These local communities can directly tap into national and EU resources earmarked for direct community mobilization.

While unintended during the design of the Regional Initiatives Fund (RIF), self-selection by minorities provided an opportunity to scale up this instrument to fight chronic poverty among hard-to-reach Roma groups and ethnic Turks. The 2001 Bulgaria Poverty Assessment (World Bank 2002) found that Roma were 10 times more likely to fall below the poverty line than ethnic Bulgarians while members of the Turkish minority were four times more likely to be poor. In 2003, the Bulgarian government, with US$40 million from the World Bank, launched a US$50 million project to provide flexible windows of financing for demand-driven community projects in the country in the period 2003–2008. The Social Investment and Employment Promotion (SIEP) Project was designed to use the capacity of RIF to reach individuals and groups of people in chronic poverty. While the new Social Investment Fund (SIF) does not follow an explicit ethnic targeting criteria, it is expected that self selection similar to that which

---

BOX 4.1 Targeting Chronic Poverty in Excluded Communities in Bulgaria

In Bulgaria, the government observed that close to two-thirds of those employed by the Regional Initiatives Fund (RIF) were ethnic minorities in the period 1998–2001 (see table below).

Beneficiaries of the Bulgarian Regional Initiatives Fund 1998–2001

	Employed by the RIF		Users of RIF-supported services	
Ethnic group	Number	Percent	Number	Percent
Bulgarians	1,196	37	117,338	53
Turks	939	29	35,397	16
Roma	642	20	33,221	15
Pomaks and others	454	14	35,481	16
Total	3,231	100	221,437	100

Source: Information provided by the Bulgarian Social Investment Fund (SIF).

occurred with RIF will take place. To increase the effectiveness of reaching out to the poor minorities, SIEP also includes resources to help communities apply for SIF financing. SIEP aims at creating sustainable capacities in poor communities to articulate local development objectives and to apply for and to use resources. SIEP and SIF, its implementing agency, were part of the 2003 National Action Plan for Inclusion presented to the EU by the Bulgarian government.

Strengthening administration

The predecessor to this book, *Labor Markets and Social Policies in Central and Eastern Europe: The Transition and Beyond* (Barr 1994), emphasized strengthening the administration of social assistance. If anything, this turned out to be more important and more difficult in real life. Region-wide, there were significant efforts to train benefit administrators and social workers.[17] Statistical systems were realigned to produce better survey-based data on social status and income dynamics to improve policy design and monitoring.

Ministries of labor and social welfare throughout the region acquired new roles as the institutional arrangements for designing, delivering, and monitoring social assistance and unemployment benefits were put in place. Social assistance requires substantial administrative capacity, in particular to implement means-tested benefits, which requires trained staff and defined processes to assess the income and assets of applicants. The change in administrative arrangements also reflected the change in underlying philosophy. In the old communist order, poverty was treated as deviance and pathology, and thus was often left to the jurisdiction of ministries of health. This was quite logical, as it was often medical determination of disability that was the way out of a situation requiring social assistance. Similarly, many poor and frail elderly were placed into hospitals, forcing nurses to play social worker roles. The emergence of open unemployment demonstrated the link between employment and poverty status and paved the way to pair social protection with labor rather than health, not necessarily at the ministerial level but at lower echelons of public administration.

The most common approach for the administration of unemployment benefits was to use the public employment service as a registration, payment, and monitoring agent. However, these offices were not well staffed, equipped, or prepared to handle this task because their original mandate was to find workers to fill jobs, not the other way around (see chapter 3). Large numbers of unemployed, coupled with few staff and limited automation, resulted in major problems making payments. When combined with a shortage of funds, which resulted in further delays of payments, the situation became chaotic in the initial stages, with related stress on the unemployed. Staffing levels to registered unemployed were often in the ratio of 1 to 400 as compared to 1 to 100 in the EU. By accession, most of the following major administrative problems had been overcome: employment service staffing, automation to register the unemployed and job applicants and job openings, automation of services to limit fraud, provision of direct links with social assistance programs, alternative service provision through NGOs and private employment services, and introduction of alternatives for payment of benefits (for example, through local banks for an agreed-on fee). This shift and refinement of administrative workload increasingly permitted employment service staff to focus on preventive and active labor services, which is a priority of the EU employment strategy.

Deinstitutionalization

Deinstitutionalization became a desirable policy objective because institutional care proved to be the costlier alternative and because the EU was paying special attention to reducing high institutionalization rates among the accession countries, especially in Bulgaria and Romania. Initial steps sought to introduce, monitor, and enforce standards in providing social assistance services and to encourage the launch of alternative community services to gradually move away from direct provision by the state.

Countries increasingly involved nonstate actors, including NGOs and community organizations, in the provision of social services. Some countries passed legislation that allows for the participation of NGOs in social policy. For example, Bulgaria's Social Assistance Act of 2002 established the regulatory framework for NGO involvement in social services. Hungary has a particularly active NGO sector; since 1989, roughly 35,000 new nonprofit organizations have been registered. It is estimated that about 15 percent of these are involved in social welfare provision, including children and youth services; large-family organizations; organizations for the physically and mentally disabled and the chronically ill; kidney and diabetes organizations; sight- and hearing-impaired organizations; elderly services and institutions; and organizations serving the homeless, refugees, and the poor and needy (Jenkins 1999).

SOCIAL SAFETY NETS UNDER ACCESSION

Neither binding nor nonbinding legislation applies to the field of social assistance, so the logic of the previous chapters cannot be fully followed here. However, increasing cooperation on social policies and a robust family policy in the old member states (see EC Directorate General for Employment and Social Affairs 2002) suggest that inclusion efforts will remain high on the social policy agenda in the new member states during and after accession. Furthermore, it is also highly likely that after the targeted poverty relief focus of the transition years, more emphasis will be given again to broader aspects of social policy.

The EU agenda: Coordination for social inclusion

While the primary *acquis* are not specific about family support or social assistance, a number of secondary *acquis* affect this area. More important, the 10 accession countries joined the EU during a period when EU countries extended their Open Method of Coordination (OMC) to eradicate poverty and social exclusion by 2010, following the decision of the Lisbon Council in March 2000 (see Communication from the Commission 2000). The Enlargement Guide for the accession countries states:

> While the funding and organization of social protection systems remain the responsibility of individual member states, the EU requires that these systems have the capacity to develop and operate sustainable and universally applicable social protection systems in line with Treaty objectives. The systems of the candidate countries must also be capable of coordinating with those systems currently operating in the EU which are themselves developing in a very dynamic way and undergoing significant reform. (EC 2003, pp. 44–45)

In this spirit, in 2003 all accession countries, including Bulgaria and Romania, whose accession was expected later, concluded individual Joint Inclusion Memoranda with the EU and prepared their National Action Plans for Inclusion. These steps will allow the new member states to proceed in lockstep with the existing 15 member states, converging their social protection systems to combat poverty and social exclusion in the framework of OMC. According to the conclusions of the Presidency of the European Council, the objective of the OMC in this respect is "simplifying and streamlining the various strands of work on social protection and social inclusion into a coherent framework within OMC" (Communication from the Commission 2003, p.17).

Practical and binding action steps of this OMC process include the following:

- Joint Report on Social Inclusion, 2004
- Revised indicators on poverty and social exclusion, 2004
- Consultation of social partners regarding the feasibility of guaranteeing a minimum income in each member state, including the new ones, following the 1992 Council Recommendation on minimum guaranteed resources, 2004 (see Communication from the Commission 2003, p. 18)

While no policy measures are binding or uniform, obligations made by the member states will shape future social policies by setting the stage for measures that will provide an adequate guaranteed minimum income to all in need—including all legal residents and their dependents, not just nationals—in a way that will help recipients find their way back to labor markets and full inclusion into society. One such step was the development of consistent poverty indicators at the Laeken European Council (box 4.2).

In the 1990s, the EU experienced some convergence of social policies: average social protection expenditures started to decline from 28.4 percent of GDP in 1996 to 27.3 percent in 2000, while at the same time such expenditures increased in real terms on a per capita basis in all member states (EU average 8.7 percent) except Finland (table 4.1). The increase was greatest in Greece (42.6 percent), Portugal (27.1 percent), and Ireland (21.4 percent) where social protection was previously lower, while the Scandinavian welfare states registered no (Finland, negative 0.1 percent) or low (Denmark, 1.8 percent; Sweden, 5.2 percent) increases.

Cash family benefits registered the steepest increase of all social protection expenditures (twice the average growth rate) in the EU between 1995 and 2000, 17.2 percent in real per capita terms followed by housing and social exclusion benefits (13.1 percent). The increase in cash family benefits was continuous during the 1990s and equaled 36 percent over the decade (see table 4.2).

The sharpest increase of cash family benefits over the decade took place in Luxembourg (156 percent), Germany (81 percent), Greece (67 percent), and Ireland (66 percent). In 2000, Luxembourg had the highest share of cash family benefits with 2.6 percent of GDP followed by Austria (2.3 percent),

---

BOX 4.2 The Laeken Indicators to Monitor Poverty and Social Exclusion

In December 2001, the Laeken European Council endorsed a set of 18 common statistical indicators—the "Laeken indicators"—to monitor progress in the fight against poverty and social exclusion. These indicators cover four important dimensions of social inclusion (financial poverty, employment, health, and education [see Dennis and Guio 2003]).

To measure poverty, the income threshold used to determine the poverty risk level was fixed at 60 percent of the national median income in each member state. Based on this measure, after all social transfers (old-age pensions, unemployment benefits, disability pensions, and so

(continued)

**BOX 4.2 The Laeken Indicators to Monitor Poverty and
Social Exclusion** (*Continued*)

forth), in 1999 15 percent of EU inhabitants were living in poverty.
(See table next page.) Adjustment of the threshold yields different poverty
percentages: if the threshold is lowered to 40 percent of national median
income, only 5 percent of EU inhabitants lived in poverty, while at
50 percent the rate was 9 percent. On the other hand, if the threshold is
raised to 70 percent, the poverty rate rises to 23 percent.

Sizable differences occurred among EU member states in the percentage of citizens living under this 60 percent poverty line. The share was
lowest in Sweden (9 percent), Denmark, Germany, the Netherlands,
and Finland (all 11 percent), and highest in Greece and Portugal (both
21 percent). Of those living in poverty in the EU, more than half—
9 percent of the population, or some 33 million persons—were below
the poverty line in at least two of the preceding three years and were
therefore subject to a persistent risk of poverty.

The effect of social transfers in the EU in reducing poverty is significant. When pensions and other social transfers are excluded from
income, 40 percent of EU families fall below the poverty line. Including
pensions in family income reduces this figure to 24 percent; including
other social transfers (unemployment benefits, invalidity payments, family allowances, for example) reduces the poverty rate to the 15 percent
level. This rate varies greatly between EU member states: social transfers
had the strongest effect in Sweden, where they dropped the poverty rate
19 percentage points, to 9 percent from 28 percent, while in Denmark
social transfers lowered the poverty rate 13 percentage points (to
11 percent from 24 percent). Such transfers had the weakest effect in
Italy (3 percentage points) and Greece (1 percentage point).

In 2001, one in eight people in the EU lived in a jobless household (see
table below). Long-term unemployment (lasting at least 12 months) is
regarded as a primary indicator of social exclusion, not only for the
unemployed person but also for that person's family. In 2001, about
3 percent of the EU's active working population fell into this category.
Again, this overall percentage conceals differences between member
states: the long-term unemployment rate measured less than 1 percent in
Luxembourg, Denmark, the Netherlands, and Austria, and was greater
than 5 percent in Greece and Italy. In addition, in 2001 2 percent of the
EU's active population had been unemployed for at least 24 months. In
that same year, 12 percent of households in which at least one person
was of working age and available for work were also classified as "jobless
households." Again, there were variations between member states: from
5 percent of households in Portugal and 8 percent in Spain to 14 percent
in the United Kingdom and 16 percent in Belgium.

**BOX 4.2 The Laeken Indicators to Monitor Poverty and
Social Exclusion** (*Continued*)

A Selection of Poverty and Social Exclusion Indicators
percent

	Monetary indicators, 1999			Nonmonetary indicators, 2001		
	Poverty rate at 60 % of national income					
	After all social transfers	*Before social transfers (income including pensions)*	*Persistent poverty rate*	*Long-term unem- ployment rate*	*Very long-term unem- ployment rate*	*Proportion of people living in jobless households*
EU-15	**15**	**24**	**9**	**3.1**	**2.0**	**12.2**
Belgium	13	25	8	3.2	2.2	16.5
Denmark	11	24	5	0.9	0.3	—
Germany	11	21	6	4.0[a]	2.6[a]	13.8
Greece	21	22	13	5.4	3.1	10.5
Spain	19	23	11	3.9	2.3	8.1
France	15	24	9	3.1	1.7	13.0
Ireland	18	30	12	1.3	0.8	10.0
Italy	18	21	11	5.8	4.3	11.9
Luxembourg	13	24	8	0.5[a]	0.2[a]	8.9
Netherlands	11	21	5	0.9	—	9.7
Austria	12	23	7	0.8	0.4	9.9
Portugal	21	27	14	1.5	0.8	5.0
Finland	11	21	5	2.4	1.3	—
Sweden	9	28	—	1.0	—	—
United Kingdom	19	30	11	1.3	0.7	14.2

Source: Eurostat 2003c.
Note: — Data not available.
a. 2000 data.

TABLE 4.1 Social protection in Europe in 2000 and as share of GDP, 1996–2000

	Social protection expenditure in PPS per capita in 2000, EU-15=100	Per capita expenditure growth for period 1995–2000 (%)	Share of social protection expenditure in GDP (%)		Distribution of social benefits, 2000 by function (%)					
			1996	2000	Old age, survivors	Sickness, health care	Family, children	Disability	Unemployment	Housing, social exclusion n.e.c.
Belgium	105	6.7	28.6	26.7	43.8	25.1	9.1	8.7	11.9	1.4
Denmark	126	1.8	31.4	28.8	38.1	20.2	13.1	12.0	10.5	6.1
Germany	114	7.9	29.9	29.5	42.2	28.3	10.6	7.8	8.4	2.6
Greece	66	42.6	22.9	26.4	49.4	26.6	7.4	5.1	6.2	5.4
Spain	60	9.7	21.9	20.1	46.3	29.6	2.7	7.6	12.2	1.6
France	110	7.0	31.0	29.7	44.1	29.1	9.6	5.8	6.9	4.5
Ireland[a]	77	21.4	17.8	14.1	25.4	41.2	13.0	5.3	9.7	5.5
Italy[b]	97	12.9	24.8	25.2	63.4	25.0	3.8	6.0	1.7	0.2
Luxembourg	150	17.9	24.0	21.0	40.0	25.2	16.6	13.7	3.3	1.2
Netherlands	114	4.6	30.1	27.4	42.4	29.3	4.6	11.8	5.1	6.8
Austria	120	10.8	29.5	28.7	48.3	26.0	10.6	8.2	4.7	2.1
Portugal	60	27.1	21.2	22.7	45.6	30.6	5.5	13.0	3.8	1.5

Finland	96	−0.1	31.6	25.2	35.8	23.8	12.5	13.9	10.4	3.5
Sweden	120	5.2	34.7	32.3	39.1	27.1	10.8	12.0	6.5	4.5
United Kingdom	98	13.8	28.1	26.8	47.7	25.9	7.1	9.5	3.2	6.8
EU-15	**100**	**8.7**	**28.4**	**27.3**	**46.4**	**27.3**	**8.2**	**8.1**	**6.3**	**3.7**
Iceland	82	29.3	18.8	19.5	31.1	39.2	11.7	13.9	1.3	2.8
Norway	132	26.5	26.2	25.4	30.7	34.2	12.8	16.4	2.7	3.3
EEA	**101**	**9.6**	**28.4**	**27.2**	**46.1**	**27.5**	**8.3**	**8.2**	**6.3**	**3.7**
Switzerland	123	13.4	26.9	28.7	51.6	24.4	5.1	12.5	2.8	3.6
Slovak Republic	34	13.1	20.1	20.0	38.4	32.9	9.3	8.0	4.6	6.8
Slovenia	66	—	26.1	26.6	45.2	30.7	9.2	9.0	4.3	1.6

Source: Eurostat 2003a, p. 3.

Note: Constant 1995 prices. Social protection expenditure and receipts are calculated in line with the methodology of the 1996 version of the ESSPROS (European System of integrated Social Protection Statistics) Manual. Expenditure includes social benefits, administration costs, and other expenditure linked to social protection schemes. PPS = purchasing power standard, an artificial currency that allows for differences in national price levels, making it easier to compare data. n.e.c. = Not elsewhere covered. EEA = European Economic Area. — = Not available.

a. The data for Ireland on occupational pensions for private-sector employees, which should come under "old age and survivors" are not available.

b. In Italy, the "old age and survivors" functions also include certain benefits that to some extent come under the "unemployment" function. Such benefits account for around 6 percent of total social benefits.

TABLE 4.2 Cash family benefits in European Union and other European countries in 2000, and growth during 1991–2000

	Cash family benefits, per capita PPS	Cash family benefits as percentage of GDP	Cash family benefits as percentage of total benefits	Cash family benefits as percentage of family and child benefits	Cash family benefits in constant prices, 1991 = 100[a]
EU	**1,361**	**1.4**	**5.5**	**67.2**	**135.8**
Belgium	2,000	2.0	7.7	84.6	116.2
Denmark	1,260	1.1	4.0	30.3	146.6
Germany	2,391	2.1	7.5	70.9	181.1
Greece	694	1.0	3.8	51.8	167.0
Spain	160	0.2	0.9	34.6	147.3
France	1,820	2.0	7.0	73.0	115.4
Ireland	1,664	1.5	11.2	85.9	166.4
Italy	581	0.5	2.0	52.2	128.6
Luxembourg	4,687	2.6	12.9	77.6	255.8
Netherlands	789	0.8	2.9	64.4	86.3
Austria	2,599	2.3	8.2	77.5	133.6
Portugal	386	0.5	2.7	48.9	115.4
Finland	1,345	1.4	5.8	45.8	119.1
Sweden	972	1.0	3.2	30.0	—
United Kingdom	1,278	1.4	5.5	78.4	120.2
Iceland	651	0.8	4.0	34.7	65.5
Norway	1,749	1.4	5.7	44.4	127.0
Switzerland	1,244	1.1	4.2	81.3	120.1
Slovak Republic	553	1.5	7.9	84.2	—
Slovenia	1,017	1.5	5.9	63.9	—

Source: Eurostat 2003b, p. 2.
Note: Expenditure on cash family benefits is calculated in accordance with the methodology of the 1996 ESSPROS Manual (European System of Integrated Social PROtection Statistics). Expenditure includes the following family and children benefits: birth grant, parental leave, family allowances, and other cash benefits. Expenditure is registered without any deduction of taxes. It does not include cash benefits paid as income replacement during maternity leave, nor does it include benefits in kind, such as day care centers (crèches, nursery facilities), accommodation (nursing homes, foster families), home help, and other benefits in kind. PPS = purchasing power standard, an artificial currency that allows for differences in national price levels, making it easier to compare data.
— Not available.
a. Indices for EU-15 are obtained by applying the respective 1995 national expenditure weightings in European currency units or euros in EU-15 to the national currency indices of each country.

Germany (2.1 percent), and Belgium and France (2 percent each) while Spain had the lowest with 0.2 percent, followed by Italy and Portugal (0.5 percent each) and the Netherlands (0.8 percent). In addition to cash benefits, EU countries provide a wide array of in-kind family benefits. These benefits are usually about one-third of the value of cash benefits, and make up another 0.4 percent of GDP (Abramovici 2002).

The only new member states in table 4.2, the Slovak Republic and Slovenia, each spent 1.5 percent of GDP on cash family benefits. This spending level placed them somewhat above the average. Also, both new member states spent more than the EU average of 5 percent of all social protection expenditure on cash family benefits (the Slovak Republic 7.9 percent, Slovenia 5.9 percent). While comparable data is not available for the other new member states, the trend in those states was opposite to the old members of the EU: family benefits decreased both in real terms and as share of GDP; however, they still remained at the higher end of the EU distribution.

Help or hindrance?

It is too early to assess the impacts and scope of OMC in the area of social assistance. A more unified approach to welfare and social policies would increase social cohesion in the EU and could be beneficial in facilitating the movement of people and goods within the EU, because similarly structured family support and social assistance packages would be available to all legal residents in each member state. A similarly structured safety net would also help link social insurance systems and extend risk pools to all countries of the EU by providing a predictable fallback of last resort. The downside is a potential loss of competitiveness by the new member states if wages grow more than productivity and benefits grow more than fiscal capacity. Also, guaranteed incomes that are too high might reduce incentives to work, save, engage in voluntary insurance arrangements, or comply with social insurance contributions. The closer a unified approach brings the guaranteed minimum to average incomes in the poorer countries, the greater the risk of downside effects in these countries. In theory, there could also emerge a reverse problem in more affluent EU states where, to keep the guaranteed minimum low to avoid encouraging welfare migration from poorer member states, protection of the poor might become inadequate.

Obviously, setting an EU-wide, guaranteed minimum income level would pose enormous fiscal problems for poorer members, especially for new member states if required to be financed entirely from domestic resources. However, moving toward a standardized approach does not mean actually equalizing benefit levels up front, because not only is fiscal capacity uneven within the EU, but price and wage levels are, too. Lower guaranteed minimum income in lower income member states would still meet the requirements of justice, equity, and inclusion, because in a lower income country a lower guaranteed minimum could provide, in principle, the same level of inclusion as a higher minimum in a higher income country.

However, if financing of guaranteed minimum incomes remains entirely country based, higher income member states will be interested in pressuring lower income members to raise their guaranteed minimum to eliminate any motivation for welfare migration.[18] This could cause significant problems for the new member states because their fiscal constraints would remain tight during the early stage of membership while in the process of adopting the euro. Enforcing a higher guaranteed minimum income (or just higher minimum wages) could also reduce the competitiveness of the new member states through both the increased tax effort needed to finance this minimum and other family support and social assistance. Social insurance benefits would likely be affected in this scenario because countries would need to raise them to maintain incentives to work and to contribute. With the higher minimum wage, reservation wages would grow and eventually wages generally would, too. Even if the current higher income member states shared part of the burden of higher guaranteed minimum income in the new member states to stem welfare migration, the adverse implications for competitiveness of the new members would still remain. The only exception is if other measures and flows increased productivity to the extent that the increased productivity offset the wage impact of higher guaranteed minimum income. Because most new member states are likely to remain at lower income levels compared to the old member states for quite some time, they are likely to be involved critically in the social policy harmonization process of the EU.

While harmonization of minimum income regimes is not yet on the agenda in the EU, most new member states have already introduced such systems (see table 4.3).

However, at the inception, these minimum guaranteed income benefits were only a small fraction of total social assistance benefits (see table 4.4).

The state of play at accession

The EU's Lisbon strategy frames the fight against poverty as an effort toward social inclusion and integration. From this perspective, equality of minorities, measures to prevent discrimination in labor markets, and ensuring access to social services are key social policy instruments, not just matters of legal equality and human rights. In 2003, all accession countries, including Bulgaria and

TABLE 4.3 Minimum income systems in selected European Union
accession countries

	Year	Name of income system	Financing	Administration
Bulgaria	1999	Guaranteed minimum income	Central and Local	Central
Czech Republic	2001	Social need benefit	Central	Local
Estonia	1999	Subsistence benefit	Central	Local
Hungary	2000	Regular social assistance	Local	Local
Latvia	2000	Low income family benefit[a]	Local	Local
Poland	2000	Permanent social assistance benefit	Central	Local
Romania	2000	Guaranteed minimum income	Central and Local	Local
Slovak Republic	2000	Minimum subsistence	Central	Local

Source: Updated from Murthi 2001; World Bank 2002.
a. The benefit level is determined by the local authority and can be paid in cash or kind.

Romania, made major efforts to introduce or amend and modernize their antidiscrimination framework laws and specific legal instruments such as the Labor Code, specifically ruling out any form of discrimination. Despite considerable progress on the legal front, much remains to be accomplished in the field of family support and social assistance to better reach all persistent pockets of poverty among minorities, especially the Roma (see Sotiropoulos 2004).

Integration of minorities

The EU also prioritized attention to minority issues as part of the Copenhagen criteria for accession. For the accession countries, this provision has focused attention on the situation of the Roma minority (see the case study in annex 4A), the most vulnerable minority group in Central and Eastern Europe (see Ringold, Orenstein, and Wilkens 2005; UNDP 2002). The status of Roma, in terms of access to political participation, and social and human rights, was reviewed and noted in each of the progress reports issued by the Commission. The issue of Roma was flagged as particularly important in the countries where Roma comprise the largest shares of the total population, including Bulgaria, the Czech Republic, Hungary, the Slovak Republic, and Romania.

The EU has supported Roma-related activities in the accession countries through its PHARE program.[19] PHARE projects have helped to meet the Copenhagen criteria and have focused on issues including education, employment, housing, and policy coordination. Between 1993 and 1999, 20 million

TABLE 4.4 Spending on social assistance schemes in European Union accession countries

		Spending (% of GDP)		Beneficiaries (thousands)	
	Year	Minimum income scheme	Total social assistance	Minimum income scheme	Total social assistance
Bulgaria	2001	0.32	1.12		
Czech Republic	1997	0.15	0.9	50	
Estonia	1997		0.6		
Hungary	1997	<0.1	0.4	27	2,287
Latvia	1996		1.3		
Poland	1999	<0.1	0.4	61	2,084
Romania	2002	0.28	0.37[a]	1,098	4,121[b]
Slovak Republic	1999		1.2 to 1.4		298

Source: Updated from Murthi 2001; World Bank 2002, 2003.
Note: Spending estimates include the cost of benefits alone and do not cover the costs of staff and other administrative expenses and institutional care.
a. 1.22 percent of GDP if including family allowances (0.69 percent) and social assistance for disabled (0.16 percent).
b. The number is 10,130 if including family allowances.

euro were allocated to Roma-linked projects across six candidate countries. After accession, support to overcome the exclusion of Roma and minorities is provided through structural funds and the EU's social inclusion process.

To address the particular issues faced by Roma, and to meet the EU's accession criteria, the Central and Eastern European countries have built institutions and passed legislation to address Roma issues. All Central and Eastern European governments have adopted Roma strategies and many have set up offices to coordinate policy development and implementation at the national level, including the Office of the Plenipotentiary for Roma Communities in the Slovak Republic, the Office of Roma Affairs in Hungary, and the National Council for Ethnic and Demographic Issues in Bulgaria.

Deinstitutionalization and Reintegration

Deinstitutionalization of social assistance services is an aspect of the inclusion agenda that is especially relevant to most accession countries because the logic of the old communist order led to higher institutionalization in these countries. The problems are especially acute in Romania and Bulgaria where deinstitutionalization became a critical part of the 2004 Joint Inclusion Memorandum and a political criterion of accession. Deinstitutionalization as a goal of accession is appropriate because institutionalized children face long-term difficulties with social integration and fall behind in developing both their human and social capital, easily leading to a cycle in which poverty and social exclusion are reproduced. Where problems with institutionalization are the greatest, Roma compose a high share of institutionalized children. Carefully crafted and well-supervised family or community alternatives are needed to reverse old practices. The accession process has already helped Bulgaria and Romania adopt child care standards and legislation from existing member states through successful twinning arrangements (Bulgaria with Austria and the United Kingdom; Romania with France, the Netherlands and Spain). Other new member states such as Hungary are EU-wide leaders in finding new community-based and foster care solutions.

The integration of people living with disabilities is another part of the inclusion agenda that will affect the provision of social assistance services in the new member states. As examined in the beginning of this chapter, in the old communist order, social assistance cases were kept in check by referring people who deviated from the average and were not fully capable of work in the rudimentary industrial structures of the times to certain categories of treatment, many of them to disability. A stepped-up effort for reintegration is taking place in all new member states in line with EU best practices, which themselves are changing rapidly. This intensifies the burden on social services in the accession countries because it is increasingly no longer acceptable to keep people with disabilities disengaged from work and society. Disabled people are seen increasingly as potentially productive individuals who can participate in the labor force with appropriate policies and social support. With declining and aging populations and with the changing nature of modern jobs, and incentives to employers to employ disabled workers (for example, in the Czech Republic), disabled people are more attractive as a reserve to expand employment.

BEYOND ACCESSION: FROM POVERTY RELIEF TO SOCIAL INCLUSION

The fact of accession does not mean that the reform agenda for social safety nets is complete—far from it.

A changing world beyond accession

Chapter 1 argues that unfolding trends in family formation and decreased employment stability exert pressure on EU policies to include a more complex mix of public and private assistance arrangements. In addition, the cohesion of the extended EU requires that new member states grow at a faster pace until they catch up with existing members. To achieve these objectives, EU countries will need to develop their family support and social assistance system with the following main facts in mind:

- The income level of new EU members will likely trail the EU average for a long time.
- Catching up with the rest of the EU will require decades of productivity growth higher than the EU average.
- The new member states face the consequences of rapid aging at a significantly lower level of income than the existing higher income members.
- Migration will become a more important factor affecting the welfare system of the new member states, first because of the expected (modest) initial out-migration from the new members to the higher income old member states, and then because of in-migration to the new members from outside the EU. Catching up with the longer-standing members will require higher growth rates and higher growth will attract and require immigrants because the work-force of the new member states is aging in much the same way as that of the existing member states. After regaining pretransition economic activity rates, and even achieving the EU's targeted 70 percent activity rate, aging and low fertility will further limit expansion of the labor force, and economic growth will require an inflow of immigrants to the new member states on a large scale.
- The EU will likely pursue further OMC and convergence of welfare regimes to increase cohesion and improve the conditions for intra-EU mobility, but the predominance of national financing is not likely to change for a long time.
- The nature of poverty in the new member states will converge toward that of the old members, toward a "chronic poverty" profile as opposed to the large and relatively quickly changing pool of transient poverty that characterized the transition. These persistent "pockets of poverty" associated with unemployment, large families on the fringes of society, low education, and adaptation difficulties of ethnic minorities are more difficult to address and require a sustained effort for activation and inclusion.

Reform directions

Achieving higher growth would require less robust welfare expenditures for the new EU states to be able to harness more resources for investment. However, retaining and attracting productive workers is easier if a solid social protection system is in place—one that provides competitive benefits compared to other member states and the rest of the world. Workers in the EU will be increasingly likely to make decisions on where to work and live on the basis of a continuum of wages, associated social insurance, and family support arrangements and available social assistance fallback options. While there seem to be no easy ways to sever these Gordian knots, improved benefit design, better financing and administration of social assistance, family benefits, and social services are essential to maintain the momentum for higher growth in all EU countries and growth higher than the EU average in the new and poorer member states.

Improving benefit design

Improving benefit design includes:

- *Balancing active and passive measures.* Work incentives need to be built into social assistance benefits to minimize poverty traps. Possibilities include building in a work requirement, capping benefit duration, and introducing an earned-income disregard for calculating benefit levels. Active measures can provide an alternative to cash benefits. Activating most social assistance benefits could increase the effectiveness of the system but at a higher cost because efforts to bring social assistance benefit recipients back to work are expensive.
- *Encouraging improved local governance and community-driven development.* Policies that help local communities articulate their interests are consistent with the principle of subsidiarity that dominates social policies in the EU and that have taken root in the new member states, too, as social safety nets and social services have become more decentralized during the transition. The emergence of Social Development Funds (SDFs) in Bulgaria and Romania and matching grants with social policy objectives in Hungary reflect the desire for a demand-driven approach to social policy and service delivery. SDFs can have multiple objectives including increasing community involvement, building social capital, generating employment, diversifying social services, and so on. Projects supported under SDFs also take widely differing approaches. This diversity of instruments and practices could be made into an advantage as the EU offers various financing windows for communities.

Strengthening finance

Rapidly aging societies will require strengthening the financing of safety nets, which may involve new mixtures of public-private solutions, especially because of pensions and long-term elderly care. The future welfare outcome of pension reforms is critically important because if the new schemes fail to provide adequate pensions, various guarantees prompt the state to pay the difference (see chapter 5). These potential payments for shortfalls are part of the social safety net and certainly reduce the fiscal scope for financing other social assistance. Regardless of guarantees, low pensions from the funded or the streamlined pay-as-you-go (PAYG) schemes would likely contribute to a higher number of social assistance claimants or a bigger shortfall from the poverty line, increasing the need for social assistance payments. Other proactive arrangements to manage social risks would also make sense. In 2003, for example, the government of Hungary announced that it would levy a 1 percent payroll tax for long-term care for the elderly starting in 2004.[20] Rapid aging of the population certainly justifies attention to this social risk, and if left unattended, the costs will fall back to the budget, draining the financing of social assistance in the future. Social insurance appears the logical answer because there are many information and insurance problems for which private insurance markets cannot provide optimal solutions[21] (see Barr 2001). Increasing payroll taxes, however, reduces competitiveness. Furthermore, if funding is through a PAYG payroll tax, and the benefit is not carefully designed, there is a potential for moral hazard. People might forgo saving on their own for this purpose, expecting that a PAYG benefit will take care of their needs. They would also likely request more long-term care services if they perceive them to be acquired rights with no additional cost involved. The shortfall again would end up draining public resources.

An improved intergovernmental financing framework needs to be in place to ensure that responsibilities and resources match. Decentralization is an attractive option because it helps empower people and their communities and is in line with the principle of subsidiarity, a cornerstone of the European social model. However, an adequate corrective transfer mechanism should be in place to offset the weaker fiscal capacity of the poorer communities where the needs are higher, otherwise decentralization undermines the effectiveness of social assistance. When local governments fail to deliver social assistance benefits due to a lack of funding, options include full to partial centralization of financing (as in Bulgaria and Romania) of these benefits. One of the risks of fiscal centralization (or recentralization) is that local governments lose the incentive to target benefits, in that they are no longer accountable for managing costs. Another possibility may be to build in incentives for the payment of benefits through matching grants.

Increasing professional and administrative capacity

Administrative capacity to implement reforms has proved to be critical. Reforms of social assistance require a division between the administration of social benefits and the delivery of social services. The social care and social work profession needs to be revitalized for service delivery. Emphasis needs to be placed on training at the university and postgraduate level and on on-the-job training.

Improving data and information systems to monitor policies and outcomes is essential for the new members to fully participate in the EU's OMC for social policy convergence and to eradicate poverty, both for the credibility of their policies and commitments and to guide their policies. This requires a management information system to monitor social benefits, and regular and improved household surveys to assess poverty and social assistance beneficiaries.

Debate on the future of family support

Chapter 1 characterized the debate on the future social protection system of the EU as a choice between a parsimonious (or residual) welfare state with a correspondingly minimal system of family support geared toward poverty relief or a more fully fledged welfare state with universal family benefits.

Arguments in favor of the parsimonious approach

With higher incomes and a more sophisticated targeting mechanism in place, proxy targeting is no longer needed. Poverty can now be targeted fairly accurately. Any redistribution from families with no or few children to families with more children would introduce unnecessary distortions in income distribution by imposing higher taxes and therefore act against investments and productivity and would tend to undermine the competitiveness of the economies of the EU. Transfers for family support would increase reservation wages and decrease motivation for employment in a period when labor supply will likely be tight as the population ages. There is no evidence that family support transfers in themselves could affect birth rates in any sustainable way, so pro-natalist incentives are a waste of public resources. Furthermore, there is no evidence either that declining population would affect economic growth in any way that would justify public intervention. An older population will merely affect the relative prices of goods and services. Facilitating migration to fill service jobs (and for elder care), if needed at all, is a better option because it increases the tax base and the overall output of the economy, while family support transfers are bound to reduce output with no proven impact on labor supply. Because having children can be perceived as a freely made individual choice for the use of available resources, there is no reason for public intervention to compensate for having children at all. Consumption smoothing could be better served by providing access to credit and mortgages so that young people who elect to have more children can acquire the goods and services (especially housing, child care, and education) they need to raise them and repay these loans when their income is higher as they age. In addition, public family support tends to crowd out private intergenerational transfers, which is a suboptimal public policy choice. Finally, because the EU will need to secure sustainable and affordable pensions and old-age care, public transfers would be better used to target poverty and market failures in these areas rather than supporting nonpoor families with children.

Arguments in favor of a more robust system of family support

In addition to Lindert's (2003) empirical observations and the general case for well-designed public transfers,[22] there are a number of specific arguments in favor of family support. Because family size will always have an impact on the risk of falling into poverty, mechanisms for family support and family allowances could be used to neutralize the impact of family size on poverty, reducing the need of stigmatizing targeted poverty relief. Universal family benefits carry no stigma and guarantee a high take-up. Family support also acts to smooth consumption between various age groups. People receive family benefits when their children are young, and are taxed to finance these benefits for others when their children grow up. This consumption smoothing occurs because people have children when they are young and their wages (and taxes paid on these wages) are relatively lower.[23] Furthermore, the state may want to compensate for the cost of having children to reduce incentives for not having children, because a decision against having children involves serious negative externalities in a period of low fertility and declining population. Family support can facilitate higher labor force participation as well. Family support in cash can make private child care services affordable, or public child care can help lower-income workers stay in the labor force. For single parents, family support could be critical in facilitating access to labor markets, smoothing consumption, and for social inclusion. Family support could also be used to make a more equitable society. A well-provided for childhood leads to a more productive adulthood, so redistribution toward young families with children is an investment in future productivity. Indeed, one can argue that if a state strives for redistribution to create a more equitable society, universal family allowances are perhaps one of the least distortionary policy options available for achieving the desired level of redistribution because there is no withdrawal when income or work status changes. Subjecting family support transfers to progressive income taxation can claw back a significant amount of the benefit at the top of the income distribution. Providing some family support for higher income groups, too, would strengthen political support to these nonstigmatizing transfers and positively discriminate against the rich with children relative to the rich without. While family support should more than compensate for the cost of child-rearing to deliver an effective pro-natalist impact (for which evidence is scant[24]), at least neutralizing the adverse impact on consumption of having children could help families make a positive decision on childrearing.[25] This decision is critical in a period of high old-age dependency and declining population. Having children is, after all, not simply a consumer choice but a decision that affects the reproduction of society.

Family support is the fastest growing social protection expenditure in the EU, and family support is a robust system both in existing and new member states, indicating that it is likely to remain an important policy instrument for the future. Welfare regimes tend to exhibit a strong path dependency for political economy reasons,[26] and this effect could become even stronger in a period of continued rapid population decline in the EU. If this is the case, it is more productive to focus the public debate on how best (most effectively and efficiently) to deliver these benefits, rather than challenge them on the basis of an unlikely public choice to dismantle them.

While the OCM is not fully extended to family policies, a European Observatory on National Policies was established in 1989 with a mandate to monitor member state family policies. This institution was renamed in 1999 to the European Observatory on Family Matters and given a somewhat broader mandate. At the same time, the European Commission stated

> Social protection should contribute to reconciling work and family life: support for families and for the possibility to reconcile work and family life is not only a question of equal opportunities for women and men, but also an economic necessity in the light of demographic change. (Communication from the Commission 1999, p. 10)

Annex 4A. Roma: Europe's Largest Minority

Dena Ringold

Three brothers ages 13, 11, and 7 spend their days at the garbage dump in Rousse, a town on the Danube in northeastern Bulgaria. They cannot afford to go to school, so they scavenge for paper and other recyclables, earning less than US$1 a day—just enough for half a loaf of bread. Their father is in jail and cannot care for the boys, who live with their bedridden grandfather.

This marginal existence is extreme but not, sadly, atypical of Roma (or gypsies), Europe's largest and most vulnerable minority. An estimated 7 million to 9 million Roma live throughout Europe, nearly 80 percent of them in the countries that joined the EU in May 2004 and the candidate countries. The accession process elevated Roma issues through the Copenhagen criteria for enlargement. However, tackling Roma poverty and overcoming stark gaps in human development remain outstanding issues in the wider Europe.

Roma were among the biggest losers in the transition. They were often the first to lose their jobs in the early 1990s, and were persistently blocked from reentering the labor force—because their skills were often inadequate, and because of pervasive discrimination. Even in the more prosperous countries of Central and Eastern Europe, Roma poverty is strikingly high, sometimes more than 10 times that of non-Roma. In 2000, nearly 80 percent of Roma in Bulgaria and Romania were living on less than US$4.30 per day, in comparison with 37 percent of the total population of Bulgaria and 30 percent of Romania. In better-off Hungary, 40 percent of Roma were living under this line, compared with 7 percent of the total population (see figure below).

FIGURE 4A.1 Poverty Rates, 2000

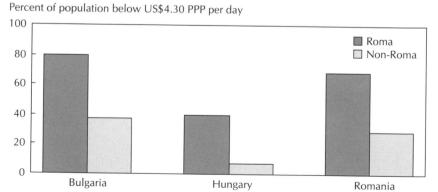

Percent of population below US$4.30 PPP per day

Source: Revenga, Ringold, and Tracy 2002.
Note: PPP = purchasing power parity; dollars are U.S. dollars.

Roma are locked in a vicious cycle of poverty and exclusion. High unemployment drives down living standards, leaving many to live in marginalized settlements without access to electricity, clean water, and other basic utilities. Lack of education keeps them out of work and limits their future opportunities. Most do not complete education beyond primary school, and few continue on to secondary school. Across countries, less than one percent of Roma participate in any form of university or post-secondary education. Of those students who are in primary school, many are stuck in inferior segregated institutions. Others are wrongly placed in schools for the mentally and physically disabled, leaving them ill-prepared for further education or employment.

Who are Roma?

Roma are a unique minority in Europe. Unlike other groups, they have no historical homeland and are found in nearly all countries in Europe and Central Asia. Current estimates indicate that between 7 million and 9 million Roma live throughout Europe, making them the largest minority in Europe. Historical records suggest they migrated from northern India into Europe in waves between the ninth and fourteenth centuries. While some groups are nomadic, the vast majority of Roma in Central and Eastern Europe have settled, some under the Austro-Hungarian and Ottoman empires, and others more recently during the socialist period.

A defining characteristic of Roma is their diversity. There are numerous subdivisions based on cross-cutting divisions, including family groups and religion. Ethnographers have identified 60 different groups in Bulgaria and similar diversity is believed to exist in other countries. In addition to ethnic differences, there is significant diversity among Roma settlements: rural or urban, assimilated or non-assimilated, as well as affiliations with different religious denominations. Some groups speak variations of the Roma language, others do not.

Estimates of the size of the Roma population differ widely. Census data are intensely disputed because many Roma do not identify themselves as such in the questionnaires. By most estimates, the share of Roma has grown to between 6 percent and 9 percent of the population in Bulgaria, Macedonia, Romania, and the Slovak Republic—shares that are likely to increase in the near future because of high population growth among Roma and decreasing fertility among the majority populations. Romania has the highest absolute number of Roma in Europe, estimated at between 1 million and 2 million. Large populations of between 400,000 and 1 million Roma live in neighboring Hungary, Bulgaria, the Slovak Republic, Turkey, and Serbia and Montenegro. In Western Europe, the largest Roma populations are found in Spain (estimated at 750,000), France (310,000), Germany (120,000), and Italy (100,000).

Roma and EU accession

Roma issues have become increasingly salient internationally since 1989, because of emerging evidence of human rights violations, and seriously deteriorating socioeconomic conditions within many Roma communities. These developments raised the attention of international organizations as well as NGOs, including the Soros Foundation and its network of Open Society Foundations. Perhaps most significantly, Roma issues have become an integral part of the EU accession process, because attention to Roma issues was adopted in 1993 as part of the Copenhagen criteria.

At the 1993 Copenhagen Summit, the European Commission included "respect for minorities" as one political criterion for the accession of new member states under the subchapter on "human rights and the protection of minorities."[27] This shaped policy toward Roma in the applicant countries. Based on the criteria, the countries of Central and Eastern Europe built institutions and legislative mechanisms, including passage of antidiscrimination legislation and the establishment of intergovernmental bodies, to coordinate Roma policies.

The European Commission's involvement in Roma issues is evolving, and accession has accelerated this process. With enlargement, Roma became the largest and most vulnerable minority in Europe, although institutional responsibility for Roma in member states within the commission has not been determined, with activities spread across different Directorates General, including Education, Health, and Employment and Social Affairs. There has been increasing demand from some members of the European Parliament and from Roma groups to appoint a focal point for Roma issues within the commission.

The commission's involvement in Roma issues has concentrated on three areas: the legal framework, including protection against discrimination; financial support, through resources from structural funds to member states for specific objectives; and a forum for policy coordination and cooperation. The EU provides support for protection of fundamental legal rights. This was most prominent during the accession process through work on antidiscrimination legislation. Roma stand to be among the main beneficiaries of EU legislation banning discrimination on grounds of racial or ethnic origin in employment, education, social security, health care, housing, and access to goods and services.

On the financing side, the new member states are moving from EU support provided through the enlargement process, to the general support mechanisms available to all member states. In the candidate countries, the main channel for

EU support for Roma-related activities has been the PHARE program.[28] Between 1993 and 1999, 20 million euro were allocated to Roma-linked projects across six candidate countries (EC Directorate General for Enlargement 1999). The total amount of PHARE funding allocated for financing Roma projects in candidate countries has risen from 11.7 million euro in 1999 to 31.4 million in 2001 (EC Directorate General for Enlargement 2002). Other parts of the EU provide smaller levels of support, including some education initiatives coordinated by the Directorate General of Education.

With accession, the new member states have access to Structural and Cohesion funds. While Roma are not explicitly mentioned in programming criteria for these funds, Roma communities will receive resources through the instruments to improve social inclusion and strengthen local development. Structural funds are targeted to underdeveloped regions, and include objectives such as combating inequalities and discrimination in the labor market, and rural development through local initiatives. For 2004–2006, the total amount programmed through the structural funds for all objectives for the 10 new member states was 15 billion euro. Bulgaria and Romania will continue to have access to PHARE resources until their expected accession in 2007.

A major challenge for the new member states, and for Roma communities in particular, will be to strengthen the capacity of local communities to identify and propose successful projects for funding, and to implement them according to EU procedures and processes. Some training programs have been initiated, but the process will take time.

The European dimension of Roma poverty provides a useful framework for policy. First, Roma are not poor only in Central and Eastern Europe, suffering from serious poverty and exclusion also in Western Europe. Second, the process of European integration offers a unique opportunity for addressing Roma poverty at a cross-national level. It also let countries learn from one another throughout the accession process. Third, because the project of creating an integrated Europe will not be completed when the latest accession treaties are ratified, the accession process offers an opportunity to institutionalize a long-term approach to reducing Roma deprivation in Central and Eastern Europe and to improving conditions for Roma in the older member states.

NOTES

1. The eight former communist countries that joined the EU in 2004 are the Czech Republic, Estonia, Hungary, Latvia, Lithuania, Poland, the Slovak Republic, and Slovenia.
2. Family benefits were usually provided through the workplace and they often looked like social insurance benefits. However, there were no or short work-history requirements

that families could meet with ease. Paid maternity leave was provided for one to three years with a reemployment guarantee in most new member states as opposed to six months to one year in old EU countries (see Dörfler 2002 and European Commission 2003).

3. Kornai (1980; 1992) provides the most penetrating analysis of the working of the old regime.

4. Almost all former communist countries tried to apply coercion to increase fertility. However, coercive measures, which included prohibition of abortion and contraception, achieved only limited results with large unintended consequences in the form of dangerous illegal abortions and a surge in the number of institutionalized children. As propaganda campaigns also failed to convince people to have more children, and as the more coercive measures were no longer possible in the somewhat more relaxed atmosphere of the 1960s and 1970s, communist authorities decided to introduce an increased set of incentives, including a large family allowance. More totalitarian regimes, such as in Ceausescu's Romania, maintained coercive measures until the fall of the regime (see Kligman 1998).

5. This large family allowance ranged between 17 percent (Poland) and 25 percent (Hungary) of average earnings, while in the EU countries the comparable benefits were usually below 10 percent of average earnings (Sipos 1994; Sipos and Tóth 1998).

6. While there were differences in housing practices across the former communist countries, access to housing was the most important determinant of family welfare differences after the number of children. In Hungary, for example, housing subsidies were equal to 6 percent of GDP at the end of the 1980s while the EU average was about 1 percent of GDP in the 1990s. For a discussion of socialist housing policies, see Turner, Hegedüs, and Tosics (1992); Renaud (1996); Hegedüs, Mayo, and Tosics (1996); Hegedüs and Tosics (1996); and Lowe and Tsenkova (2003).

7. Fertility dropped earlier in most accession countries than in the older member states of the EU and certainly much earlier than could be expected on the basis of per capita income. Some countries, such as Hungary, have experienced negative population growth for over two decades—partly due to a larger than expected drop in fertility and smaller than usual improvement in mortality.

8. This education philosophy was originally developed by Soviet educator Makarenko (1967) in the 1920s and was then adapted by the communist regimes in Central and Eastern Europe.

9. Palubinskas (2003) and Borsody (1993) provide a model and comprehensive analysis of how the Party-state transformed civil society to its objectives.

10. The evolving typologies describe four welfare regimes—liberal welfare, Scandinavian social democratic, Continental European conservative, and Southern European familiastic—with different sets of goals and policy instruments. For detailed discussions of Western welfare states, see Deacon (2000), Esping-Andersen (1999), Ferge (2001), Ferrera (1996, 1998), and Kazepov (2003).

11. There have been significant variations in the structure and operation of the welfare system in the Central and Eastern European countries and the countries of the former Soviet Union. These variations could possibly be explained by social and cultural differences among the countries that were embraced by the old communist order. With this repressive order removed as the most powerful organizing principle, these social and cultural variations have started to play a much more prominent role in shaping the new welfare system of the countries that emerged after the collapse of communism.

12. Deacon argues that because of "path dependency," the new EU countries are in the process of creating a new variant of the Western European welfare state that would combine a Bismarckian style social insurance with Scandinavian style state financing (Deacon 2000).

13. In the 1990s, the number of children in institutions grew from 1.1 million to 1.3 million in Central and Eastern Europe and the former Soviet Union (Tobis 2000 and UNICEF 2001).

14. Family benefits offset the labor market disincentive effects of other social policies (early retirement, disability, and so forth) only partially because the overall employment rate of the new member states dropped significantly during the transition (below 50 percent) and since the mid-1990s it remains well below the EU average (see chapter 3 and Tóth 2004).

15. Subsidiarity means that decisions are delegated to the level where issues emerge so that only unresolved problems are elevated to the next hierarchical level.

16. Social investment funds are instruments created to mobilize local communities to carry out programs that have high potential to improve local conditions. These programs usually have strong antipoverty components and mobilize the poor to improve their conditions. Increasingly, these programs are demand driven and represent an important bottom-up approach to mobilization and interest articulation.

17. Social administrators are trained to determine eligibility and to effect payment of social benefits on the basis of set criteria with no or little discretion. Social workers apply a holistic approach to each case of social assistance with a clear objective of maximizing social inclusion. In principle, social workers have a great degree of discretion in designing individual plans to return to work or for justifying income support.

18. Pressures to increase the minimum wages in the new EU member states can be expected with or without the introduction of an EU-wide guaranteed minimum income regime, driven by concerns about competitiveness, jobs, and migration in richer member states. Introducing an EU-wide mechanism for guaranteed minimum income subjected to OMC could be an effective instrument for increasing minimum wages in new member states.

19. Since 1989, the EU has provided support for Central and Eastern European countries. The main instrument through which this assistance is provided is the PHARE Program, under the responsibility of the Directorate General for Enlargement. In 1993, PHARE support was reoriented to focus more on the needs of countries applying for EU membership, including an expansion in support to infrastructure investment. In 1997, PHARE funds were again reoriented to focus entirely on the preaccession priorities highlighted in each country's Accession Partnership agreements. PHARE funding is distributed as grants rather than loans.

20. The government of Hungary later withdrew this decision because there was no public support for increasing payroll taxation.

21. Rapid progress in medicine will likely affect long-term care related probabilities in significant ways. However, both the magnitude and the direction of these changes are unpredictable. This high uncertainty usually leads to more expensive products and lower coverage in private insurance markets (see Barr 2001).

22. Lindert (2003) discusses and proves that there are five main reasons why arguments against welfare transfers are weak. First, the costly forms of transfers usually imagined have not been practiced by real world welfare states. Second, better tests con-

firm that the usually imagined costs would be felt only if policy had strayed out of sample, away from any actual historical experience. Third, the tax strategies of high-budget welfare states are more pro-growth and less progressive than has been realized. Fourth, the work disincentives of social transfers are designed to shield GDP from much reduction, if any. Fifth, there are some positive growth and well-being benefits of high social transfers in the context of how democratic cost control relates to budget size.

23. Family support thus appears more a "piggy bank" function of the welfare state—ensuring mechanisms for redistribution over the life cycle, rather than the "Robin Hood" function—the provision of poverty relief, the redistribution of income and wealth, and the reduction of social exclusion (Barr 2001).

24. Gauthier and Hatzius (1997) analyzed the total fertility rate from 1970 to 1990 based on aggregate data from 22 industrial countries, using a model that includes indicators of maternity leave (duration and benefits-to-earnings ratio) and child benefits in addition to other fertility determinants. Their results suggest that fertility may be positively related to child benefits, while there are no significant effects of maternity leave. Most evident is probably the effect of the so called "speed premium" in Sweden, which, as expected, has encouraged mothers to have their second and third child sooner (see Oláh 1996; Berinde 1999). This corroborates the earlier findings of Hoem (1993) based on individual-level register data. An interesting additional finding from Sweden by Oláh is that women are more likely to have a second baby if the father took parental leave with the first child, suggesting that features that encourage active participation from the father in child care may stimulate fertility. In Israel, fertility has increased substantially (from about three to six children per woman) among ultra-orthodox Ashkenazi and Israeli-born Jews. Manski and Mayshar (2002) argue that this pattern could have been generated by the joint effects of private preferences for childbearing, preferences for conformity to group fertility norms, and the major child-allowance program introduced by the Israeli government in the 1970s.

25. Catherine Hakim (2003) suggests the debts required to finance home purchase are resulting in women delaying childrearing. She surveyed 2,345 couples of working age in Britain about their work-lifestyle patterns and preferences. She found that two-thirds of wives paying off their own homes are working, with one-third working full time. In contrast, fewer than half of wives in public rented homes work, and only 15 percent work full time. But putting off having children easily drifts into permanent childlessness.

26. Kazepov (2003) observes that convergence appears to occur in the European welfare regimes within a framework of path dependency, i.e. at the level of parametric changes. If this is true, family support would likely remain robust for a long period of time even if the general direction would be a thinning of the system.

27. These political conditions were determined during the European Council meeting of June 1993. According to the concluding document, "membership requires that the candidate country has achieved stability of institutions guaranteeing democracy, the rule of law, human rights and respect for and protection of minorities" (Conclusions of the Copenhagen European Council 1993).

28. While having a special focus on Roma issues, some of the projects are not targeted solely at Roma, and may include other ethnic minorities or disadvantaged groups. As a result, these figures do not represent the amount spent *exclusively* in support of Roma. For a more detailed breakdown of PHARE funding for Roma by sector and project title, for

Bulgaria, the Czech Republic, Hungary, Poland, Romania, the Slovak Republic, and Slovenia, see European Commission 2003.

REFERENCES

Abramovici, Gérard. 2002. "Social Protection: Expenditure on Cash Benefits and on Benefits in Kind." *Statistics in Focus,* Theme 3—16/2003, Luxembourg: Eurostat.

Barr, Nicholas, ed. 1994. *Labor Markets and Social Policy in Central and Eastern Europe: The Transition and Beyond.* New York: Oxford University Press.

———. 2001. *The Welfare State as Piggy Bank: Information, Risk, Uncertainty, and the Role of the State.* Oxford: Oxford University Press.

Berinde, D. 1999. "Pathways to a Third Child in Sweden." *European Journal of Population* 15(4): 349–78.

Borsody, Stephen. 1993. *The New Central Europe: Triumphs and Tragedies.* Boulder, CO: Eastern European Monographs.

Communication from the Commission. 1999. "A Concerted Strategy for Modernising Social Protection." COM/99/0347/final. Brussels: Commission of the European Communities.

Communication from the Commission. 2000. "Building an Inclusive Europe." COM/2000/0079/final. Brussels: Commission of the European Communities.

Communication from the Commission. 2003. "Communication from the Commission to the Council, The European Parliament, The European Economic and Social Committee and the Committee of the Regions: Mid-Term Review of the Social Policy Agenda." COM/2003/0312/final. Brussels: Commission of the European Communities.

Council of Europe. 1992. *The European Social Charter.* Strasbourg: Council of Europe.

Deacon, Bob. 2000. "Eastern European Welfare States: The Impact of the Politics of Globalisation." *Journal of European Social Policy* 10(2): 146–61.

Deacon, Bob, Michelle Hulse, and Paul Stubbs. 1997. *Global Social Policy: International Organizations and the Future of Welfare.* London: Sage Publications.

Dennis, Ian, and Anne-Catherine Guio. 2003. "Poverty and Social Exclusion in the EU after Laeken-part 1." *Statistics in Focus,* Theme 3, Eurostat, 8/2003, Brussels: European Communities.

Dörfler, Sonja. 2002. *Family Benefits in Selected EU Accession Countries: Poland, Slovakia, Hungary.* Vienna: Austrian Institute for Family Studies. English excerpts from Dörfler, Sonja. 2002. *Familienpolitische Leistungen in ausgewählten europäischen Staaten außerhalb der Europäischen Union.* ÖIF-Working Paper No. 30 (in German).

Esping-Andersen, Gøsta. 1999. *Social Foundation of Post-Industrial Economies.* Oxford and New York: Oxford University Press.

EC (European Commission). 2003. *Enlargement of the European Union: Guide to the Negotiations Chapter by Chapter.* Brussels: European Commission.

EC (European Commission), Directorate General for Enlargement. 1999. *EU Support for Roma Communities in Central and Eastern Europe—Enlargement Briefing.* Brussels: European Commission Directorate General for Enlargement, Enlargement Information Unit.

EC (European Commission), Directorate General for Enlargement. 2002. *EU Support for Roma Communities in Central and Eastern Europe—Enlargement Briefing.* Brussels: European Commission Directorate General for Enlargement, Enlargement Information Unit. http://europa.eu.int/comm/enlargement/docs/pdf/brochure_roma_may2002.pdf.

EC (European Commission), Directorate General for Employment and Social Affairs. 2002. *Family Benefits and Family Policies in Europe.* Brussels: European Commission Directorate General for Employment and Social Affairs.

Eurostat. 2003a. *European Social Statistics: Social Protection—Expenditures and Receipts 1991–2000.* Luxembourg: Eurostat.

Eurostat. 2003b. *Social Protection: Cash Family Benefits in Europe.* Theme 3—19/2003, Luxembourg: Eurostat.

Eurostat. 2003c. http://europa.eu.int/comm/eurostat/.

Ferge, Zsuzsa. 2001. "Welfare and 'Ill-Fare' Systems in Central Eastern Europe." In *Globalization and European Welfare States: Challenges and Change,* eds. R. Skyes, B. Palier, and P. Prior. Houndmills-Basingstoke, Hampshire: Palgrave Publishers Ltd.

Ferrera, Maurizio. 1996. "A New Social Contract? The Four Social Europes: Between Universalism and Selectivity." Working paper, European University Institute, Florence.

Ferrera, Maurizio. 1998. "The Four Social Europes: Between Universalism and Selectivity." In *The Future of the European Welfare State: A New Social Contract?* eds. M. Rhodes and Y. Many. Basingstoke: Macmillan.

Ferrera, Maurizio, and Martin Rhodes. 2000. "Recasting European Welfare States: An Introduction." *West European Politics,* Special Issue on Recasting European Welfare States 23(2): 1–10.

Fox, Louise. 2003. "Safety Nets in Transition Economies: A Primer." Social Protection Discussion Paper Series No. 0306. Washington, DC: World Bank.

Gauthier, A. H., and J. Hatzius. 1997. "Family Benefits and Fertility: An Econometric Analysis." *Population Studies* 51(3): 295–306.

Hakim, Catherine. 2003. *Models of the Family in Modern Societies.* Aldershot, UK and Burlington, MA: Ashgate.

Hegedüs, J., and I. Tosics. 1996. "Housing in Transition." In *Housing Policy in Europe,* ed. P. Balchin. New York: Routledge.

Hegedüs, J., S. Mayo, and I. Tosics. 1996. "Transition of the Housing Sector in East-Central European Countries." *Review of Urban and Regional Studies* 11(1): 101–36.

Hoem, J. M. 1993. "Public Policy as the Fuel of Fertility." *Acta Sociologica* 36(1): 19–31.

Jenkins, Robert M. 1999. "The Role of the Hungarian Nonprofit Sector in Postcommunist Social Policy." In *Left Parties and Social Policy in Postcommunist Europe,* eds. L. J. Cook, M. A. Orenstein, and M. Rueschemeyer. Boulder, CO: Westview Press.

Kazepov, Yuri. 2003. "Local Policies Against Poverty: The Role of Social Assistance and Activation Measures in Europe." Institute of Sociology, University of Urbino.

Kligman, Gail. 1998. *The Politics of Duplicity: Controlling Reproduction in Ceausescu's Romania.* Los Angeles: University of California Press.

Kornai, János. 1980. *Economics of Shortage.* Amsterdam: North Holland.

———. 1992. *The Socialist System: The Political Economy of Communism.* Princeton: Princeton University Press; and Oxford: Oxford University Press.

———. 1995. *Highway and Byways: Studies on Socialist Reform and Post-Socialist Transition.* Cambridge: MIT Press.

Lindert, Peter. 2003. "Why the Welfare State Looks Like a Free Lunch." NBER Working Papers No. w9869, National Bureau of Economic Research, Cambridge, MA.

Lowe, S., and S. Tsenkova, eds. 2003. *Housing Change in Central and Eastern Europe.* Aldershot: Ashgate Publishing Limited.

Makarenko, Anton. 1967. *The Collective Family: A Handbook for Russian Parents.* Garden City, NY: Anchor Books, Doubleday & Company Inc.

Manski, Charles F., and Mayshar Joram. 2002. "Private and Social Incentives for Fertility: Israeli Puzzles." NBER Working Papers No. w8984, National Bureau of Economic Research, Cambridge, MA.

Milanovic, Branko. 1998. *Income, Inequality and Poverty during the Transition from Planned to Market Economy.* Washington, DC: World Bank.

Murthi, M. 2001. "Minimum Income Systems and Social Assistance in EU Accession Countries: An Overview." Paper prepared for the International Seminar on "Improving Minimum Income Systems in the EU." February 9–10, 2001, Faculty Club, Leuven, Belgium.

Oláh, Livia, Sz. 1996. "The Impact of Public Policies on the Second-Birth Rates in Sweden: a Gender Perspective." *Stockholm Research Reports in Demography,* no.98., Stockholm University, Stockholm.

Palubinskas, Ginta T. 2003. "Democratization: The Development of Non-Governmental Organizations (NGOs) in Central and Eastern Europe." *Public Administration and Management: An Interactive Journal* 8(3) www.pamij.com.

Ravallion, Martin, and Michael Lokshin. 1999. "Subjective Economic Welfare." Development Research Group Working Paper 2106, World Bank, Washington, DC.

Renaud, Bertrand. 1996. "Housing Finance in Transition Economies." Policy Research Working Paper 1565, World Bank, Washington, DC.

Revenga, A., D. Ringold, and W. M. Tracy. 2002. "Poverty and Ethnicity: A Cross-Country Study of Roma Poverty in Central Europe." World Bank Technical Paper No. 531, World Bank, Washington, DC.

Ringold, Dena, Mitchell A. Orenstein, and Erika Wilkens. 2005. *Roma in Expanding Europe: Breaking the Poverty Cycle.* Washington, DC: World Bank.

Sipos, Sándor. 1994. "Family Benefits and Social Assistance." In *Labor Markets and Social Policies: The Transition and Beyond,* ed. N. Barr, Washington, DC: Oxford University Press for the World Bank.

Sipos, Sándor. 2004. "Integrating and Empowering the Poor and the Excluded: The Roma and Other Pockets of Poverty." Washington, DC: World Bank.

Sipos, Sándor, and István György Tóth. 1998. "Poverty Alleviation: Social Assistance and Family Benefits." In *Public Finance Reform during the Transition: The Experience of Hungary,* eds. Lajos Bokros and Jean-Jacques Dethier, Washington, DC: World Bank.

Sotiropoulos, Dimitri. 2004. "After the Transition: Poverty, Inequalities and Welfare Systems in Eastern Europe." *Italian Journal of Social Policy* 1(1).

Tobis, David. 2000. *Moving from Residential Institutions to Community-Based Social Services in Central and Eastern Europe and the Former Soviet Union.* Washington, DC: The World Bank.

Tóth, István György. 2004. "Assessing the Effects of Economic Transition on Income Distribution: The Case of Hungary, 1987–2001." Paper presented at the Fifth Annual Global Development Conference "Understanding Reform," New Delhi, India, January 28, 2004.

Turner, B., J. Hegedüs, and I. Tosics. 1992. *The Reform of Housing in Eastern Europe and the Soviet Union.* New York: Routledge.

UNDP (United Nations Development Programme). 2002. "The Roma in Central and Eastern Europe: Avoiding the Dependency Trap." A Regional Human Development Report, Bratislava: UNDP Regional Bureau for Europe and the Commonwealth of Independent States.

UNICEF. 2001. "A Decade of Transition." MONEE Regional Monitoring Report No. 8, Florence: Innocenti Research Center.

World Bank. 2002. *Bulgaria Poverty Assessment,* Report Number 24516. Washington, DC: World Bank.

World Bank. 2003. *Romania Poverty Assessment,* vol II. Report 26169-RO. Washington, DC: World Bank.

$$5$$

PENSIONS

Nicholas Barr and Michal Rutkowski

T his chapter explores options for reforming pension systems, starting with
problems specific to the accession countries,[1] then extending to problems
that are generic to the wider Europe, and beyond. The chapter is almost
entirely about old age pensions. It omits disability pensions and the finance of
long-term care, both for reasons of space and because they are not of primary
salience for European Union (EU) accession. That does not mean that they are
unimportant.[2] Pensions raise highly controversial issues, particularly over the
best way to organize them. The chapter brings out the various disputes where
relevant, and the latter part debates different points on the spectrum of reform
options.

THE LOGIC OF TRANSITION: PENSIONS

The first part of the chapter explores the chain of logic that runs from the nature
of the inherited system, through the impacts of transition, to necessary reform
directions.

The inherited system

Pension systems under communism had their roots in two of the stylized facts
set out in chapter 1: the key role of the enterprise in finance and administration

of pensions, and permanent employment as the norm for most people. A typical pension system had the following features:

- Entitlement was based on formal employment in a state-owned enterprise.
- Records of contributions at an individual level were weak or nonexistent.
- Pensions were generous: the normal retirement age was low, it was possible to receive old age pension while continuing to work, and access to disability pension was relatively easy.
- The system was fragmented, with different retirement ages for different groups, ranging from miners and steelworkers to ballet dancers. For some groups, for example, miners in Poland, the early retirement privilege was combined with a more generous benefit formula than elsewhere in the system.
- Pensions bore little relation to contributions, and the entire pension contribution was paid by the employer. Both factors were distortionary, as this chapter discusses.
- Pensions were financed on a "pay as you go" (PAYG) basis, and administered by a specialized social security institution.[3]

As in other parts of the social sectors, these arrangements made sense under the old economic order.

Basing the system on formal employment in state-owned enterprises was logical, because formal employment was in effect the only employment, and there was virtually no unemployment. Almost everyone worked in state-owned enterprises, so this was a natural basis for organizing pension entitlement.

Individual contribution records were not necessary because, with full employment, it was reasonable to assume that every worker had a full contribution record.

The generosity of the system was logical, given the underlying premises. The low retirement age was a victory of socialism. Easy access to pension while continuing to work had two roots. Wages under central planning were low, hence not market clearing, reducing the supply of labor; separately, firms with soft budget constraints but hard output targets faced incentives to hoard labor, increasing the demand for labor. As discussed in box 1.1, these mutually reinforcing factors led to persistent labor shortages. Generous provisions for combining pensions with work were one response to those labor shortages.

Easy access to disability pension was another outcome of the prevailing incentive structure. The fact that the entire contribution was generally paid by employers, rather than shared between worker and employer, was seen as another victory of socialism. The problem is that if the entire contribution is paid by the employer, particularly when employers face a soft budget constraint, everyone—workers and employers—thinks benefits are paid by someone else; so neither workers nor employers have any incentive to economize on pension spending. This third-party payment problem is not unique to the communist system. As discussed in chapter 6, parallel issues arise with fee-for-service medical care financed by insurance.

The fragmented nature of the system resulted, at least in part, from undemocratic and nontransparent politics. Favored groups had lower retirement ages or higher pensions, or both, largely based on political considerations—journalists, miners, and school teachers, all powerful lobby groups, being examples.

The distortionary nature of the system was not surprising, either. Marxist ideology largely ruled out incentives as a legitimate way of analyzing society. Thus, little attention was given to incentive structures. Although the proper relation between contributions and benefits can be debated, in most of the communist countries they were unrelated and, given the fragmented nature of the system, often with arbitrary variation across different groups of workers. On top of this, the entire contribution was paid by the employer. In a market economy this should not matter, because the incidence of the contribution would be shared between worker and employer.[4] In the communist system, however, the soft budget constraints created an upward bias in benefit spending. Thus, pensions with a distortionary formula giving no incentive to contribute were just one of many examples of adverse incentives permeating all aspects of economic life.[5]

The system was PAYG both for direct ideological reasons and because there were no financial assets that pension funds could hold. The system was usually administered by a specialized institution, and financed by payroll taxes paid to an extra-budgetary fund that was expected to remain in balance.

The impact of transition

The effects of the early transition on the pension system were predictable.

Effects of early transition

FALLING OUTPUT. The economic shock described in chapter 2 had a profound impact. The decline in gross domestic product (GDP) of more than 30 percent between 1991 and 1994 (table 2.1) led to an almost equally rapid fall in the real value of a pension. The fall in pensions, however, was smaller than the fall in wages during the same period.

DECLINING CONTRIBUTIONS. Declining social insurance contributions resulted from falling output. Output fell fastest in the state sector, where most taxes and contributions had been collected, with two ill effects. The contributions base declined: open unemployment increased, and so did nonparticipation (that is, people dropped out of the labor force or, at least, dropped out of the formal labor force). In addition, the revenue yield from a given contributions base declined as state-owned enterprises, facing collapse, delayed or defaulted on contributions; the revenue yield also declined in the face of fraud. Thus, contributions from the state sector fell sharply. Employment and self-employment in the private sector started to grow, but tax enforcement in the early transition was weak or nonexistent, so contributions from the emerging private sector were initially small.

RISING NUMBERS OF BENEFICIARIES. For humanitarian reasons and to ward off political pressures, responses to rising unemployment included policies to allow older workers to retire early to make room for younger workers, and easier access to disability pensions. The retirement age, already low, was further reduced in the early years of transition.

Inevitably, these forces exerted downward pressure on the level of pensions and upward pressure on already high payroll contribution rates. The social security contribution grew from about 25 percent of payroll in the early 1990s to about 35 percent at the end of the decade.

EMERGENCE OF A PRIVATE FINANCIAL SECTOR. An emerging private financial sector was a somewhat later development. Stock exchanges were created, and life insurance companies and mutual funds developed. In markets that were often poorly regulated, some mutual funds and life insurance companies started offering products called "pensions." Private pensions are discussed in greater detail later in the chapter.

Resulting problems

Pension arrangements were relatively well suited to the old economic order, characterized by stable employment in state-owned enterprises facing soft budget constraints. For precisely that reason the system was systematically ill suited to a market economy, where a person may work in the public sector, or in the private sector, or may be self-employed; where people may experience periods of unemployment or nonparticipation; and where enterprises operate in a competitive environment and thus face hard budget constraints. The resulting problems were not surprising.[6]

HIGH PENSION SPENDING. Pension spending was high for several reasons. First, pensions were generous, in the early transition offering a high replacement rate (that is, a generous ratio of benefits to earnings). Second, the retirement age was low and in many cases pensions were granted before retirement age was reached. In Poland in 1990, for example, one-third of expenditure on old age pensions was on individuals below normal pensionable age. Third, combining pension with work was easy, and in some countries years of work *while receiving pension* counted as years of service, adding to pension entitlement. As noted, these arrangements are understandable given pervasive labor shortages, but their cost was high.

Disability pensioners and recipients of benefits connected with work injury and occupational diseases benefits were also numerous. Safety at work was a neglected area, so many people had genuine and serious health problems. In addition, as with pensions, access to benefits was relatively easy, in part because the authorities typically had little power to police entitlement. Rising unemployment added further to the number of invalidity pensioners, as a humane way of allowing older workers, in effect, to retire early.

LOW PENSIONS. The logic is compelling: a low retirement age and unpoliced access to disability pensions led to large numbers of beneficiaries, leading to high pension spending, and in turn to downward pressure on pensions generally and on the minimum pension in particular. The effect of the low retirement age was like trying to spread a small piece of butter onto a huge slice of bread.

The problem arose, more specifically, because the minimum pension was often not tied to a poverty line (because communism denied the existence of poverty, there was no official poverty line), but to the average wage or the minimum wage. With minimum pension tied to the average wage, it fell if real wages fell, which is exactly what happened during the early transition. Indeed, the whole purpose of the incomes policies that often accompanied the early transition was to ensure that wages did not rise as fast as prices. In cases where the minimum pension was linked to the minimum wage, the minimum wage always became highly political, and when subsidies on basic commodities were being reduced, the level of the minimum pension was politicized even further.

High pension spending combined with low pensions illustrates graphically the systemic problem of ineffective targeting discussed in chapter 1. Problems did not stop there.

ADVERSE INCENTIVES. The large payroll deduction that paid for benefits created problems both before and after the start of the reforms. As noted earlier, the third-party payment incentive created upward pressure on benefit spending when enterprises faced soft budget constraints; and when enterprises started to face hard budget constraints as reforms started to take hold, the high rate of deduction adversely affected their solvency and thus their ability to compete internationally.

UNDERPOWERED ADMINISTRATION. The use of enterprises as the primary vehicle for collecting pension contributions and for administering some other benefits (family allowances, for example) made sense in a world with stable employment and soft budget constraints, but could not readily extend to private firms and self-employed workers, or to a regime with hard budget constraints. State administration of benefits, however, was woefully underpowered during the early transition: records were generally of the pencil-and-paper variety[7]; and the main method of getting pensions to recipients was cash through the postal system.

Few countries kept records of individual social insurance contributions—with full employment it was reasonable to assume that on retirement everyone had fully contributed. Individuals approaching retirement, with help from their employer, assembled a dossier of their entire work history to establish their contribution record. Such arrangements are clearly incompatible with an economy in which workers change jobs frequently and experience periods of unemployment.

Resulting reform directions

Reform directions in the early transition were those that made the pension system compatible with a market economy.

Early transition

WEATHERING THE SHOCK. An early step was to index pensions to cope with high inflation. Initially pensions were tied to changes in wages, thus protecting pensioners' incomes relative to those of workers. When real wages started to fall, many countries moved to ad hoc indexation and then to price indexation to protect pensioners against erosion of their living standards. Some countries (Latvia) introduced flat-rate pensions, that is, the same pension for everyone, as a transitory measure during a period of high inflation.

Other reforms began somewhat later, with a longer time horizon.

IMPROVING INCENTIVES. It was essential to improve incentives, both to limit labor market distortions and to reduce the number of pensioners. After the initial shock, policies included increasing the number of years used to calculate pension entitlement (not basing pension on final salary, for example), and moving toward a higher pensionable age, the same for men and women. Latvia went the farthest by introducing a notional defined contribution (NDC) pension system in 1996 in which benefits (once the system is fully phased in) will be linked to lifetime contributions and life expectancy at retirement age. See box 5.1 for a brief description of NDC pensions.

BOX 5.1 Notional Defined Contribution Pensions

Notional Defined Contribution (NDC) pensions have four central elements:

- A contribution of some percent of a person's earnings is credited to a notional individual account, that is, the state "pretends" that there is an accumulation of financial assets.
- The cumulative contents of the account are credited periodically with a notional interest rate, usually equal to the rate of growth of total wages, WL in equation 5.1 (see page 151).
- At retirement the notional account is converted into an annuity.
- The value of a person's annuity is calculated on the basis of his or her accumulation of notional capital and on the cohort's life expectancy at the age of retirement.

Thus, NDC pensions are organized on a PAYG basis, but mimic defined-contribution pensions in that benefits bear an actuarial relationship to contributions.

STRENGTHENING ADMINISTRATION. Reform directions included, first, increasing contribution revenues by starting to build institutions capable of collecting contributions cost effectively from private and public employers and from self-employed workers. Second, such systems had to be able to maintain individual contribution records and to accommodate flexible work arrangements (a mixture of employment and self-employment, for example). New management and information systems had to be built to support these collection and recordkeeping requirements.

ENSURING POLITICAL SUSTAINABILITY OF REFORM. The great political challenge was to break the vicious circle of lower expected pensions and decreasing contribution compliance. Future pensioners needed to see that there was a "light at the end of the tunnel," and the government needed to provide reassurance by restoring their belief in the sustainability of the system. This partly explains the popularity of funded pensions and notional defined contribution systems, described later in this chapter.

Second wave reform directions

The countries of Central and Eastern Europe faced economic, administrative, and political challenges; but they also had opportunities. Over time financial sector development in the advanced reformers opened options for voluntary private pensions. Because long-term savings products were offered for sale in all countries, irrespective of the state of financial market development, regulation of such pensions was essential—a conclusion that stands whatever position one takes about mandatory private pensions, discussed below. Thus, along with strengthening the administration of public pensions, another administrative challenge was to build the capacity to regulate and supervise financial and insurance markets.

In the most advanced reformers, financial sector developments, reliable institutions, a growing economy, low inflation, and other preconditions made it possible to consider adding a mandatory funded element to their pension systems. By the time of EU enlargement in 2004, such schemes existed in Estonia, Latvia, Poland, Hungary, and Bulgaria, their sizes ranging from 2 percent of payroll in Bulgaria and Estonia to 7 percent to 8 percent in Poland and Hungary.

PENSIONS UNDER ACCESSION

In parallel with the imperatives of transition, pension systems were also influenced by the requirements of accession. This section outlines the main drivers of change and includes a summary of the state of play at accession.

Technical preconditions

In the accession countries, pension regimes need to comply with at least three sets of conditions that apply to the economy as a whole—directly binding legislation, indirectly binding legislation (especially the Stability and Growth Pact), and non-binding cooperation under the Open Method of Coordination (OMC). Some external restrictions also apply, including international conventions.

Binding legislation

Binding EU legislation on pensions is limited, because social security lies within the competence of member states. Binding legislation covers the portability of pension rights as part of the free movement of people, the freedom to establish pension funds, and a directive on Institutions for Occupational Retirement Provision, a provision on capital movements, and procedures for the elimination of tax discrimination.

Indirectly binding legislation

Indirectly binding EU legislation derives from the Stability and Growth Pact. Public spending generally and public pension spending in particular should be compatible with fiscal sustainability, which is primarily a macroeconomic constraint. In this context, the pension systems in long-standing member states are highly relevant to the new entrants.

Public pension spending in the advanced industrial countries falls into two groups. Across the older member states, average pension spending in 2000 was 10.4 percent of GDP according to the Economic Policy Committee (2001) and 11.7 percent according to the OECD (2002). The comparable figure for the richer non-European OECD countries—Australia, Canada, Japan, the Republic of Korea, New Zealand, and the United States—was about 5.3 percent of GDP, roughly half. Within the EU, only Ireland (4.6 percent) and the United Kingdom (5.5 percent) had levels similar to the non-European OECD countries.

Despite their much lower levels of income, public pension spending in the Central and Eastern European countries was close to the EU average, and higher in Poland and Slovenia.[8] The only exception was Romania, at 5.1 percent of GDP.

The gap between the high- and low-spending countries is not the result of differences in the age structure of the population, but has three causes. First, the EU countries generally have a low effective retirement age, partly because of incentives to early retirement and partly because of past labor market policies that deliberately allowed older workers to retire early as a response to rising unemployment. Second, high pension spending arises because benefit levels, as measured by the replacement rate (that is, the ratio of a person's pension to his or her income when working), tend to be generous. Third, public pension spending tends to be higher in countries in which public pensions receive little supplementation from private schemes. As discussed in chapter 1, all three characteristics apply with even more force to the inherited pension regimes in the accession countries.

Nonbinding cooperation under OMC

The Lisbon strategy[9] highlighted the challenge of an aging population and its implications for sustainable and adequate pensions. As a result, the Gothenburg meeting of the European Council in June 2001 laid the groundwork for the application of the OMC[10] to pensions. The process of applying the OMC to pensions was finally launched by the Laeken European Council in December 2001.

OBJECTIVES. The process refers to three general aims of pension systems, which break down into several more specific objectives.

- *Adequate to meet social objectives.* Specifically pensions should help to prevent social exclusion, to maintain living standards, and to strengthen solidarity.

- *Fiscally sustainable.* Specifically, pension design should help to increase employment, to prolong working lives, and to consolidate public finances. Further objectives include adjusting the parameters of pension schemes and developing funded pensions.
- *Responsive to changing societal needs.* Pension design should foster labor market flexibility, gender equality, transparency, and adaptability.

THE PROCESS. The pursuit of those aims is organized as a collaborative effort between the Social Protection Committee (SPC) and the Economic Policy Committee (EPC) of the European Commission.[11] The EPC has developed a model to forecast the budgetary impact of population aging in member states. The first comprehensive results of this common forecasting exercise were published in November 2001 (EPC 2001), and the first set of reports from member states were submitted to the Commission in September 2002. The draft joint report written on the basis of these documents was adopted by the Commission in December 2002 and by the Brussels European Council meeting in March 2003. In its midterm review of the social policy agenda in June 2003, the European Commission emphasized that

> [t]he modernization of social protection systems is a crucial aspect of the reform of the European social model. The long-term sustainability and quality of social protection systems, particularly in the face of an ageing population, is . . . crucial. (European Commission 2003, p. 8)

For that reason,

> [t]he Commission is intensifying from 2003 onwards the monitoring of legislative and policy developments in the ten acceding countries with a view to ensure their best preparation for membership. In the employment and social area, this includes efforts with regards to legislation, social dialogue, preparation for the participation in the European employment strategy and in the open method of co-ordination in the areas of social exclusion and pensions. (European Commission 2003, pp. 20–21)

THE HOPES. The Open Method of Coordination is a step toward translating common pension policy objectives into national policy objectives and specific national targets, and toward the future use of comparable indicators. The tactic may lead to more robust approaches in the longer term, making pension systems more similar, despite being subject to the principle of sovereignty. This approach may be necessary given the scale of the problem and the power of supra-national reform if domestic reform faces the continuing political difficulties discussed in chapter 2.

External restrictions

Both newer and older members of the EU must meet a range of international standards, often deriving from International Labour Organization conventions. Convention 102, for example, specifies that the basic pension system should have a replacement rate of at least 40 percent. Because most EU countries do not have mandatory funded pensions, it falls to the accession countries to argue that such pensions should be counted for the purpose of fulfilling the requirements of the convention.

Eurostat plays an important role in this context through the definitions it adopts. Under current rules, mandatory private pensions are not regarded as part of the social security system unless most of the participants benefit from government guarantees to the private system; thus only *failed* private pensions (that is, those that are unable to deliver an adequate pension) count as social security. Whatever view one takes about pension reform, this cannot be right.

EU impact: Helpful to pension reform?

Chapter 1 asked whether EU conditionality was unambiguously helpful to transition. In the case of pensions, with little binding conditionality beyond the maintenance of macroeconomic stability, the problem of conflicting objectives does not arise. Indeed, the arguments in the next section suggest that pension reform in some of the accession countries has gone beyond that in the longer established member states.

The state of play at accession

Accession countries do not need to copy EU pension systems. They may have different systems in recognition of different initial conditions and a more urgent timetable for reform. However, they have to prove that their pension systems meet the objectives laid out in the OMC, that is, in broad terms, that they are adequate, sustainable, and support societal needs.

The status of pension reforms

It is useful to distinguish two approaches to reform—parametric and systemic (Rutkowski 2002). A parametric reform seeks to rationalize the pension system by increasing revenues and reducing expenditure, at the same time encouraging voluntary private pension arrangements. Policies to increase revenues include increasing the contribution rate (although counterproductive if taken too far) or action to enforce better compliance with contribution conditions. Policies to reduce spending on PAYG pensions all involve cutting benefits. One approach is to raise the earliest age at which a person is eligible for a pension, but without any increase in the level of pensions, thus reducing lifetime benefits but not the monthly pension. Other methods reduce the monthly pension, either explicitly or by making the indexation provisions less generous, or by curtailing privileges to particular groups. Policies to develop voluntary pension funds include tax advantages, tripartite agreements (that is, between representatives of workers, employers, and government), improved administration, and better public information. Parametric reforms of this type have been adopted in Austria, Belgium, the Czech Republic, France, Germany, Greece, and Slovenia.

Other countries decided on systemic reform, introducing a mandatory funded second-tier pension along with major reform of the PAYG pension and expanded opportunities for voluntary retirement saving. This approach, sometimes referred to as a "three-pillar reform," was adopted by Bulgaria, Croatia, Denmark, Estonia, Hungary, Latvia, Poland, the Slovak Republic, and Sweden. The parametric and systemic approaches are discussed in greater detail later in this chapter.

The distinction between the two approaches cuts across the divide between old and new member states. Both types of reformers can be found on either side of the disappearing fence. However, systemic reformers are more common among the accession countries and, in addition to those mentioned above, others may follow—Romania and perhaps Lithuania and the Slovak Republic. Among older EU member states, it is hard to find new systemic reformers.

Difficulties in reforming pensions

Attempts to reform pensions in Western Europe have often stalled because of strong political opposition to changes to what the electorate regards as an entitlement. State pensioners oppose any reduction in the generosity with which pensions are indexed and any increase in the taxation of pensions. Workers close to pensionable age oppose changes in the pension formula or retirement age that make the system less generous. Beneficiaries of special privileges defend their positions. Political resistance is particularly strong in countries with mature PAYG systems, where pensions are high and support for current programs intense. Thus, current and future beneficiaries object to proposals to diminish their actual or potential benefits and resist proposals for reform.

In contrast, some of the accession countries were successful in breeding "winners" in the reform process (often young professionals) who actively supported pension reform. Such support was strong, it can be argued, both because of the technical merits of pension reform in transition economies (see "Debates about Strategic Choices," below) and because the political economy of pension reform in those countries was more conducive to change. The inherited PAYG systems did not command the confidence of workers. Broken promises during times of high inflation in the early 1990s, ad hoc indexation, and a series of arbitrary changes in the pension formula left workers with the impression that the defined benefit formula did not contain much that was defined. At the same time, educational advances and rapid development of the financial sector strengthened a new group of young professionals who wanted to promote more radical changes in public policy, including pensions, believing that they would benefit from those changes, along with the majority of the population. This group was influential among younger people.

A new enlarged EU increased the exchange of information. Thus, the new member states offered interesting examples for the older member states.

BEYOND ACCESSION: LONGER WORKING LIVES?

Old and new member states face common challenges—demographic change, socioeconomic change, and changed labor market conditions. Some of the resulting reform directions are not contentious. Others, however, are controversial, in particular the debate between those who favor systemic reform—particularly a move to actuarial pensions—and those whose major priority is parametric change, in particular raising the age at which pension is first paid. In short, the need for reform is indisputable, but countries face strategic choices about the form it should take.

A changing world

Notwithstanding controversy about the exact shape of reform, broader economic and social changes make reform inevitable.

Demographic change

Keeping existing pension arrangements unchanged, the demographic component in pension spending will increase sharply as aging continues. The total fertility rate has been below its replacement level (approximately 2.1) in the West since the 1970s and in Central and Eastern Europe since the 1980s, with few signs of a rebound. Over the next 50 years, life expectancy is projected to increase by about four years for women and five years for men. Assuming an increase in the total fertility rate to 1.8 and a slower increase in life expectancy than in the past, the old-age dependency rate (that is, the ratio of pensioners to workers) in the EU-15 is projected to rise from 27.7 percent in 2000 to 53.4 percent in 2050. Projections for the accession countries are similar (United Nations 1998). Without reform, the effect will be roughly to double pension spending by 2050.

Of course, such a sharp increase in spending will not necessarily happen. Some reform measures reducing benefits per capita have already been enacted, with others under consideration. Separately, employment rates may increase: labor market policies could reduce unemployment; labor force participation by women may increase; and the labor force participation of older workers could increase. As a result of such policies, the system dependency ratios (the ratio of beneficiaries to contributors) may not deteriorate as much as the old-age dependency ratio.

On the basis of such trends, the country projections for 2000–2050 put forward by the Economic Policy Committee of the EU (EPC 2001) suggest that average EU pension spending will increase from 10.4 percent of GDP in 2000 to a peak of 13.6 percent around 2040, although with wide variation across countries (projected to fall from 5.5 to 4.4 percent in the United Kingdom, but almost doubling in Spain from 12.6 to 24.8 percent). This projected 30 percent increase in average pension spending compares with a pure demographically induced increase of some 70 percent.

Socioeconomic changes

Along with these demographic pressures, pension systems also need to accommodate socioeconomic changes, notably increasing female labor force participation, changing family structures, increased diversity of employment patterns, and the need for lifelong learning.[12]

FEMALE LABOR FORCE PARTICIPATION. Women's participation in the labor force has increased substantially in the EU countries in recent decades. In the communist countries it was substantial, but decreased during the transition. Although there are differences among EU countries (female labor force participation in 2000 was 53 percent in Italy, whereas in Denmark it was 83 percent, almost equal to the rate for men) a further increase is projected for all countries. Projections for the EU as a whole suggest that women's participation will increase from 67 percent to 77 percent, while that for men will remain broadly constant at around 85 percent. To date, changes in female labor force participation have been reflected in the pension benefit structure hardly at all.

CHANGING FAMILY STRUCTURE. Benefit rules largely continue to reflect the traditional pattern of a working husband and child-caring wife who needs a widow's pension to protect her old age. However, eligibility for an old age pension based on marriage is complicated by rising divorce rates (about 50 percent of marriages do not survive), particularly when divorce occurs in mid life. To ensure gender neutrality, eligibility to a survivor's pension has been extended to male spouses and the budgetary consequences addressed in some countries by restricting the amount paid, for example, through an income test. Only a few countries have yet established independent pension rights for spouses. In many, benefit traps for women still exist, that is, incentives work against a woman rejoining the labor market or remarrying if that would force her to give up her existing entitlement to a survivor's pension.

GREATER DIVERSITY OF EMPLOYMENT PATTERNS. More diverse employment patterns include a reduction in full-time salaried employment and an increase in part-time employment, self-employment, home-based employment, and temporary employment. Such trends can be attributed to constraints, for example globalization and competitive pressures, that make full-time employment less dominant than before, or to individual choice, including choices about retirement. Whatever the reason, people without full-time jobs tend to fare badly under many pension schemes, which are based on a model of full-time employment. Reform needs to accommodate diverse work arrangements.

LIFELONG LEARNING. Many pension schemes are still based on a strict separation of education, work, and retirement leisure. However, the need for lifelong learning requires pension arrangements in which mixing the three activities is encouraged, not impeded—for example, going back to college after years of work, bringing forward (retirement) leisure, or taking up work again after retirement (say, from ages 70 to 72). Such flexibility is discouraged in most pension schemes.

Changing labor market conditions

The debates about labor market flexibility are set out in chapter 3. Although greater wage flexibility and migration are necessary responses to a more competitive environment, it is open to discussion how far such reform should go. Although minimizing avoidable impediments to mobility is desirable, governments throughout the EU are demonstrably unwilling to harmonize tax and benefit systems. Within that constraint, pension arrangements should seek to accommodate labor mobility across jobs, professions, and countries. This requirement has not yet been met. In many European countries, different pension rules for public and private sector workers impede mobility between the sectors. Mobility across countries exists to some extent for public schemes, although in reality such portability is often only partial; full portability for corporate and voluntary funded pensions is still under discussion. Thus, the EU does not have a coordinated pension system, let alone the harmonized pensions that character-ize other areas integrated under a common currency, including Brazil, Canada, Switzerland, and the United States. These federations or confederations exhibit many differences at state or provincial levels (including taxes or short-term social benefits), but share a common feature—each has a retirement income scheme.

Less contentious reform directions

Some of the responses to these common pressures arouse little controversy.

Objectives

The broad objectives of pension reform set out in the Lisbon process are gen-erally accepted.

- Sustainability of pension systems is implicitly mandated by the Stability and Growth Pact, reinforced by demographic and competitive pressures, and by the Lisbon strategy, under which pensions should encourage employment, prolong working life, and consolidate public finances. However, agreement about the objective of sustainability does not rule out differences of opinion about how to achieve it (discussed below in the section on Debates about Strategic Choices) or about how to define it. Sustainability refers to the capac-ity to maintain a pension system over the long term; but, what matters for many purposes is total public spending rather than its pension component— if pension spending is thought to be too high one response is to advocate reduced pension spending, another is to seek reductions in other spending.
- Adequacy is one of the core objectives mandated by the Lisbon summit. Again, there is agreement in principle, but with room for debate about what an adequate pension means. The debate, in turn, will depend on two factors: first, views about fiscal sustainability and second, whether pensions are thought of only as poverty relief, or also as providing consumption smooth-ing. The Lisbon process, with its emphasis on preventing social exclusion, endorses the role of pensions in consumption smoothing.
- Among the mandates of the Lisbon summit are that pension systems must be supportive of competitiveness and core social objectives. The way pensions are constructed should assist labor mobility, support varied employment patterns, and accommodate more fluid family structures.

There is also widespread agreement on a range of policy directions.

Promoting growth

As discussed earlier in this chapter, the proponents of systemic change argue that a shift from PAYG to funded pensions will promote economic growth, an issue debated in the next section. Growth also derives from a range of other sources.

To illustrate subsequent discussion in simple terms, consider a balanced PAYG scheme, in which

$$sWL = PN \qquad (5.1)$$

where
s = the PAYG social security contribution rate
W = the average real wage
L = the number of workers
P = the average real pension
N = the number of pensioners.

Policies to raise output increase the productivity of each worker, thus raising W, or increase the number of workers, thus increasing L. Policies to increase the productivity of each worker include

- more and better capital equipment;
- improving the quality of labor through education and training.

Policies to increase the number of workers from each cohort include

- increasing labor supply, for example through better child care facilities and tax regimes that support part-time employment;
- raising the age at which pension eligibility starts;
- importing labor directly;
- importing labor indirectly by exporting capital to countries with a young population.

Changes in each of these variables cannot, of course, be considered in isolation. Raising the age at which pension eligibility begins increases L and reduces N; but with an actuarial system it also raises P. Similarly, any increase in output has to come from somewhere—longer hours of work, or more workers, or higher investment. These interactions between variables will be discussed where relevant. Equation 5.1, however, is not intended as a fully specified model of pension finance, but to highlight the larger forces and thus to help tease out policy directions that assist pension finance. Note also that these policies are largely independent of the PAYG versus funding debate in the next section.

Assisting sustainability and adequacy

Alongside the objective of promoting growth, other goals are to ensure sustainability and adequacy. Again, there is a range of options. The direct approach is to reduce future spending, PN in equation 5.1. However, excessive reliance on reducing P may aggravate pensioner poverty, thereby violating the adequacy objective, or it may create political pressures, or both. As argued in the later section on Debates about Strategic Choices, a more desirable policy is to reduce N by raising the earliest pensionable age. This approach, taken on its own, aims to keep taxation broadly constant, thus imposing the burden of adjustment on pensioners. It is important to be clear about what is not being said. Sustainability, however defined, does not mean that state pension spending should be minimized; nor does an aim of keeping tax rates broadly constant rule out some increases. However, as discussed earlier, pension systems in the transition countries generally absorbed a much higher fraction of GDP than in OECD countries, with projected spending incompatible with macroeconomic constraints such as the Stability and Growth Pact and with other claims on resources, notably those that increase output growth. Such levels of spending, if nothing were done, would require very high rates of taxation—with adverse incentives both for labor supply and for compliance with taxes and social security contributions.

An alternative approach seeks to finance higher future pension spending by reducing other expenditure. One way is to reduce public debt now; thus governments in the future would spend less on interest repayments, freeing resources for PAYG pensions. This policy levels out taxation to a point between present levels and those that would apply in the future in the absence of any policy change—a form of tax smoothing. The cost of change is thus spread across generations of taxpayers. Another approach is to set aside resources now, for example, building up a surplus on the state PAYG scheme. The three approaches can, of course, be combined, for example paying off some debt to assist fiscal smoothing, and raising earliest pensionable age to share some of the burden with pensioners.

Another option for containing pension costs is through Notional Defined Contribution (NDC) pensions of the sort outlined in box 5.1. NDCs are run on PAYG lines, but mimic defined-contribution pensions in that a person's pension bears a fairly exact actuarial relation to his or her lifetime contributions. The NDC approach reduces pension spending if it has the effect of reducing the overall level of pensions. Projections for countries that have introduced NDC pensions, including Italy, Poland, and Sweden, show that such reform, even if implemented slowly as in Italy, can reduce future deficits. As table 5.1 shows, Dang and others (2001) project that a shift to NDC pensions in those countries keeps pension spending relatively unchanged in the long run notwithstanding rising numbers of pensioners relative to workers.[13]

TABLE 5.1 Change in old age pension spending 2000–2050 in selected European Union countries

	Total old age spending 2000 (% GDP)	Total old age spending 2050 (% GDP)	Change 2000–2050
Italy	14.2	13.9	−0.3
Poland[a]	10.8	8.3	−2.5
Sweden	9.2	10.8	1.6
OECD average	7.4	10.6	3.2

Source: Based on Dang, Antolin, and Oxley 2001.
a. Includes old-age spending and "early retirement" spending (including disability pensions for persons over age 55 and preretirement benefits).

Encouraging labor supply

Overwhelming evidence indicates that badly designed schemes—public or private, funded or PAYG—create adverse incentives, both during working life and with respect to the retirement decision. However, over the decades, employers have designed pensions explicitly to keep their workers (to impede mobility) and to encourage them to retire early (reducing labor supply). Thus, there may be a conflict between the private objectives of firms and national objectives such as encouraging labor-force participation, the latter being a plausible objective given the pressures of population aging.

Accommodating demographic pressures

It follows from earlier discussion that a large range of policies to contain demographic pressures, especially longer life expectancy, are available. It is possible to

- increase output, thus increasing W in equation 5.1;
- reduce the average pension, P;
- increase the retirement age, thus reducing N and increasing L;
- take steps now to reduce future nonpension spending, making it possible to increase s without any increase in overall taxation;
- set aside resources now to meet future needs, thus avoiding the need to increase s. Policies under this head may include private pension accumulations.

Accommodating socioeconomic change

One option for accommodating socioeconomic change is to adapt pensions so that each spouse has his or her own pension entitlement. Another approach is through a tax-funded citizen's pension (box 5.2). A mandatory funded scheme requires joint life annuities, that is, pensions should cover both husband and

---

BOX 5.2 A Citizen's Pension

Although the primary purpose of pensions is consumption smoothing (enabling people to redistribute from their younger to their older selves), pensions also act to reduce poverty among the elderly, especially as they typically constitute a dominant source of income at retirement. A strong case can be made for a universal, tax-funded pension payable to anyone over a given age. Given the importance of increasing labor-force participation, that given age should be fairly high (for example, 68) and should increase over time to reflect increasing life expectancy.

---

wife. Continuing analysis is needed in this area (see Barr 2001, chapter 9 for an early start).

In sum

What do these alternatives for meeting accession objectives tell us about pensions policy? Three specific policy directions follow about which, at a strategic level, it is hard to disagree.

Take action to ensure that the state pension is adequate at a minimum for poverty relief, and does not and will not make fiscal demands that cannot be met. All of the policy directions discussed previously have a role in this mandate. Two points are fundamental. First, sustainability should not be regarded as important for theological reasons, but because unsustainable public spending reduces growth. Although there is controversy about the definition of public spending that is "too high," there is no disagreement about the principle. Second, if a state pension system is unsustainable, the *only* solution is to make it sustainable: privatization in itself is no panacea to short-term fiscal problems, even if it can be a part of a broader move toward sustainability.

Improve incentives. Pension design should encourage workers to comply with contribution conditions, ideally paying contributions throughout their working lives. It can also be argued (and is so argued in the next section) that population aging requires pensions that incorporate incentives to encourage later rather than earlier retirement. At a minimum, pension design should avoid inefficient incentives to early retirement of the sort described by Gruber and Wise (1998). NDC pensions are thought to have advantages from those perspectives, although they are not unique in that respect (see Barr 2005).

Introduce voluntary private pensions and regulate them effectively. Regardless of the arguments about mandatory private pensions, at least some people will wish to make additional voluntary provision for their old age. Private institutions should facilitate such consumption smoothing, perhaps with tax advantages to offer encouragement, but with a ceiling for such advantages for reasons of progressivity. In the interests of consumer protection in technically complex areas, it is essential that regulation is both well designed and effectively enforced. Enforcement challenges, in particular, should not be underestimated.

Debates about strategic choices

There is agreement about the core problem—acute resource pressures on pension systems—and about the policy directions in the previous section. However, there is considerable controversy of at least two sorts about other proposed solutions: do such policies really address the problem; and, if they do, is the cure worse than the disease? The controversy thus poses a series of strategic questions for both the older member states and the accession countries. The two groups do not necessarily have to make identical choices.

This section begins with a brief overview of the main debates. It then addresses what we regard as the central question: what is the primary reform direction? This question, which encapsulates the debate about parametric change versus systemic change, boils down to a debate about the balance between introducing diversity into pension systems, that is, introducing a mix of PAYG and funding, and concentrating on pensionable age. Both ends of the debate are explored.

The issues for debate

The following discussion is intended to illustrate the range of the debate and the flavor of some of the arguments, but with no attempt to survey the terrain fully.[14]

Writers who favor systemic change argue that a funded element has a number of advantages. These are listed below and then analyzed to see whether each stands up. Such writers argue that a move to funded pensions can

- contribute to higher savings and financial market development, thus assisting growth;
- reduce public pension spending;
- reduce distortions to decisions about labor supply and retirement;
- improve individual security by diversifying pension risks;
- make pensions less vulnerable to government failure.

How valid are these arguments?

Does funding necessarily increase growth rates? The argument is that a move to mandatory funded pensions increases a country's rate of saving, thereby increasing investment and thus output. Several counterarguments can be made. First, the link through saving to investment to increased output, although sound in principle, does not hold in all circumstances. Indeed, the experience of communism in its latter days is a striking demonstration that high rates of investment do not necessarily lead to high growth rates. What matters is the quality of the decisions connecting saving with productive investment. Additionally, funding does not necessarily increase saving: people may respond to a mandatory requirement to save through funded pensions by reducing their voluntary saving (see Mackenzie, Gerson, and Cuevas 1997; Gale 1998).

As discussed in box 5.3, one of the central variables is future output. PAYG and funding are both financial mechanisms for organizing claims on that output. Thus, it should not be surprising that both fare similarly in the face of output shocks. Because future output is uncertain, all pension schemes face uncertainty.

A separate way in which a move to funding could enhance growth is through its contribution to financial market development (Holzmann 1999). This argument is relevant to the accession countries, which had undeveloped financial markets at the start of transition. Pension funds in those countries quickly became major financial institutions and generated demand for other financial services and for a well functioning regulatory framework. This argument may apply in countries capable of putting into place such regulation, but with two potential caveats. First, policy makers should not underestimate the importance of sound regulation, nor the challenge it poses. Second, introducing mandatory pensions in countries in which financial markets are still developing is not without risk—different countries will have differing attitudes toward such risk.

Does private funding necessarily reduce public pension spending? The argument is that if people save for their old age through private schemes, it becomes possible to change the balance of pension finance from public toward private, reducing public pension spending. This is, of course, an option in steady state, when private pensions are mature.

Introducing funding, however, is not easy. The transition to funding makes explicit the implicit debt of unfunded schemes, deriving from the original gift to the start-up generation. A move to funding makes it necessary to repay that debt by continuing to pay benefits to those currently entitled to a PAYG pension, while allowing workers to make contributions to funded

BOX 5.3 The Simple Economics of Pensions

The economics of pensions can be confusing because the literature tends to focus on financial aspects such as analysis of portfolios of financial assets. Discussion here simplifies matters by concentrating on the essential economic issues—the production and consumption of goods and services.

There are two (and only two) ways of seeking security in old age (Barr 2001). It is possible, first, to *store current production* by storing part of current output for future use. Although this is the only way Robinson Crusoe could guarantee consumption in retirement, the method in practice has major inefficiencies: it is costly; it does not deal with uncertainty, for example, about how one's tastes or constraints might change; and it cannot be applied to services deriving from human capital, medical services being a particularly important example. With few exceptions, organizing pensions by storing current production on a large scale is therefore not a realistic option.

The alternative is for individuals to exchange current production for a *claim on future production.* There are two broad ways in which a worker might do this: by saving part of wages each week, the worker could build up a pile of *money* (or other assets) which he or she would exchange for goods produced by younger people after retirement; or the worker could obtain a *promise*—from his or her children, or from government—that the worker would be given goods produced by others after retirement. The two most common ways of organizing pensions broadly parallel these two sorts of claim on future output. Funded schemes are based on accumulations of financial assets, PAYG schemes on promises.

Given the deficiencies of storing current production, the *only* way forward is though claims on future production. Thus, the central variable is the level of output after the worker has retired. The point is fundamental: pensioners are not interested in money, but in consumption—food, clothing, heating, medical services, seats at sporting events, and so on. Money is irrelevant unless the production is there for pensioners to buy.

The big issue is: are pensions safe? Pensions are about future entitlements. The future is an uncertain business. Thus, no pension scheme can be completely safe. Pensions are based either on promises (PAYG) or piles of financial assets (funded): in the former case, government can change the provisions of the social security act; in the latter it can appropriate the assets, either through policies specific to pensions (removing some tax privileges, for example) or broader policies (inflation, perhaps).

schemes. Financing PAYG pensions from taxation will involve one or more of the following:

- Reducing pensions (imposing the cost of transition on pensioners)
- Increasing payroll deductions (imposing the cost of transition on workers)
- Reducing other public spending (imposing the cost on citizens through reduced public services)
- Increasing government borrowing (imposing the costs on current and future taxpayers who have to finance the interest and repayment of principal)

To the extent that a move to funding increases output, there might also be an offset in the form of additional tax revenues. Some commentators argue that the most appropriate form of finance is through government borrowing, because future taxpayers will benefit from the new pension system. On the face of it, the increase in explicit debt is exactly matched by a reduction in implicit debt of PAYG promises. Several problems occur in this line of argument: it oversimplifies by treating explicit and implicit debt as symmetrical; as a practical matter, any decline in implicit debt is not an offset against higher explicit debt in conventionally cast public accounts; finally, and perhaps most fundamentally, funding pensions through increased government debt does nothing to increase savings and hence will not promote growth.

In short, introducing funded pensions in a country that already has a mature PAYG system will generally *increase* short-term budgetary pressures. If workers' contributions go into their individual pension accounts, they cannot be used to pay for the current pensions of the older generation.

A separate line of argument is that introducing a funded element might make it politically easier to make necessary cuts in excessive spending on state pensions. As Leszek Balcerowicz, the former Deputy Prime Minister and Minister of Finance of Poland, once put it, "I am not entirely sure whether our pension reform will really deliver on all its promises. However, as long as it gives me another serious argument to reduce unnecessary spending now, I support it."[15]

Do funded schemes always have better labor market effects? In discussing the impact of pensions on labor market decisions, it is helpful to distinguish two statements that are sometimes blurred: badly designed pensions cause labor market distortions, and fully actuarial pensions minimize such distortions. Although the first statement is true, the second does not follow.

Indisputably, badly designed pensions—public or private, funded or unfunded—cause labor market distortions with respect to both retirement decisions and responses earlier in life (see Gruber and Wise 2002). Both state and private schemes can provide inefficient incentives to early retirement; and many employer schemes encourage labor immobility (public schemes, being universal, do not have this problem). The bottom line is that labor supply depends on pension design, not on whether a scheme is private or public, PAYG or funded.

The second statement raises separate issues. Some writers argue that fully actuarial pensions, whether private defined contribution or publicly organized NDC (see box 5.1), minimize labor market distortions. Two questions follow. First, do fully actuarial benefits indeed minimize labor market distortions? They might—depending on the model—in an idealized theoretical world; but that is not the case in a world with information problems, missing markets, and other distortions such as progressive taxation (see, for example, Diamond 2002). Second, is the result optimal, that is, in a less than ideal world, is minimizing (as opposed to containing) distortions the correct aim? The argument implicitly assumes, for example, that all that matters is labor supply. What really matters, however, is economic welfare. It may be, for example, that a defined-benefit pension reduces labor supply at the margin; but if the loss of utility resulting from lower output is more than offset by the utility gain resulting from greater certainty about consumption smoothing, then defined-benefit arrangements may be welfare improving, notwithstanding reduced labor supply. At a minimum, the welfare gains from greater certainty should be compared with any costs of reduced labor supply. Thus, the argument that fully actuarial pensions are optimal is, at best, oversimplified.

Do funded pensions diversify risk? In recent discussions, the argument for an element of funding is usually based more on diversifying risk than on any intrinsic advantages of funding. The argument, known as "security through diversity" (Góra and Rutkowski 2000), is that a mix of pension arrangements does the following:

- Diversifies the financial base. Other things being equal, state schemes depend on the performance of the wage base (WL in equation 5.1), whereas funded schemes are based on the rate of return over time to financial assets, r. The reasoning is that if WL and r are not fully correlated, the standard risk-spreading argument suggests that a person can reduce his or her pension risk by holding a diversified pension portfolio, partly PAYG, partly funded.[16]
- Diversifies administration. Having experienced firsthand the political or policy risks inherent in public pension schemes, workers in the accession countries may be receptive to the idea of spreading their risks between public- and private-sector institutions.[17] However, gains from diversified administration (for example, greater individual choice) need to be considered along with the likelihood of higher administrative costs and increased regulatory complexity.

● Allows smaller countries to diversify their collective pension risks onto a larger economic base. Again, though, this argument should not be relied on too heavily. If, to reduce risk, a country (say Bulgaria) holds a significant fraction of its pension savings in, for instance, Germany, Bulgarian savings end up financing investment in Germany rather than in Bulgaria.

The argument about risk does not end there. PAYG and funded schemes are both vulnerable to macroeconomic shocks and to demographic shocks; and both depend critically on effective government, and are therefore vulnerable to political shocks. Private pensions face additional risks, including management risk: management may be honest but incompetent, or deliberately fraudulent. In addition, there are investment risks and annuities market risks. Under a defined-contribution scheme, two people with identical earnings histories may end up with very different pensions, a point painfully illustrated by the performance of the stock market in the early 2000s. "Benefits depend on the returns on assets (which are stochastic and with the right stochastic process in dispute) and on the pricing of annuities (which is also stochastic and also subject to dispute . . .)" (Diamond 2001, p. 76).

Thus, the risk-spreading argument is more complex than it appears: private pensions may or may not diversify risk; they do introduce additional risks; and any increase in funded benefits requires an immediate increase in contributions. Additionally, if one accepts the argument that funded pensions diversify risk, it should be clear that it is as much a defense of the state pension as of private pensions. Thus, the risk-diversification argument—which points to a mix of pension institutions—is logically incompatible with the view that the state pension should be minimized.

Does private funding reduce the risk of government failure? Examples abound of government failure in the form of PAYG schemes built on fiscally irresponsible promises, coupled with an inability to collect contributions. Results include inflationary pressures and political instability. However, private pensions are also vulnerable. They depend critically on a government's macroeconomic capacity, because fiscal imprudence leads to inflation that can decapitalize private funds. They depend equally on a government's microeconomic capacity—a major challenge is the design and implementation of effective regulation of financial markets and insurance markets, on which private pensions depend. Although such regulatory capacity need not be fully established at the start of a scheme, it must be in place soon after, to protect growing balances in people's pension accounts. While international diversification may provide some support to this end, the problems are not trivial.

A related claim is that pensions based on private property rights are safer from government depredations. It is, of course, true that governments can (and do) break their PAYG promises, and that private property is in principle better protected. In practice, however, without infringing on property rights or acting illegally, governments can and do appropriate part of the returns of pension funds, either by requiring fund managers to hold low-yielding government financial assets, or by reducing any tax privileges (the United Kingdom budget of July 1997 is an example of the latter). Indeed, it can be argued that PAYG schemes are less vulnerable, because the only pot of money is the current year's contributions, that is, the flow of contributions, not the stock; therefore there are fewer assets for the state or private actors to pillage than in funded schemes, where the stock of accumulated contributions is much larger.

It is also argued that political pressure to repair ravages to a state scheme are stronger than those to rectify adverse outcomes in private schemes. Ultimately the matter is empirical, but the counterargument is that the larger the share of the population with private pensions and the greater the fraction of pension income derived from private sources, the greater the political pressure on government in the face of disaster. In short, just as state pensions involve implicit debt, private schemes can rest on implicit guarantees.

The case for systemic change

The elements in the debate will have different weights in different countries depending, among other things, on differences in political preferences and in economic and institutional constraints. A central question for the wider EU is whether the arguments for systemic reform, that is, a move toward a multipillar system, or at least a switch to an NDC regime, are stronger for the accession countries than for the older members of the EU. The core arguments of the proponents of systemic reform include the following:

- Individual accounts strengthen incentives to make pension contributions. Although not a strong argument in the older member states, it is acutely relevant to the accession countries where enforcement of taxes and contributions is still being built up, in part because there was little or no taxation of individual income under communism.
- Under the right fiscal conditions, funding can increase saving and investment. Again, this argument is potentially more relevant to the accession countries than to the older member states, where access to borrowing is less constrained.
- Funded accounts can accelerate the development of capital market institutions and increase the efficiency with which capital is allocated, thus improving growth rates. Again, this issue is more pertinent to the accession countries.

As indicated, these arguments might be more relevant in the accession countries than the older member states. Savings in the former are scarce and capital markets not fully developed, suggesting that a mandatory funded element might yield greater benefits than in the older member states. The high share of informal labor markets points to the important role of incentives to comply with contribution requirements. The pension commitments in the accession countries are somewhat lower, making the transition costs smaller.

There are also political economy arguments. The desire in the accession countries to reach living standards closer to those in the older member states might create the political will for more investment and somewhat less consumption. Separately, parametric reform can create political difficulties because it requires governments to deliver bad news (in the form of lower current or future pensions or higher current or future contributions). A systemic reform, in contrast, can incorporate bad news for some workers (a less generous state pension) with good news for other (often younger) workers. Thus, a larger package that combines parametric and systemic reforms may be politically easier. That argument, however, is far from watertight. Under some governments, simple parametric reforms might be more credible.

Introducing a system with a mandatory funded element, however, carries with it complex challenges.

- Financial markets must be sufficiently developed.
- Public and private administrative and supervisory capacity must be sufficient.
- There must be a fiscally feasible strategy to deal with the transition costs.
- There must be sufficient political will to see through long-run reforms.

These constraints, however, should not prevent countries from improving both the poverty relief and consumption-smoothing aspects of their PAYG pension systems, or from introducing fully funded elements on the basis of collective agreement. Reform in Germany (lowering the level of the PAYG pension) may be a useful guide to other EU countries and to the accession countries that decide not to take up the challenges of changing the system.

The current trend—a more willing embrace of systemic reforms in EU accession countries than in older member states—may be explained by the former countries' desire to grow quickly to catch up with EU countries. To some extent, the willingness to engage in systemic reforms, which emphasize personal accountability, private savings, and so forth, is because the accession countries have undergone a profound crisis leading to a major ideological shift; the longer-established EU member countries for the most part have not.

Parametric change: The case for raising pensionable age

Equation 5.1 suggests that in a PAYG system there are four ways of improving the finance of pensions.

Reduce the living standards of pensioners (reduce P). Pensions could be explicitly cut, or the formula could be adjusted in more subtle ways, making pension indexation less generous, or a combination of the two. Reducing pensioner living standards is a valid approach, but taken too far it can create pensioner poverty (as in the United Kingdom in the early 2000s) and will be politically unpopular.

Reduce the living standards of workers (by increasing s). Reducing the living standards of workers has its own problems, first, because increased contributions can create adverse incentives—emigration is the extreme case—putting growth at risk. Second, reducing workers' living standards is likely to be politically unpopular.

Increase output. Output can be increased by raising labor productivity (increasing W) and by increasing the number of workers by increasing employment rates (increasing L). Higher labor productivity makes it possible for a smaller but more productive workforce to support a larger pensioner generation. Relevant policies include more and better capital per worker and additional investment in education and training. Funding of pensions, to the extent that it increases the quantity and quality of capital, contributes to growth through this route.

Raising employment rates can be pursued by increasing domestic participation rates, by importing labor directly (allowing more immigration), and by importing labor indirectly (by exporting capital to countries with a young population). Even a small increase in participation, if sustained over a period of years, can have a dramatic impact on pension finance.

Raise the age at which pension eligibility starts. Raising the earliest age at which a person is eligible for his or her pension, but with a less-than-actuarial increase in pensions, is a specific way to increase participation. Later retirement increases L and simultaneously reduces N—it is not double counting to include both.

With funded pensions, these four generic policy directions—reducing pensioner demand or worker demand, increasing output, or raising pensionable age—are equally applicable (although the links are more complex than equation 5.1 suggests). Because of its power and also because of its inevitability, the last policy merits more detailed discussion.

People today live much longer than 100 years ago—a wonderful outcome. Talk about the "problem" of population aging grotesquely misses the point. The problem is not that people are living longer but that they are retiring too early.

In considering the forces that drive pension spending, two issues interact:

- People are living longer; thus they receive a pension for longer. At a given real pension this increases the total cost of providing for each pensioner.
- The high birth rates of the late 1940s and the 1960s were followed by lower birth rates; as a result of falling fertility, the population is aging, raising the age dependency ratio.

It should be noted that longer life expectancy makes it harder to finance pensions even in the absence of declining fertility; the main effect of the latter change is to make the problem worse.

The first two policies to accommodate these pressures—reducing the real pension or increasing contributions—are useful instruments for marginal adjustments, but beyond a certain point have major costs in both equity and efficiency terms. On their own they are inadequate for a system with significant longer-term imbalances, either because of unsustainable past decisions, as in many of the accession countries, or because of demographic "blips." Output growth, by increasing the supply of goods, makes it easier to finance pensions. The relevant policies include reducing current consumption to finance increased investment in physical and human capital, and action to increase the supply of labor. Output growth, with some adjustments to contributions and benefits, can address small changes in fertility. Longer-term structural pressures because of sustained increases in life expectancy, however, are a different matter. To address rising life expectancy this section argues that the most efficient and equitable policy is to raise the average retirement age with less than full actuarial compensation, to accommodate aggregate resource pressures, but to offer choice over retirement, to accommodate individual preferences.

This policy direction is largely inescapable. The earliest pensions incorporated a retirement age that was old relative to life expectancy (65 in the 1898 New Zealand pension, 70 in the 1906 UK legislation). Life expectancy has increased on a fairly linear trend for about 150 years. As yet, there is no evidence that the curve is flattening.

There are two counterarguments to the proposition that earliest pensionable age must rise. First, countries are richer and can afford more leisure. This is true, but it is also true that with rising incomes, people have growing expectations about living standards in old age. Thus, the case for raising pensionable age arises where the combined effects of increased life expectancy and expectations about living standards in old age dominate growth effects. In the richest countries (see Diamond and Orszag [2004a; 2004b] on the United States) it may be possible to get by with adjustments to contribution and benefit levels. In most countries, however, the mix of growth rates, rising life expectancy, and expectations about living standards in retirement is increasingly creating fiscal strain. It is right to embrace increasing life expectancy with open arms, but wrong to believe in a nominal retirement age fixed at 65 forever. By the time that people live to be 110 (not that implausible nor that far away) they will work for 45 years (age 20 to 65) and then be retired for another 45. In most countries, therefore, along with the other policy directions, raising pensionable age is an inescapable consequence of increasing life expectancy. That conclusion stands independently of demographic trends and of arguments about PAYG versus funding.

A second counterargument is that it is unnecessary to increase the minimum pensionable age, instead leaving it to people's choices in the face of an actuarial budget constraint. If people live longer, the actuarially adjusted pension they will get at age 65 will decline, encouraging them to work longer. This would be true in a world of rationality and perfect information. However, if people have a personal discount rate higher than the interest rate used for actuarial adjustment, they will tend to retire as soon as possible, with progressively larger actuarial adjustments as life expectancy increases. In the limit, this pulls everyone down to the minimum pension—pensions may be able to provide poverty relief, but fail to provide consumption smoothing. One of the conclusions in Gruber and Wise (1998; 2002) is that many people retire as early as they are allowed. "The collective evidence from all countries combined shows that statutory social-security eligibility ages contribute importantly to early departure from the labor force" (Gruber and Wise 1998, p. 161). Thus, a minimum age at which a person may first receive pension is an important element in pension design.

As well as being good macroeconomic policy, raising earliest pensionable age also has advantages in terms of social policy. Not everyone wants to retire earlier. The 1978 amendment to the 1967 Age Discrimination in Employment Act in the United States was not a top-down measure motivated by budgetary control, but a legislative response to grassroots activism by people who resented compulsory retirement. In addition, the policy contains pension spending not by reducing living standards in old age, but by reducing the duration of retirement. Even those who eagerly anticipate retirement would generally prefer the latter option.

In operational terms, this suggests that a well-designed pension scheme should have five elements:

- An earliest pensionable age that makes it possible to provide a genuinely adequate state pension. This is the variable most under strain in all countries.
- A subsequent earliest pensionable age that increases with rising life expectancy in a way that is rational and transparent, so that people know long in advance when (in broad terms) they will be able to retire. Pensionable age should

not necessarily fully mirror rising life expectancy; pensionable age could rise by, say, six months for each year of extra life expectancy, or in some nonproportional way. The relationship between earliest pensionable age and life expectancy needs more detailed study. None of the OECD countries yet has such arrangements.

- An incentive structure that increases a person's pension roughly actuarially for each year that he or she delays retirement beyond earliest pension age.
- A flexible labor market that allows people to move from full-time work toward full retirement along a phased path of their choosing, and pension arrangements that support such flexibility. Final-salary schemes would need adjustment to make them compatible with part-time work.[18] Other options include allowing people who work beyond minimum pensionable age to draw, for example, half their pension, while increasing their pension entitlement for the deferred half (Sweden has such an option). The topic raises complex issues and, again, is an area in need of further study. This is uncharted territory, even in most OECD countries.
- Public understanding of the simple economics of pensions. This element is lacking everywhere.

CONCLUSION

What policies should the older and newer members of the EU adopt?
  Certain measures are not controversial. They include policies to

- improve the sustainability and adequacy of the state pension;
- improve incentives in connection with contributions and retirement decisions;
- introduce voluntary funded pensions and regulate them effectively.

  Three further sets of policies are more controversial:

- *Move toward a defined-contribution framework,* as the best way to improve incentives. The basis of this argument is the communist inheritance in which there was virtually no relationship between contributions and benefits.
- *Increase earliest pensionable age and put in place arrangements to support flexible retirement.*
- *Diversify the system by introducing mandatory funded pensions.* A core controversy is whether—and when—countries should introduce mandatory funded pensions, as opposed to the noncontroversial policy of introducing a framework for voluntary schemes. The minimum prerequisites are an adequate regulatory framework and sustained political support.

These various policy directions, both parametric reform and systemic reform, can, of course, be combined, with a greater or lesser emphasis on each. In summary, there is a sufficient set of noncontroversial pension reforms to keep European politicians busy for many years. It is likely, however, that some countries will venture into more controversial areas, building their own policy packages to reflect their individual country experiences and goals. Even if those ventures involve risks, as long as they also facilitate absolutely needed noncontroversial reforms, they will probably meet the minimum standard of a "good reform," as the experience of some transition economies shows. Ultimately, any reform will be judged in hindsight: a well-designed, well-timed, and well-executed controversial reform will over time lose its controversial edge; in contrast, a poorly designed, badly timed and ineffectively executed noncontroversial reform may eventually show the reformers as irresponsible. In the case of pensions, perhaps more than in other areas, the choices are wide.

NOTES

1. The eight former communist countries that joined the EU in 2004 are the Czech Republic, Estonia, Hungary, Latvia, Lithuania, Poland, the Slovak Republic, and Slovenia.
2. For fuller discussion of long-term care insurance, see Barr (2001, chapter 5). On disability pensions see Bloch and Prins (2001).
3. PAYG pensions are paid (usually by the state) out of current tax revenues. In contrast, in funded schemes, pensions are paid from a fund built over a period of years from the contributions of the members.
4. It is a standard proposition in economic theory that taxes are not paid where they are legally placed, but are generally shared between buyer and seller depending, among other things, on the relative price elasticities of demand and supply.
5. The point about incentives is fundamental, and explains why behavior that, from the outside, appears illogical was in reality deeply logical. For example, shortages under communism were endemic. As a result, the customer was the enemy of the supplier; anything bought at the official, controlled price reduced the stock available to the supplier for sale at black market prices. Thus, poor service was not the result of laziness, but an entirely rational response to the prevailing incentive structure.
6. For fuller discussion, see Barr (1994).
7. In 1990, social security institutions and local employment offices in Poland and Lithuania did not even have calculators, let alone computers.
8. Slovenia's pension spending, nearly 15 percent of GDP, vies with that of Austria and Italy for highest in the world.
9. See chapter 1.
10. The Open Method of Coordination is defined in box 1.3.
11. The two committees are composed of the top civil servants from the Ministries of Social Affairs and the Ministries of Financial and Economic Affairs in member states.
12. For more detailed discussion, see Holzmann, Orenstein, and Rutkowski 2003.

13. NDC pensions arouse both interest and controversy. See Holzmann and Palmer 2005.
14. Writers who are enthusiasts of a move toward mandatory, funded private pension arrangements include Feldstein (1996), Góra and Rutkowski (2000), and Holzmann (2000). For more skeptical views, see Barr (2000), Gillion (2000), Hemming (1999), and, in a United States context, Diamond and Orszag (2004a; 2004b). On pension reform in Central and Eastern Europe see the symposium in *International Social Security Review* (2001), Augusztinovics and others (2002), and Schmähl and Horstmann (2002). On Latin America, see Mesa-Lago and Müller (2002), and Gill, Packard, and Yermo (2005).
15. Conversation with Michal Rutkowski in late autumn 1996.
16. Correlation coefficients for time series of wage growth and equity returns were not significantly different from zero in Germany, Japan, the United Kingdom, the Netherlands, and the United States (Holzmann 2000).
17. This was used effectively as a political argument in the Polish reform, under the label "security through diversity." See Rutkowski (1998); Chlon, Góra, and Rutkowski (1999).
18. Suppose that at age 65 a worker moves to a less demanding and hence lower paid job, or moves to part-time work. In a simple final-salary scheme this would dramatically reduce his or her pension.

REFERENCES

Augusztinovics, Mária, Robert Gál, Ágnes Matits, Levente Máté, András Simonovits, and János Stahl. 2002. "The Hungarian Pension System before and after the 1998 Reform." In *Pension Reform in Central and Eastern Europe, Volume 1: Restructuring with Privatization: Case Studies of Hungary and Poland,* ed. Elaine Fultz, 25–93. Geneva: ILO.

Barr, Nicholas. 1994. "Income Transfers: Social Insurance." In *Labor Markets and Social Policy in Central and Eastern Europe: The Transition and Beyond,* ed. Nicholas Barr, 192–225. New York and Oxford: Oxford University Press for the World Bank.

Barr, Nicholas. 2000. "Reforming Pensions: Myths, Truths, and Policy Choices." Working Paper WP/00/139, International Monetary Fund, Washington, DC. http://www.imf .org/external/pubs/ft/wp/2000/wp00139.pdf.

Barr, Nicholas. 2001. *The Welfare State as Piggy Bank: Information, Risk, Uncertainty and the Role of the State.* Oxford and New York: Oxford University Press.

Barr, Nicholas. 2005. "Notional Defined Contribution Pensions: Mapping the Terrain." In *Pension Reform through NDCs: Issues and Prospects for Non-Financial Defined Contribution Schemes,* eds. Robert Holzmann and Edward Palmer. Washington, DC: World Bank.

Bloch, Frank S., and Rienk Prins, eds. 2001. *Who Returns to Work & Why?: A Six-Country Study on Work Incapacity and Reintegration.* New Brunswick: Transactions Publishers.

Chlon, A., M. Góra, and M. Rutkowski. 1999. "Shaping Pension Reform in Poland: Security through Diversity," Social Protection Discussion Paper 9923, World Bank, Washington, DC.

Dang, Thai-Thanh, Pablo Antolin, and Howard Oxley. 2001. *The Fiscal Implications of Ageing: Projections of Age-related Spending,* Economics Department Working Paper No. 305. Paris: OECD.

Diamond, Peter A. 2001. "Comments on Rethinking Pension Reform: 10 Myths about Social Security Systems." In *New Ideas About Old Age Security: Toward Sustainable*

Pension Systems in the 21st Century, eds. Robert Holzmann, Joseph E. Stiglitz, with Louise Fox, Estelle James, and Peter R. Orszag, 76–9. Washington, DC: World Bank.

Diamond, Peter A. 2002. *Social Security Reform.* Oxford and New York: Oxford University Press.

Diamond, Peter A., and Peter R. Orszag. 2004a. *Saving Social Security: A Balanced Approach.* Washington, DC: The Brookings Institution.

———. 2004b. "Saving Social Security." *Boston Review,* April/May. http://www.boston review.net/BR29.2/diamondorszag.html.

EPC (Economic Policy Committee of the European Commission). 2001. "Budgetary Challenges Posed by Ageing Populations: The Impact of Public Spending on Pensions, Health and Long-Term Care for the Elderly and Possible Indicators of Long-Term Financial Sustainability of Public Finances." EPC/ECFIN/655/01-EN final. Brussels: European Union.

European Commission. 2003. *Communication from the Commission to the Council, The European Parliament, The European Economic and Social Committee and the Committee of the Regions: Mid-Term Review of the Social Policy Agenda.* COM (2003) 312 final. Brussels: European Union.

Feldstein, Martin S. 1996. "The Missing Piece in Policy Analysis: Social Security Reform." *American Economic Review* 86(2): 1–14.

Feldstein, Martin S., and Horst Siebert, eds. 2002. *Social Security Pension Reform in Europe.* National Bureau of Economic Research. Chicago, IL: University of Chicago Press.

Gale, William. 1998. "The Effects of Pensions on Wealth: A Re-Evaluation of Theory and Evidence." *Journal of Political Economy* 106(1): 706–23.

Gill, Indermit, Truman Packard, and Juan Yermo. 2005. *Keeping the Promise of Old Age Income Security in Latin America.* Stanford: Stanford University Press.

Gillion, Colin. 2000. "The Development and Reform of Social Security Pensions: The Approach of the International Labour Office." *International Social Security Review* 53(1): 35–63.

Góra, Marek, and Edward Palmer. 2004. "Shifting Perspectives in Pensions," Institute for the Study of Labor (IZA) Discussion Paper No. 1369, Bonn, Germany.

Góra, Marek, and Michal Rutkowski. 2000. "The Quest for Pension Reform: Poland's Security through Diversity," Working Paper 286, William Davidson Institute, Ann Arbor, MI.

Gruber, Jonathan, and David Wise. 1998. "Social Security and Retirement: An International Comparison." *American Economic Review* 88(2): 158–63.

———. 2002. "Social Security Programs and Retirement Around the World: Micro Estimation," NBER Working Paper No. W9407, National Bureau of Economic Research, Cambridge, MA.

Hemming, Richard. 1999. "Should Public Pensions be Funded?" *International Social Security Review* 52(2): 3–29.

Holzmann, Robert. 1999. "Financing the Transition," Pension Reform Primer Paper, World Bank, Washington, DC.

———. 2000. "The World Bank Approach to Pension Reform." *International Social Security Review* 53(1): 11–34.

Holzmann, Robert, and Edward Palmer, eds. 2005. *Pension Reform through NDCs: Issues and Prospects for Non-Financial Defined Contribution Schemes.* Washington, DC: World Bank.

Holzmann, Robert, Michal Rutkowski, and Mitchell Orenstein. 2003. *Pension Reform in Europe: Progress and Process.* Washington, DC: World Bank.

International Social Security Review. 2001. 54(2-3): 3–230.

Mackenzie, G. A., Philip Gerson, and Alfredo Cuevas. 1997. "Pension Regimes and Saving," Occasional Paper 153, International Monetary Fund, Washington, DC.

Mesa-Lago, Carmelo, and Katharina Müller. 2002. "The Politics of Pension Reform in Latin America." *Journal of Latin American Studies* 34(3): 687–715.

Müller, Katharina. 2001. "The Political Economy of Pension Reform in Eastern Europe." *International Social Security Review* 54(2-3): 57–79.

OECD (Organisation for Economic Co-operation and Development). 2002. "Fiscal Implications of Ageing: Projections of Age-Related Spending." Economics Department Working Paper 305, OECD, Paris.

Rutkowski, Michal. 1998. "A New Generation of Pension Reforms Conquers the East—A Taxonomy in Transition Economies." *Transition* 9(4): 16–19.

———. 2002. "Pensions in Europe: Paradigmatic and Parametric Reforms in EU Accession Countries in the Context of EU Pension System Changes." *Journal of Transforming Economies and Societies (EMERGO)* 9(1): 2–26.

Rys, Vladimir. 2001. "Transition Countries of Central Europe Entering the European Union: Some Social Protection Issues." *International Social Security Review* 54(2-3): 177–89.

Schmähl, Winfried, and Sabine Horstmann, eds. 2002. *Transformation of Pension Systems in Central and Eastern Europe.* Cheltenham and Northampton, MA: Edward Elgar.

United Nations. 1998. *World Population Prospects: The 1998 Revision.* New York: United Nations.

6

HEALTH CARE

Alexander S. Preker and Olusoji O. Adeyi

Prior to the breakup of the Soviet Union, most of the communist countries had well-developed health systems, although many were collapsing
after decades of neglect and were suffering from underinvestment, low productivity, and low quality of care. The rising unemployment rates and social
adjustments associated with the economic recessions of the 1990s made this
situation worse.

The resulting excess morbidity and mortality continues to place a heavy
burden on the economies of the new democratic states. Increases in out-of-
pocket spending on drugs and health care providers have slowly eroded the
financial protection against illness that the population enjoyed during the communist era. On top of the obvious economic and human costs of sick leave, disability pensions, and medical expenses, individuals who die in middle age
represent a significant loss of human capital.

This chapter summarizes the transition from centrally planned health care
to more client-oriented service delivery systems. It describes the poor health
conditions of the accession countries and other challenges to integration.
Finally, the chapter looks forward to the implications of social integration in
Europe, beyond the transition and the *acquis,* including a brief discussion on
ways to improve aggregate health status of the population and protect individuals from the impoverishing effects of illness under a new social contract within
the EU.

Trends in health and health care in the accession countries[1] tell an interesting story and pose difficult challenges to social integration for EU policy makers.

THE LOGIC OF TRANSITION: HEALTH CARE

The communist system was described using five stylized facts in chapter 1: low wages, generous social benefits, lifetime employment, central planning, and totalitarian governments. The resulting communist health systems had many of the inefficient features of state-owned enterprises (World Bank 1996). Some of these features include

- state monopoly over most health sector activities;
- lack of functioning labor markets, capital markets, and insurance markets;
- state monopoly over financing and ownership of most health services;
- rigid public bureaucracies with little management flexibility;
- pervasive responsiveness to demand and little scope for dynamic evolution.

The inherited health care system

The World Health Organization (WHO) has described the objectives of the health sector as (World Health Organization 2000)

- improving health;
- protecting the population against the impoverishing effects of illness;
- responding to the legitimate expectations of the population regarding how they are treated by health providers and the quality of services received.

Using this description, the communist socioeconomic system led to both successes and failures in the health sector (Preker and Feachem 1996). In some areas, such as priority setting, management of scarce resources, infectious disease control, and health care financing, state involvement in the health sector had a number of positive effects. Free and equitable access by the whole population to a comprehensive range of health care benefits was one of the social benefits that allowed firms to continue to pay workers low wages (Preker and Feachem 1994). No other region in the world, not even Europe or China, has ever succeeded in providing such extensive coverage of comprehensive health care to a population of similar size. Because equity in access to affordable health services appears to be one of the most important determinants of health status at upper income levels, preserving this positive legacy should be a high priority.

During the early years of communism, rapid economic growth, expansion in the social sectors (health, education, and culture), and more readily available food, shelter, and employment led to significant improvements in living standards and health status in many of the socialist states. Officially, there was no unemployment and no poverty. Hence there was no need for sophisticated targeting mechanisms to secure access by the poor to essential social services such as health care. In comparison with earlier periods of physical destruction, economic hardship, starvation, and homelessness in countries like Estonia, Latvia, Lithuania, Poland, and the Soviet Union, the 1950s were characterized by improvements in human well-being and health status.

By the early 1970s, countries such as Czechoslovakia and Hungary had mature health systems. Compared with developing countries with similar per capita gross domestic product (GDP), or even compared with the industrial countries, the health sectors of the new accession countries were well endowed in basic physical infrastructure, trained staff, and education programs. Structurally integrated networks of hospitals, clinics, and other clinical facilities, based on the Soviet health care model, secured universal access to curative health services throughout the region. Patients had their first point of contact with the lower tiers of the health system through individual outpatient departments of hospitals, polyclinics, diagnostic departments, emergency services, community health centers, rural health centers, and industrial health services. With varying degrees of effectiveness, doctors working in these settings acted as gatekeepers, treating what they could and referring more difficult cases to higher levels of care. University hospitals and national specialist institutes capable of providing advanced technological interventions formed the tip of this pyramid. A highly structured system of hygiene and epidemiology stations focused on the control of infectious diseases, but in a command and control fashion and without the population-based approaches of modern public health functions.

In other areas, however, where there was a need for an entrepreneurial spirit and innovation (research and development of new pharmaceuticals and medical technology, for example) or where there was a need to be responsive to patients, the system failed.

The former health policies and services of the accession countries were remarkably ineffective in promoting good health or preventing illness and disability from known and avoidable causes during the communist era. While the health of the people in Western Europe has improved steadily, for people in the accession countries, it has stagnated and for those in the former Soviet Union it has deteriorated sharply, as demonstrated by the high morbidity and mortality rates among adult males (McKee and Shkolnikov 2001).

The belching chimneys of the state-owned enterprises and outdoor pollution contributed to worsening health prior to the transition (Bobak 2000). However, lifestyle-related cerebrovascular diseases and cancer were the main causes of the emerging mortality gap between the accession countries during the communist era and Western Europe (Eberstadt 1990; Bobak and Feachem 1992; Eberstadt 1993). People depended on the omnipotent state to solve their health problems while household and community participation in health promotion was ignored (Makara 1994).

Impact of the transition on health and health care

As described in chapter 1, three core socioeconomic objectives of the transition were to

- improve living standards;
- secure greater individual freedom;
- allow a return of the countries from the former communist bloc to the community of democratic nations.

The early phase of the transition—from central planning to a market economy and from totalitarian to more democratic government—had a number of negative consequences, many of which were anticipated (Barr 1994). The resulting high unemployment and fiscal pressures had a profound impact on health and the health sector throughout the region. At the political level, the transition led to a call for greater individual participation in health-seeking behavior and choice of health care through a democratic process. At the economic level, it led to a new incentive system and competitive market pressures in the allocation of scarce resources. At the organizational and institutional level, it led to greater private ownership and market-oriented institutional structures.

The deterioration in health created some difficult challenges for policy makers trying to reform the health sector. Many of these challenges were a direct consequence of the three major effects of the transition discussed in chapters 1 and 2 of this volume, including: a drop in output of from 20 percent to over 50 percent of GDP—on a scale not seen since the Great Depression of the 1930s; an end to job security; and widening income distribution.

In contrast with Russia and the Central Asian Republics, however, this initial economic downturn was relatively transient in most of the accession countries. As a result, most of these countries had begun to recover by the mid-1990s. Although the speed of recovery varied, all the accession countries must meet required economic stability and growth criteria before joining the EU. This has resulted in an easing of both the initial pressures on health status from economic causes and the fiscal pressures on the health sector.

Rising mortality patterns

Serious debate has taken place on the origins of the increase in adult mortality during the early transition years in the accession countries and its possible link to the collapse in economic output and rising unemployment (Goldstein and others 1996; Adeyi and others 1997; McKee, Adany, and MacLehose 2004). On aggregate, there was a significant drop in life expectancy in the mid-1990s in Eastern Europe and the former Soviet Union (see figure 6.1).

Stress may have been a major factor (Valkonen 1982; Makinen 2000; Stone 2000; Moller-Leimkuhler 2003). Political turmoil (Bobak and others

FIGURE 6.1 Average life expectancy at birth for the Europe and Central Asia region

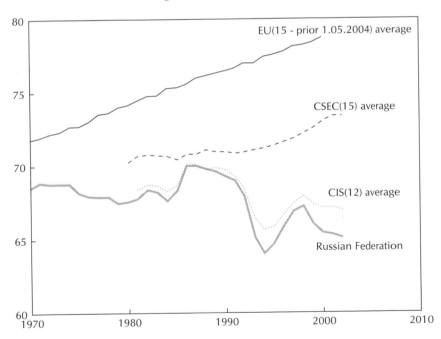

Source: WHO Health for All Database.
Note: EU-15 = countries of the EU as of April 2004; CSEC = Central and Southern European Countries; CIS = Commonwealth of Independent States, which consist of Armenia, Azerbaijan, Belarus, Georgia, Kazakhstan, the Kyrgyz Republic, Moldova, the Russian Federation, Tajikistan, Turkmenistan, Ukraine, and Uzbekistan.

1997), loss of income security (Catalano 1991), unemployment (Hanke and others 2001), inequity (McKee 2002), and poverty (Marmot and Bobak 2000) have all been shown to be positively correlated with increased mortality during the early transition. The observed rise in adult mortality during the early transition may also have been caused by an increase in smoking (Balabanova, Bobak, and McKee 1998; McKee and others 1998), consumption of alcohol (McKee and Britton 1998; Bobak and others 1999; McKee, Shkolnikov, and Leon 2001), violence (Walberg and others 1998; Chervyakov and others 2002), and accidents (Koradecka 2001).

With the exception of a potential HIV/AIDS crisis and the continued challenges of coming to grips with lifestyle-related risk factors such as smoking, unhealthy diets, sedentary lifestyles, and unsafe sexual practices, the mortality decline observed during the early transition reversed itself in most of the accession countries during the 1990s.

Decrease in tax-based funding in the face of growing expenditures

An immediate effect of the collapse in output was a reduction in public funding available to all the social sectors (World Bank 1996). Although health and other social expenditures were relatively protected as measured by share of GDP devoted to these sectors during the early transition, real expenditures still dropped substantially in many of the accession countries. This situation was worse in the Baltic countries and Romania and Bulgaria than in the Czech Republic, Hungary, Poland, and the Slovak Republic, where the contraction in GDP was less pronounced (Goldstein and others 1996).

Parallel to this drop in revenues, liberalization of the economy and labor markets put additional expenditure pressures on the main health sector cost drivers (pharmaceuticals, equipment, energy, and wages). The pharmaceutical and medical equipment sectors opened up to foreign competition and competitive pricing, leading to changes in both the quality and range of available products, and to a significant increase in expenditure on those areas (Kanavos 2004). Wage increases in other sectors of the economy and comparisons with health care income in Western Europe put upward pressure on health labor market expenditures (Jakubowski and Hess 2004). The energy crisis of the 1990s further compounded expenditure pressures on the health sector due to the large and inefficient physical structures of many hospitals (Nanda and others 1993). Finally, increased mobility of the population and exposure to Western European health systems raised expectations about the quality and range of health services available to accession country patients (McKee, MacLehose, and Albreht 2004).

As in Western Europe, downward pressures on the funding base and upward pressures on expenditures are likely to pose a long term challenge in the health policy of many accession countries.

Resistance to reform followed by institutional collapse

Despite expenditure pressures, service providers were able to resist change during the early phase of the transition. First, the massive buildup of physical infrastructure in the health sector during the communist years left the sector with considerable excess capacity. Second, investment in capital stock, and expenditures on maintenance, the supply of drugs, and many consumables could be cut without initial perceivable changes in the health system (Preker 1996).

During the mid-1990s, despite the looming crisis in the health of the population and several years of reforms in health care financing, the health sector was left with excess capacity in physical infrastructure and staff compared with the rest of the world, including Western Europe. Notably, the accession countries were slow in reforming the governance arrangements of their hospital sector in line with reforms seen elsewhere in the world (Harding and Preker 2000; Jakab, Preker, and Harding 2002; McKee and Healy 2002; Jakab, Preker, and Harding 2003; Preker and Harding 2003).

These factors led to a pernicious erosion in the quality of health services available through the public sector. The infrastructure of health services deteriorated, there were chronic shortages of drugs and certain critical surgical supplies, and staff morale declined.

Policy response

The policy responses to these negative aspects of the transition can be grouped into two phases: short term crisis management in the face of the collapse in economic output, unbridled liberalization of labor markets, and political pluralism; and longer term effects of stabilization and adjustment in the economy, labor markets, and political system.

Short-term crisis management

The primary response was survival. With dwindling tax-based resources, loss of income security, and rising expenditures being the most visible effects of the early transition, it was not surprising that financing reforms took precedence over the less obvious deterioration in health status and infrastructure of the service delivery system. Most of the accession countries were slow to react to the evolving mortality crisis that accompanied the transition (Makara 1994; McKee and Jacobson 2000).

The preferred solution to dealing with the funding crisis throughout the region, not just in the accession countries, was to make the health sector less reliant on tax revenues by diversifying the sources of health care financing to include a payroll tax and user fees or copayment for some goods and services (Preker, Jakab, and Schneider 2002).

This initial response in health care financing was only partially successful. The countries that shifted to a mixed source of financing that included both general revenues and contributory payroll taxes did better in terms of overall spending than countries that continued to rely only on general revenue financing (Goldstein and others 1996). However, rising unemployment, erosion of the wage base, and increases in informal sector employment during the early transition made payroll taxes an unstable source of financing for the health sector. Hence, all the accession countries that shifted to partial reliance on payroll taxes for financing health care continued to rely on the treasury and general revenues to meet the shortfall from the new health insurance funds.

Longer term effects of stabilization and adjustment

Once the economic and political context began to stabilize, most of the accession countries turned their attention to more medium-term reform objectives. These objectives focused on

- reorientation of public health policy toward an engagement by individuals and families in seeking healthy lifestyles;
- diversification in the source of health care financing;
- introduction of new incentives in the allocation of scarce resources;
- restructuring and downsizing the service delivery system;
- strengthening the governance and management of providers.

Some countries, such as the Czech Republic, Hungary, and Poland opted for a "big bang" approach to the economic restructuring process. Others followed a more moderate path. In all instances, however, the elixir of rapid liberalization of demand, supply, prices, and wages, combined with continued fiscal constraints and resistance to structural reforms, contributed to the deterioration of health services.

For example, removal of centralized state control over the health sector and the rapid introduction of unregulated competitive markets sometimes led to the emergence of significant market failure. In the Czech Republic, ownership of most health care facilities was quickly transferred to local communities.

Substantial parts of the former national health service were decentralized or privatized, especially pharmaceutical products, medical equipment, supplies, ancillary services, and ambulatory health services (private offices, clinics, pharmacies, and diagnostic centers). Many health care providers, such as general practitioners, consultant specialists, dentists, and pharmacists working outside the hospital subsector no longer saw themselves as public employees but rather as entrepreneurs in private practice. Patients saw themselves as consumers of health care, demanding services in return for the taxes or social insurance contributions they were paying.

Instead of the emergence of a constructive partnership between the public and new private sector (Harding and Preker 2003), unrestrained privatization within an excessively relaxed regulatory framework led to unscrupulous profiteering and pillage by health care providers who used equipment bought for public facilities in their private clinics (Saltman, Busse, and Mossialos 2002). Throughout the region, the sudden removal of constraints on freedom of choice led patients and health care providers to shop around indiscriminately, wasting valuable resources and further straining an already overutilized health service.

Most of the accession countries were unprepared for this overshoot in economic liberalization in the health sector (Preker 1994). They were also unprepared for the sudden rejection of the old political system. Weak management capacity and collapse of the old institutional framework often left health care facilities with a void in governance arrangements and led to a popular perception of confusion. Purges of the *nomenclatura,* and a "witch hunt" for previous card-carrying communists decapitated the Ministries of Health and many health care institutions in Poland, the Czech Republic, and the Slovak Republic, leaving them without experienced senior staff. Medical doctors with little training or experience in management assumed key administrative posts in Ministries of Health, hospitals, and other institutions, creating a policy vacuum in which poorly prepared and contradictory reform proposals were often presented to parliament at the same time. Excessive decentralization and a breakdown in referral networks in countries such as the Czech Republic, the Slovak Republic, and Hungary led to expensive overlaps, because every community hospital wanted its own neurosurgical unit and the latest technological equipment.

Not surprisingly, many of the accession countries experienced a significant backlash against these negative transition effects during the mid-1990s, complicated by the fact that each successive minister tried to distance himself or herself from the unpopular policies of the previous government (World Health Organization 1993; Saltman, Figueras, and Sakallarides 1997). Although the new accession countries bring this legacy with them as new members of the EU, most of the older members are currently experiencing a similar crisis in the funding and provision of health services for their populations.

HEALTH CARE UNDER ACCESSION

In October 2002, the European Commission recommended that 10 new member states be included in the union as of June 2004: Cyprus, the Czech Republic, Estonia, Hungary, Latvia, Lithuania, Malta, Poland, the Slovak Republic, and Slovenia. Romania and Bulgaria hope to accede in 2007. This inclusion in the EU by some of the former communist countries is both a great political achievement and a great opportunity for the new member states to "catch up" with European standards in health, health care financing, and the quality of health services.

This section summarizes the various legislation, recommendations, and coordination mechanisms that have relevance for health and the health sector; the support that the candidate countries received from the EU in helping them through the accession process; and a summary of the degree to which the accession process met with the expectations of member countries and policy experts.

Compliance with the conditions of accession

Although member states retain primary jurisdiction over health policy, the process of enlargement of the EU has already had major implications for national policy making related to health and the health sector through three processes: mandatory requirements, nonbinding requirements, and voluntary convergence through other coordination mechanisms for social policy (see box 6.1). In the latter case, member states have to comply with numerous technical norms, procedural obligations, and other elements that affect national health care systems.

Legislation with direct relevance to health sector

The following summarizes the major mandatory requirements imposed on new member states during the enlargement process of the EU (McKee, Mossialos, and Baetens 2002; Mossialos and McKee 2002; McKee and others 2004). Although early policy makers envisaged limited competence of the EU over health and health policy, its influence has progressively increased.

Compliance with underlying treaties. The *acquis communautaire* is the "rule book" that consolidated the agreements contained in the underlying body of legislation and treaties dating back to the 1957 treaty of Rome. International

---

BOX 6.1 Mandatory Requirements, Nonbinding Requirements, and Voluntary Convergence

Legislation with Direct Relevance to Health Sector
- Underlying treaties (treaty of Maastricht of 1993 and treaty of Amsterdam of 1997)
- Judgments of the European Court of Justice
- The *acquis communautaire*

Other Legislation with Indirect Relevance for Health Sector
- The Copenhagen Criteria of 1993
- The Stability and Growth Pact
- European Social Charter of 1989
- European Charter of Fundamental Rights of 2000

Recommendations and Coordination Mechanisms
- European Council Recommendations of 1992
- Open Method of Coordination of 2000
- Convergence with European Social Policy and Adoption of Other Agreements

---

provisions that open borders and allow free movement often need some provision to counterbalance the risk of spreading diseases from one country to another. Early health provisions under the European Commission quickly expanded beyond previous minimalist provisions. Article 3(o) of the 1993 treaty of Maastricht stipulated that the "Community will contribute to the attainment of a high level of health protection for its citizens." Article 129 spells out the community's involvement in health policy and public health, and Article 129(a) on Consumer Protection has several health-related elements. Health safety issues also come up under several other articles related to the free movement of goods, services, and persons; under articles related to transport, occupational accidents and hygiene, and imports; and in relation to articles on agriculture, fisheries, and the environment.

Most of the health-related provisions were carefully circumscribed to avoid contravening existing restrictions on harmonizing legislation. Yet, the treaty of Maastricht clearly specified that health protection should be part of the community's social policies in the case of "major scourges" such as cancer, HIV/AIDS, other communicable diseases, injuries, pollution-related diseases, rare diseases, and health data. Four criteria had to be met before the community could take action:

- There had to be a significant health threat for which preventive action would be effective.
- The resulting action had to supplement or promote other policies such as the operation of an internal market.
- The act had to be consistent with prior agreements such as WHO resolutions.
- The action had to be one that a member state alone could not achieve.

Although there were concerns at the time of the treaty of Maastricht about the degree to which the EU was increasing its involvement in health, the treaty specified the EU's competence over public health and public health issues related to the movement of goods, services, people, and capital across boarders. Additionally, it touched on health issues related to research, agriculture, the environment, food production, and other areas of social policy.

Article 152 of the 1997 treaty of Amsterdam expanded on some provisions, but it continued to frame the EU's involvement in health and health policy in a cautious way and deferred many critical issues to the competence of national governments. It tried to explicitly limit EU competence in relation to curative health services by requiring that community action in public health fully respect the organization and delivery responsibilities of member states over health services and medical care. The treaty of Nice (2001) had no additional health provisions.

Decisions by the European Court of Justice. Parallel to these explicit health conditions under the establishing treaties, the application of European law in some of the nonhealth–related areas rapidly impinged on a wide range of health-related areas.

First, many of the inputs needed to produce health services are subject to free movement among the EU member countries (pharmaceuticals, equipment, consumables, labor, knowledge, capital, and so forth). Hence the production, import, export, wholesale distribution, and retail sale of these goods and services are subject to European law, thereby giving the EU considerable competence over many areas relating to the delivery of health services.

Second, in 1998—under provisions of freedom of movement of people—the European Court of Justice upheld the right of individuals to protection and reimbursement of ordinary expenses incurred during travel (eyeglasses and orthodontic treatment) that they would have enjoyed in their own countries without the need for prior approval. Previously, such rights were restricted to emergency care. Patients that wanted to be treated and reimbursed for preexisting conditions had to secure prior authorization from their insurance programs.

These and subsequent rulings by the European Court of Justice effectively extended the scope of European law into the areas of health services and health insurance (social and voluntary).

Compliance with relevant chapters of the acquis. These disparate competencies of the European Community were pulled together under major chapter headings in the *acquis communautaire.* Chapter 13 on social policy and chapter 23 on consumer and health protection are the most relevant to health and the health sector. They pull together the various health competencies that evolved under Article 129 of the treaty of Maastricht and Article 152 of the treaty of Amsterdam.

In addition, several other chapters have significant implications for the health sector, notably, chapters 1 through 4 on the free movement of goods (pharmaceuticals, medical equipment, medical supplies, and other essential consumables such as food and supplies, and so on), persons (patients, clinical staff, and managers,), services (clinical, nonclinical, and financial), and capital (investment in public and private hospitals, clinics, and diagnostic services, and so forth). Chapters 5, 6, 15, and 16 on company law, competition policy, and small and medium enterprises have important implications for voluntary private health insurance, private hospitals, clinics, and diagnostic centers and anything else produced in the private sector for the health care supply chain.

Furthermore, chapters 7, 8, and 22 on agriculture, fisheries, and environmental policies have important public health and safety implications. Chapter 12 on statistics has implications for health policy in terms of monitoring and evaluation; chapter 17 on science and research has implications for the biomedical research complex; and chapter 18 on education and training has implications for the training of doctors, nurses, and allied health workers.

As a result of the unavoidable impact of many of the chapters of the *acquis communautaire* on the health sector, the balance in competency between national governments and the EU over health policy needs to be clarified. This work is currently in progress.

These and other mandatory requirements created a framework for the EU in both public health and health service delivery during the enlargement process. They also set the tone for a shared competency over European health policy between national governments and the EU, not unlike the division of responsibilities one finds in many federal states such as Australia, Canada, Germany, and the United States.

Other legislation with indirect relevance for the health sector

This section summarizes other mandatory requirements that are nonbinding for the health sector but have significant implications for health policy.

Compliance with the Copenhagen criteria. The Copenhagen criteria provided the underlying socioeconomic principles for convergence among accession countries. It stated that "countries in central and eastern Europe that so desire shall become members of the European Union" and that "accession will take place as soon as an applicant is able to assume the obligations of membership by satisfying the economic and political conditions required" (European Commission 1993). Accession countries were required to meet

- political criteria—"stability of institutions guaranteeing democracy, rule of law, human rights and respect for minorities";
- economic criteria—"existence of a functioning market economy as well as the capacity to cope with a competitive pressures and market forces within the Union; a functioning market economy";
- administrative criteria, including the ability to take on the obligations of the *acquis communautaire.*

The Copenhagen criteria are relevant to the health sector in a number of areas in addition to the specific requirement of the *acquis communautaire* discussed above. Health systems must respect minorities such as people with physical handicaps as well as socially excluded groups such as the Roma population in some of the accession countries. Health systems must also be consistent with "a functioning market economy," which raises issues about competition among providers and insurance programs.

Compliance with the Stability and Growth Pact. The Stability and Growth Pact deals with inflation, interest rates, budget deficits, national debt, and exchange rates among member states. Three of the Convergence Criteria are of particular relevance to the health sector, notably ensuring that: short term-term deficits do not exceed 3 percent of GDP for any prolonged period of time; national debt does not exceed 60 percent; and inflation does not exceed 1.5 percent above the average inflation rate in the three EU countries with the lowest rates of inflation.

Given that most of the member states rely heavily on public financing for the health sector and that health expenditure ranges from 6 percent to over 10 percent of GDP, maintaining affordable health polices will be important to the fiscal balance in most countries. Furthermore, because the inflation rate in the health sector of most of the member countries is greater than the consumer inflation index, the health sector contributes to upward inflationary pressures.

A concrete example of this occurred on March 13, 2000, when the European Council examined the updated stability program of Portugal for the period 2000–2004. Although the council noted with satisfaction that the Portuguese economy had been growing at rates above the EU average, the fiscal balance had been secured mainly through domestic demand-driven growth that had offset significant overspending in the health sector and a strong increase in the government's wage bill. Performance in the health sector was therefore the target of criticism related to the country's macroeconomic policies.

A clear tension arises between EU policies that foster escalation in health expenditures, that is, allowing patients to shop around in member countries for goods and services that may be restricted in their own countries for cost containment reasons, and macroeconomic constraints.

Countries such as the United Kingdom, which have new health expenditure policies aimed at "catching up" with European spending levels in response to popular dissatisfaction with the existing quality of health services, will have to find ways to reconcile such domestic health policies with the realities of their membership in the EU. Countries such as Germany and France that have recently gone through a difficult fiscal period are experiencing significant pressure to include reform of social benefits as part of their efforts to get fiscal policies under better control. The political backlash against the United Kingdom not following through on commitments to increase spending and Germany and France wanting to reform spending downward is a serious constraint to effective implementation of such policies.

Compliance with the European Charter of Fundamental Rights. The 2000 European Charter of Fundamental Rights states that "everyone has the right to access to preventive health care and the right to benefit from medical treatment" and that the Union "recognizes and respects this entitlement to social security benefits and social services providing protection in cases such as maternity, disability, illness, industrial accidents, dependency or old age."

Although rights-based approaches to health policy do not have a strong track record unless backed by adequate financial resources and functioning service delivery systems, they do provide a framework for the underlying principles for a European health policy, which will be discussed in the next section.

Compliance with the European Social Charter of 1989. The European Social Charter of 1989 has several recommendations related to health. Included among them are that all workers have a right to safe and healthy working conditions; children and young persons have the right to special protection; everyone has the right to the highest attainable standards of health; and those without adequate resources have the right to social and medical assistance.

Recommendations and coordination mechanisms

This section summarizes some of the voluntary convergence that has occurred in European health policy during the enlargement process.

Because health policy is influenced by many socioeconomic and political factors in addition to technical considerations, even after significant convergence policy makers felt that it was desirable for member states to retain considerable national diversity in areas such as health and other social policies.

Despite this desire, over time the influence of a European brand of health policy has exerted a significant influence in many of the member states through both deliberate efforts to foster coordination and more spontaneous policy convergence.

Adoption of European Council Recommendation of 1992. In the area of health, the European Council Recommendation of 1992 (European Commission 1992) called for convergence in the following areas:

- under conditions determined by each member state, to ensure for all persons legally resident within the territory of the member state access to necessary health care as well as to facilities seeking to prevent illness;
- to maintain and, where necessary, develop a high-quality health care system geared to the evolving needs of the population, and especially those arising from dependence of the elderly, to the development of pathologies and therapies and the need to step up prevention;
- to organize where necessary the rehabilitation of convalescents, particularly following illness or accident, and their subsequent return to work;
- to provide employed persons forced to interrupt their work owing to sickness with either flat-rate benefits or benefits calculated in relation to their earnings in their previous occupation, which will maintain their standards of living in a reasonable manner in accordance with their participation in appropriate social security schemes

Adoption of Open Method of Coordination. The Open Method of Coordination (OMC)—agreed on at the Lisbon European Council in March 2000 and elaborated upon at subsequent summits—was intended to provide a framework for member states to modernize European social policy in incremental ways through voluntary participation in a wide range of programs of common interest. Rather than being forced to adhere to mandatory social policies that would not be universally accepted, the OMC strives to achieve a gradual convergence in health policy through social dialogue among member states.

The Laeken European Council (December 2001) laid the foundation for a European health policy. It adopted three common objectives for European health care systems (the methods proposed for implementing these recommendations were close to the OMC already in use in the areas of social inclusion and pensions):

- Guaranteed access for all to good quality health care
- Improved transparency and quality of health care systems
- Ensured financial viability of the health care systems

Convergence with European social policy and adoption of other agreements. Other recent developments that impact health include convergence with European social policy related to the health sector, such as respect for solidarity, equity, access, and quality of care; and national adoption of other EU policies.

Meeting expectations: Has the enlargement process worked?

Feedback from accession countries and the opinions of selected experts indicate the extent to which they think the enlargement process has met or failed to meet expectations. During the accession process, most of the new member countries received extensive technical assistance from the EU's PHARE and other programs to align their health policies more closely with those of the older member states.

Feedback from accession countries and the opinions of selected experts indicate the degree to which they think the enlargement process has met or did not meet expectations.

Expectations of new accession countries

In the months prior to accession, key informants from the Ministries of Health (or other responsible ministry, such as Ministry of Social Affairs) of the candidate countries participated in a study on the perceived challenges and benefits of joining the EU (McKee, MacLehose, and Nolte 2004).

Perceived challenges for the health system included a need to control for the risk of expenditure escalation, a need to control the demand for health services, and a need to harmonize health care legislation. Other challenges for the health system included quality standards, health system performance, equity, and the pharmaceutical sector. Issues related to professional mobility and patients' rights—a major preoccupation of the *acquis communautaire*—ranked lowest.

Perceived challenges for population health included a need to enhance the role of public health and to improve policies on prevention, and a need to address the socioeconomic determinants of poor health status. Issues related to the threat of communicable diseases related to increased free movement of patients and of professionals—another major preoccupation of the *acquis communautaire*—ranked relatively low.

Perceived benefits to the health care systems included a potential improvement in quality of facilities and services, more evidence-based policies, and enhanced public participation in the health care system. Once again, the potential benefits from free movement of patients and professionals ranked low. Perceived benefits to population health included an increased focus on public health, strengthening of regulations, and improved quality and access to health services. Again, patient rights ranked quite low.

Perceived neglected areas included the unresolved tension between national and European-level health policy, and concerns for environmental health, food safety, and communicable disease control. Development of common policies for mental health and chronic diseases ranked low.

The study also revealed that issues that were not seen as important by Ministries of Health were often the subjects of greatest concern among policy makers drawn from a wider constituency.

Opinions of selected experts

Article 129 of the treaty of Maastricht and Article 152 of the treaty of Amsterdam took a minimalist approach to health policy, reflecting the fact that supporters of intergovernmentalism (with member states retaining national control over many competencies) prevailed during the enlargement process.

The resulting policy of containment in the health and health policy area was not successful for three reasons: (a) several treaties established a clear competence by the EU in several critical areas of health policy; (b) there was significant spillover from other areas of European Community policy (agriculture, fisheries, environment, industries, competition, and so forth); and (c) there was inevitable "policy creep" during the EU enlargement process (McKee, Mossialos, and Baetens 2002; Mossialos and McKee 2002).

The result of this process, which is summarized in the *acquis communautaire,* is a fragmented and incoherent health policy that is bureaucratic and confusing for both the EU and its member states. Given that both the EU and its member states are and will probably continue to be extensively involved in health policy, it may be logical to adopt a much more explicit multilevel governance arrangement (Cram 1996) for the health sector along the same lines as that found in complex federal states such as Australia, Canada, Germany, or the United States. Policy options for such power sharing are explored in the next section.

BEYOND ACCESSION: THE FUTURE OF HEALTH POLICY

Accession to the EU has been an important and positive punctuation mark in emerging health policy in Europe. However, the health criteria *acquis commu-*

nautaire were minimalist, capturing neither the full richness of recent health policy developments in Europe nor the future challenges that face member states in this sector. Following accession to the EU, both the new and old member states face a large unfinished agenda that cannot be adequately addressed through the fragmented health policy framework that emerged through the enlargement process.

This section summarizes areas of convergence and divergence in health policy during the past few years. It highlights some of the reform directions on which there is broad agreement, and it presents the debate in areas where there is less agreement over future policy direction.

Recent trends in health policy

Health policy in Europe has been in flux during the past 50 years, influenced by new directions both from within the sector itself and from significant spillover effects in other sectors. More than any of the other social sectors, the health sector is a microcosm of the underlying society—ranging from financing, insurance, and capital, to industrial organization and management of complex multiproduct firms, to production in the supply chain for pharmaceuticals, medical equipment, and other goods. The health sector cannot remain an enclave unto itself, isolated from broader socioeconomic and political events. Three trends during recent decades have had a profound impact on the health sector—population aging, rapid technological change in medicine, and increased mobility of individuals.

In the health sector, people play a unique role. Patients are simultaneously objects of and an integral part of the production process itself, consumers of services, providers of care, contributors to financing (as taxpayers), and governors of the policy making process (as voters). Human behavior is therefore central to the performance of any health system. Much has been learned during the past 50 years about health and other social policies that facilitate health-enhancing behavior changes in democratic societies. The required changes in the customs and norms of the underlying society take time and are not easily influenced by formal legislative processes.

Within the EU member countries

During the past few decades, as health policy makers were confronted by many of the same challenges, they tried to learn from each other. This resulted in a significant convergence in some of the major health policy trends in Europe even before the 1957 treaty of Rome and gradual enlargement of the EU. The following are the key elements of this policy convergence (World Health Organization 1993; Saltman, Figueras, and Sakallarides 1997; World Health

Organization 1997; McKee, Mossialos, and Baetens 2002; Mossialos and McKee 2002; McKee, MacLehose, and Nolte 2004):

- universal coverage
- progressive financing
- equitable access to services
- comprehensive range of benefits
- portability within national boundaries

This policy convergence extends beyond the EU to most Organisation for Economic Co-operation and Development (OECD) countries (Preker 1989). Even in the United States, Mexico, and Turkey, which have not yet achieved all of these goals, there is a significant policy thrust in the same direction.

Many of the health-related articles under the treaty of Maastricht and treaty of Amsterdam and summarized in the *acquis communautaire* were inspired by these trends in policy convergence rather than the other way around.

Beyond the EU borders

Diversity in health policy in the EU and other countries occurs largely due to differences in the balance between public and private roles in funding and service delivery, in the degree of cross subsidies, in the split between mandatory and voluntary affiliation, and in the scope of benefits.

Redefining the roles of the state and private providers, while maintaining universal coverage and equitable access and entitlement to a comprehensive range of benefits, has been an increasingly prominent theme throughout the world since the mid-1990s (Musgrove 1996; Preker and Harding 2000). This is equally true for the accession countries (World Health Organization 1993; Saltman and Figueras 1997; World Health Organization 1997).

During the 20th century governments of all European countries became central players in the health sector, often engaging in both the financing and provision of a wide range of care. Today, most OECD countries have achieved universal access to health care through a mix of public and private financing arrangements and providers (Preker 1989). The United States, Mexico, and Turkey are the only OECD countries that have not achieved universal access to health care.

Proponents of such involvement by the public sector in health care have argued the case on both philosophical and technical grounds. In most societies, care for the sick and disabled is considered an expression of humanitarian and philosophical aspirations.

However, not only moral principles or arguments about the welfare state warrant collective intervention in health. The past 100 years is rich with examples of how the private sector and market forces alone failed to secure efficiency and equity in the health sector. Economic theory provides ample justification for such an engagement, on both theoretical and practical grounds, to secure

- *efficiency*, because significant market failure exists in the health sector— information asymmetrics; public goods; positive and negative externalities; distorting or monopolistic market power of many providers and producers; absence of functioning markets in some areas; and frequent occurrence of high transaction costs (Bator 1958; Arrow 1963; Atkinson and Stiglitz 1980; Evans 1984; Musgrave and Musgrave 1984; Rice 1998);
- *equity*, because individuals and families often fail to protect themselves adequately against the risks of illness and disability on a voluntary basis due to shortsightedness (free riding) and characteristic shortcomings of private health insurance (moral hazard and adverse selection)(Van Doorslaer, Wagstaff, and Paci 1993; Barer, Getzen, and Stoddart 1998).

During the 1980s and 1990s, the trend moved in a different direction (Young 1986). The Reagan and Thatcher eras ushered in a growing willingness to experiment with market approaches in the social sectors (health, education, and social protection). This was true even in countries such as the United Kingdom, New Zealand, and Australia that historically had been bastions of the welfare state. As with the previous rise in state involvement in health care, the recent cooling toward state involvement in health care and enthusiasm for private solutions has been motivated by both ideological and technical arguments (Donahue 1989; Herzlinger 1997).

The political imperative that has accompanied liberalization in the accession countries contributed to a global sense of urgency to reform inefficient and bloated bureaucracies and to establish smaller governments with greater accountability (Preker and Feachem 1994; Preker 1996). However, it would be too easy to blame ideology and economic crisis for the recent surge in attempts to reform health care systems by exposing public services to competitive market forces, downsizing the public sector, and increasing private sector participation (Enthoven 1978; Enthoven 1988).

In reality, the welfare state approach failed to address many of the health needs of populations across the world (World Bank 1993, 1996, 1997, 2000; World Health Organization 1993, 1997, 2000, 2001). Hence the dilemma that policy makers face throughout the world—although state involvement in the health sector is clearly needed, it is typically fraught with public sector production failure (Wolf 1979; Peacock 1980; Wilson 1989; Vining and Weimer 1990; Osborne and Gaebler 1993; Manning 1998). The solutions many countries are exploring involve the achievement of public objectives through various combinations of public and private means (Donahue 1989).

Broadly agreed on reform directions

Health systems are useful only to the extent that they improve health outcomes, provide protection from catastrophic costs, and empower households to participate in improving their own health. This section presents some of the reform directions on which there is broad agreement.

Closing the morbidity and mortality gap between member states and the accession countries

Significant gaps still exist in health outcomes among the accession countries and the older members of the EU. In addition, there are variations among countries in the capacities of their health systems to protect the health of the population, improve health outcomes, and protect individuals from catastrophic costs. New or reemerging infectious diseases have transborder importance and will challenge systems for surveillance and coordination across countries.

The public health challenge of the accession countries in all of these areas are well known (Asvall and Alderslade 2002). Because public health is an area in which the EU has clear competence, it has been easier to make progress in developing a new public health strategy than to address some of the challenges related to health care financing or the performance of the service delivery system where competence is less well defined and often retained by member states.

The new EU health strategy. On May 16, 2000, the European Commission presented a proposal for a new public health strategy. It consisted of several important linked elements: (a) an action program for public health; (b) other measures such as health promotion and disease prevention; and (c) discussion of the health implications of activities and policies in other sectors. Particular attention was drawn to aging, mental health, nutrition, action on tobacco, and health-oriented alcohol policies (Piha 2000).

Since 2000, the Commissioner for health and consumer protection has allocated 300 million euros to implement key reforms in both public health and other areas that directly affect health, such as environmental hazards, pharmaceuticals, and so forth.

To close the mortality and morbidity gap between the old and new member states, attention is still needed in several key areas: cerebrovascular disease, cardiovascular disease, cancer, HIV/AIDS and other communicable diseases that have been on the rise, and drug dependency. Reforms in many of these areas are well under way, including

- a focus on the control of risk factors: tobacco consumption, excessive alcohol, sedentary lifestyles, and unhealthy diets (McKee and others 1998; Shkolnikov and others 1999; McKee and Jacobson 2000; McKee, Shkolnikov, and Leon 2001; Shkolnikov, McKee, and Leon 2001);
- strengthening of epidemiological surveillance networks, specialized public health laboratories, and prevention programs, especially in light of new and emerging infections such as bovine spongiform encephalopathy/Creutzfeldt Jakob disease (BSE/CJD), severe acute respiratory syndrome (SARS), and drug resistant tuberculosis;
- a methodical approach to HIV/AIDS control, with emphasis on the prevention of generalized epidemics through targeted, nonstigmatizing prevention among the high-risk core transmitter groups (such as needle-sharing injecting drug users and commercial sex workers) and the bridge populations (such as the sex partners of the high-risk core transmitters) (World Bank 2003a; 2003b).

Addressing inequalities in health outcomes. During the communist era, the concept of inequities in socioeconomic status was not widely accepted, because in principle there were no social class distinctions. Monitoring and exploration of the origins of inequities was not carried out routinely prior to the transition (Knight and others 2003). The relatively poor health status of minority groups such as the Roma population, therefore, received little attention. Understanding and addressing the origins of such social exclusion must now receive greater attention by EU policy makers (Koupilova and others 2001).

An immediate consequence of the enlargement process is that inequities in and among member states will increase. Estonia, Hungary, Latvia, and Lithuania rank particularly poorly among the accession countries in aggregate health status (see table 6.1). See also box 6.2 for a discussion on the impact of international development goals on health in the EU.

Balancing revenues and expenditures

The Stability and Growth Pact imposes a strict fiscal constraint on the health and other social sectors in all the EU countries, not just the new member states. Securing a more sustainable source of health financing and improved expendi-

TABLE 6.1 Health inequities, 1999

	Probability of dying (per 1,000)				Life expectancy at birth (years)	
	Under age 5		Between ages 15 and 59			
	Males	Females	Males	Females	Males	Females
Accession countries						
Bulgaria	21	16	242	98	67.4	74.7
Czech Republic	6	6	174	75	71.5	78.2
Estonia	14	9	316	114	65.4	76.5
Hungary	11	8	295	123	66.3	75.2
Latvia	20	14	328	122	64.2	75.5
Lithuania	15	12	286	106	66.9	77.2
Malta	10	6	111	46	75.4	80.7
Poland	12	11	226	88	69.2	77.7
Romania	29	22	285	119	65.1	73.5
Slovak Republic	11	8	216	83	69.2	77.5
Slovenia	6	5	170	76	71.9	79.4
Older member states						
United Kingdom	7	6	109	67	74.8	79.9
France	8	6	144	61	75.2	83.1
Germany	6	5	127	60	74.3	80.6
Portugal	10	7	164	66	71.7	79.3
Spain	6	5	122	49	75.4	80.2

Source: World Health Organization 2000.

ture control has become a key priority throughout the EU. Many of the new health insurance funds were established with a significant difference between the anticipated expenditures and the revenues that could be raised through payroll taxes alone.

Since the mid-1990s, most of the accession countries shifted from reliance on general revenues to social health insurance as a primary source of funding for the health sector (Preker, Jakab, and Schneider 2002). Many rely on high contributions from the working adults to cover the cost of health care for the rest of the population. This leads to excessively high payroll taxes, underreporting by employers, and tax evasion by the self-employed. An explicit subsidy to cover the cost of services used by the noncontributing part of the population (children, youths, unemployed, disabled, and retired) would go a long way toward addressing the revenue side of the resulting structural deficit. Strengthening the contribution collection compliance of many of the new social health insurance funds is also needed.

BOX 6.2 How Relevant are International Development Goals to Health in the EU?

In 2000, the international community adopted the Millennium Development Goals (MDGs) as the basis for international development policies (World Bank 2004a). Covering a range of sectors, the MDGs have the advantage of providing common, objectively verifiable measures of progress in world development. Yet the application of this common framework to diverse settings can create challenges. A particular example is the application of health goals to the countries of the Europe and Central Asia region, including the EU accession countries. A recent study examined how appropriate the health-related MDGs are for the countries of Europe and Central Asia by assessing the impact of achieving them on one of the widely used measures of aggregate health status: life expectancy at birth (Rechel, Shapo, McKee and the Health and Nutrition Group of the World Bank's Europe and Central Asia Region 2004). The study looks at the consequences of reaching the fourth and fifth MDGs, relating to infant, child (one to four years old), and maternal mortality. The report also explores other indicators that might be more relevant to the countries of this region. Four scenarios were considered: (a) reducing infant, child, and maternal mortality rates to the levels envisaged by the MDGs; (b) reducing infant, child, and maternal mortality rates to average EU levels; (c) reducing infant, child, and maternal mortality rates to the lowest levels in the subregion; and (d) keeping infant, child, and maternal mortality rates constant, and reducing mortality rates from cardiovascular disease and external causes of death to EU levels. The effects of the calculations on life expectancy at birth were then compared.

For the whole of Europe and Central Asia, the fourth scenario, focusing on adult mortality, had the greatest impact on life expectancy at birth, resulting in an average gain of 7.75 years, and reaching 10.09 years in the Russian Federation (table below). In contrast, reaching the MDG targets for infant, child, and maternal mortality resulted in an average gain of only 0.68 to 1.24 years, depending on whether national registration data or World Bank estimates of infant and child mortality were used for the countries of Central Asia and the Caucasus. Reducing infant, child, and maternal mortality to EU levels resulted on average in a gain of 0.85 to 1.97 years; while reaching the best subregional values for these indicators resulted in an average gain of 0.58 to 1.09 years.

The MDGs are important because they drive the choice of policies supported by the international community. Overall, the study confirmed the importance of adapting the health-related MDGs to the countries of Europe and Central Asia, placing greater emphasis on

(continued)

BOX 6.2 How Relevant are International Development Goals to Health in the EU? (*Continued*)

adult mortality. The choice of goals at a global level is largely determined by what data are available. The absence, in many developing countries, of data on adult mortality thus precludes the use of life expectancy at birth as a global measure. It does not, however, preclude its use where data do exist and, as this analysis shows, specific measures of adult mortality such as deaths from cardiovascular disease and external causes are appropriate additional measures of progress in improving health in this region. These findings refer to aggregate health outcomes. The study does not examine variations in infant, child, and maternal mortality across income social groups within the EU accession countries, a matter that is important for the equity dimension of health outcomes.

Source: World Bank 2004b.

Impact on life expectancy of reducing adult mortality rates to EU levels

	Increase in life expectancy		
	Overall gain in life expectancy	*Change due to reduction in injuries and violence*	*Change due to reduction in cardiovascular disease*
Eastern European EU accession countries			
Slovenia	1.36	0.73	0.63
Poland	3.30	0.56	2.74
Czech Republic	3.50	0.47	3.03
Hungary	4.29	0.73	3.56
Slovak Republic	4.65	0.39	4.26
Bulgaria	6.57	0.22	6.36
Estonia	6.72	2.28	4.44
Romania	6.85	0.51	6.34
Latvia	7.20	2.33	4.87
Lithuania	7.47	2.35	5.13
Subregional average	**4.75**	**0.65**	**4.10**
South Eastern Europe			
Albania	3.10	0.40	2.70
Croatia	3.54	0.40	3.14
Macedonia, FYR	4.84	0	4.84
Subregional average	**3.67**	**0.31**	**3.36**

BOX 6.2 How Relevant are International Development Goals to Health in the EU? (*Continued*)

	Increase in life expectancy		
	Overall gain in life expectancy	*Change due to reduction in injuries and violence*	*Change due to reduction in cardiovascular disease*
Central Asia and Caucasus			
Armenia	4.36	0	4.36
Tajikistan	5.19	0	5.19
Kyrgyz Republic	5.67	1.15	4.52
Georgia	6.39	0	6.39
Azerbaijan	6.47	0	6.47
Uzbekistan	7.98	0.23	7.75
Kazakhstan	8.63	1.83	6.81
Turkmenistan	9.70	0.34	9.36
Subregional average	**7.37**	**0.56**	**6.81**
Remaining countries of the former Soviet Union			
Moldova	7.36	1.20	6.16
Belarus	7.52	2.39	5.13
Ukraine	8.67	1.71	6.96
Russian Federation	10.09	3.40	6.70
Subregional average	**9.58**	**2.91**	**6.68**
Overall Europe and Central Asia average	**7.75**	**1.82**	**5.93**

Source: Rechel, Shapo, McKee and the Health and Nutrition Group of the World Bank's Europe and Central Asia Region 2004.
Note: Data refer to latest available years; no recent data available for Bosnia and Herzegovina, Serbia and Montenegro, and Turkey.

On the expenditure side, there is a need for more effective cost containment policies, especially in areas such as pharmaceuticals and human resources. Cost containment techniques are well known in both of these areas (Mossialos and Le Grand 1999). Although there is general agreement at the policy level on the need for labor adjustment policies and downsizing of the hospital sector, such reforms are politically sensitive and often encounter considerable resistance from both the medical profession and the general population (Reamy 1998; Lovkyte and Padaiga 2001).

Integration of the European health care market

Integration of labor markets, products, services, and capital of member states has already had a profound spillover effect on the health sector, even if direct competence by the EU over the specific health care markets was omitted from the treaty of Rome. Many of the policy directions emerging from judgments by the European Court of Justice are fragments and incomplete.

Although it may be desirable for this process to remain incremental in nature and harmonization is proscribed by the *acquis communautaire,* from time to time it will be necessary to pass legislation to resolve conflicts or fill undesirable gaps in the regulatory framework. The impetus for such reform is likely to come from member states.

Debates on difficult policy options

Various policy analysts have identified several potential problem areas arising out of the current *acquis communautaire:* the unresolved tension between individual choice and the need for coherent public health policies; the tension between the need to introduce more market-oriented policies and a commitment to solidarity; and a tension between the desire for a coherent European policy framework but reluctance to transfer too much responsibility to the EU.

Consumer choice

In democratic societies, individuals have the freedom to lead either healthy or unhealthy lifestyles. Households must engage in health-seeking behavior—the communist era demonstrated that the state cannot do this for them. Because so much of health has to do with individual behavior, what incentives are needed to stimulate health-seeking behavior? For example, when social insurance is used to pay for health care, society as a whole pays for the bad habits of some of its members. Should individuals who smoke, overeat, or drink heavily, pay a higher health insurance premium than those who do not, in the same way that they would pay a higher life insurance premium? Could car insurance companies be made to pay for the cost of emergency care at the time of road accidents so that part of this cost can be passed back to the bad drivers? Should individuals pay a copayment on the services that they use to discourage excessive consumption? How will the EU handle the question of genetically modified foods, in view of its relevance to health, consumer choice, state stewardship, public information (food labels, for example), and free trade? These issues are stimulating a lively debate as countries are facing increasing pressures to keep health insurance premiums at affordable levels and health care expenditure under control.

Market-oriented policies

THE ROLE OF VOLUNTARY HEALTH INSURANCE. Average spending on health in the EU-15 is around 8.5 percent of GDP while average expenditure in the accession countries is around 4.5 percent of GDP. Money is not everything, but closing the gap in health status will require a significant increase in the funding allocated to both the intersectoral and health sector programs that address the key causes of morbidity and mortality.

Many of the accession countries are now faced with a binding constraint on their public budgets due to the Stability and Growth Pact. As is evident from the rising out-of-pocket expenditure on health care, many households are often both willing and able to pay for some health care beyond the benefits provided through the public sector. Yet, out-of-pocket spending is inefficient for health care financing, both in terms of risk pooling and providing a steady income stream for health care providers. It can also pose a significant burden on the poor.

Encouraging households to channel some of the out-of-pocket payment through supplementary or complementary health insurance is therefore a policy option that many of the accession countries have already begun to explore. Voluntary health insurance for part of the population could also provide "head room" in the public budget that would allow scarce public resources to be better targeted to low-income groups and other vulnerable populations who may not be able to afford the current payroll taxes under the mandatory social health insurance programs or the out-of-pocket charges.

However, there are many forms of insurance, each with its own advantages and disadvantages (Mossialos and Thomson 2002). Because one of the European Commission's responsibilities is to protect consumers, regulation of this emerging voluntary health insurance market clearly needs to be a high priority for the future. Such regulations could be used to shape the insurance market toward managed care options, limit abusive profiteering, prevent fraud and abuse, and ensure that the licensed insurers provide value for money. Current regulations of private health insurance in the EU are weak (Maynard 1999; OECD 2004).

OWNERSHIP AND GOVERNANCE REFORMS. The transition from centralized planning to a market economy was about changes in incentives, ownership, and governance. It was about scarce resources being allocated by market pressures rather than by bureaucratic dictate.

In the health sector this led to privatization of many aspects of the supply chain (pharmaceuticals, medical equipment, supplies, insurance, capital, and even the labor market) as well as part of the service delivery system (many ambulatory clinics, diagnostic centers, and ancillary services). It also led to a corporatization of many hospitals (Jakab, Preker, and Harding 2003).

As with health insurance, each approach to delivering health care has its advantages and disadvantages. This process is not complete. Once again, because one of the commission's responsibilities is to protect consumers, regulation of this emerging private service delivery system clearly needs to be a high priority for the future, especially because an increasing number of patients may try to shop around for the best quality of care and as staff seek out employment opportunities that may be better than in the countries where they were trained.

Sharing of competence over health sector between the EU and member states

Finally, the division of responsibility over the many aspects of health, the health care delivery system, and health care financing involves not just technical competence but also the politics of integration versus national autonomy.

As in many other federal states, the dividing line is likely to be between population-based public health and curative services, with the former being assigned to the aggregate supranational level of the European Commission and the latter being assigned to the national level of the member states. Anxieties about SARS gave added political urgency to plans to create a United States–style European Center for Disease Prevention and Control. The agency would enhance surveillance, coordinate common responses, and set up and maintain a network of reference laboratories with EU member states, candidate countries, and international organizations such as WHO.

However, as has been seen in the spillover from competence in other sectors and the slow "mission creep" in the explicit role of the European Commission, this is likely to be an evolving story as it is in many federal states. The pendulum may swing back and forth a few times before it finally settles at an equilibrium state as both sides push the limits of their respective competences.

NOTE

1. The eight former communist countries that joined the EU in 2004 are the Czech Republic, Estonia, Hungary, Latvia, Lithuania, Poland, the Slovak Republic, and Slovenia.

REFERENCES

Adeyi, O., G. Chellaraj, E. Goldstein, A. Preker, and D. Ringold. 1997. "Health Status During the Transition in Central and Eastern Europe: Development in Reverse?" *Health Policy and Planning* 12(2): 132–45.

Arrow, K. W. 1963. "Uncertainty and the Welfare Economics of Medical Care." *American Economic Review* 53(5): 940–73.

Asvall, J., and R. Alderslade. 2002. "Europe." In *Critical Issues in Global Health,* eds. C. Koop, C. Pearson, and M. Schwarz, 37–46. San Francisco: Jossey-Bass.

Atkinson, A. B., and J. E. Stiglitz. 1980. *Lectures on Public Economics.* Maidenhead: McGraw-Hill.

Balabanova, D., M. Bobak, and M. McKee. 1998. "Patterns of Smoking in Bulgaria." *Tobacco Control* 7(4): 383–5.

Barer, M. L., T. E. Getzen, and G. Stoddardt, eds. 1998. *Health Care and Health Economics: Perspectives on Distribution.* Chichester, West Sussex, England: John Wiley and Sons.

Barr, N. 1994. *Labor Markets and Social Policy in Central and Eastern Europe.* New York and London: Oxford University Press.

Bator, F. 1958. "The Anatomy of Market Failure." *Quarterly Journal of Economics* 72(3): 351–79.

Bobak, M. 2000. "Outdoor Air Pollution, Low Birth Weight, and Prematurity." *Environmental Health Perspectives* 108(2): 173–6.

Bobak, M., and R. G. A. Feachem. 1992. "Health Status in the Czech and Slovak Federal Republic." *Health Policy Planning* 7(3): 234–42.

Bobak, M., M. McKee, R. Rose, and M. Marmot. 1999. "Alcohol Consumption in a National Sample of the Russian Population." *Addiction* 94(6): 857–66.

Bobak, M., Z. Skodova, Z. Pisa, R. Poledne, and M. Marmot. 1997. "Political Changes and Trends in Cardiovascular Risk Factors in the Czech Republic, 1985–92." *Journal of Epidemiology and Community Health* 51(3): 272–7.

Catalano, R. 1991. "The Health Effects of Economic Insecurity." *American Journal of Public Health* 81(9): 1148–52.

Chervyakov, V. V., V. M. Shkolnikov, W. A. Pridemore, and M. McKee. 2002. "The Changing Nature of Murder in Russia." *Social Science & Medicine* 55(10): 1713–24.

Cram, L., ed. 1996. *Integration Theory and the Study of the European Policy Process.* London: Routledge.

Donahue, J. D. 1989. *The Privatization Decision: Public Ends, Private Means.* New York: Basic Books.

Eberstadt, N. 1990. "Health and Mortality in Eastern Europe, 1965–85." *Communist Economies* 2(3): 347–71.

———. 1993. "Mortality and the Fate of Communist States." *Communist Economies and Economic Transformation* 5(4): 499–517.

Enthoven, A. 1978. "Consumer Choice Health Plan." *New England Journal of Medicine* 298(13): 709–20.

———. 1988. *Theory and Practice of Managed Competition in Health Care Finance.* New York: North-Holland.

European Commission. 1992. "Council Recommendation of 27 July 1992 on the convergence of social protection objectives and policies." 92/442/EEC. Brussels: European Commission.

European Commission. 1993. *EU Enlargement—A Historic Opportunity.* Brussels: European Commission. http://europa.eu.int/comm/enlargement/intro/criteria.htm.

Evans, R. G. 1984. *Strained Mercy.* Toronto: Butterworth.

Goldstein, E., A. S. Preker, O. Adeyi, G. Chellaraj. 1996. "Trends in Health Status, Services and Finance: The Transition in Central and Eastern Europe." vol 1. Technical Paper Series No. 341, World Bank, Washington, DC.

Hanke, W., M. J. Saurel-Cubizolles, W. Sobala, and J. Kalinka. 2001. "Employment Status of Pregnant Women in Central Poland and the Risk of Preterm Delivery and Small-for-Gestational-Age Infants." *European Journal of Public Health* 11(1): 23–8.

Harding, A., and A. S. Preker. 2000. "Understanding Organizational Reforms: The Corporatization of Public Hospitals." Health, Nutrition, and Population Discussion Paper, World Bank, Washington, DC.

———. eds. 2003. *Private Participation in Health Services.* Health, Nutrition, and Population Series. Washington, DC: World Bank.

Herzlinger, R. 1997. *Market Driven Health Care: Who Wins, Who Loses in the Transformation of America's Largest Service Industry.* Reading, MA: Perseus Books.

Jakab, M., A. S. Preker, and A. Harding. 2002. "Linking Organizational Structure to the External Environment: Experiences from Hospital Reform in Transition Economies." In *Hospitals in a Changing Europe,* eds. M. McKee and J. Healy, 70–202. Buckingham: Open University Press.

———. 2003. "The Missing Link? Hospital Reform in Transition Economies." In *Innovations in Health Service Delivery: The Corporatization of Public Hospitals,* A. S. Preker and A. Harding. Washington, DC: World Bank.

Jakubowski, E., and R. Hess. 2004. "The Market for Physicians." In *Health Policy and European Union Enlargement,* eds. M. McKee, L. MacLehose, and E. Nolte, 145–156. Buckingham: Open University Press.

Kanavos, P. 2004. "European Pharmaceutical Policy and Implications for Current Member States and Candidate Countries." In *Health Policy and European Union Enlargement,* eds. M. McKee, L. MacLehose, and E. Nolte, 240–264. Buckingham: Open University Press. 240–264.

Knight, T. M., C. A. Birt, I. Bocsan, and L. E. Armitage. 2003. "The Public Health Function in Central and Eastern Europe." *Public Health* 117(2): 98–105.

Koradecka, D. 2001. "Occupational Safety and Health in Small and Medium-Sized Enterprises During Social and Economic Transformation." *International Journal of Occupational Safety and Ergonomics* 7(1): 3–14.

Koupilova, I., H. Epstein, J. Holcik, S. Hajioff, and M. McKee. 2001. "Health Needs of the Roma Population in the Czech and Slovak Republics." *Social Science and Medicine* 53(9): 1191–204.

Lovkyte, L., and Z. Padaiga. 2001. "Physician Workforce Reform in Lithuania: An Inevitable Transition." *Cahiers de Sociologie Demographie Medicales* 41(3–4): 347–68.

Makara, P. 1994. "Policy Implications of Differential Health Status in East and West Europe. The Case of Hungary." *Social Science and Medicine* 39(9): 1295–302.

Makinen, I. H. 2000. "Eastern European Transition and Suicide Mortality." *Social Science and Medicine* 51(9): 1405–20.

Manning, N. 1998. *Unbundling the State: Autonomous Agencies and Service Delivery.* Washington, DC: World Bank.

Marmot, M., and M. Bobak. 2000. "International Comparators and Poverty and Health in Europe." *BMJ* 321(7269): 1124–8.

Maynard, A. 1999. "Towards an Integrated Health Care Policy in the European Union?" *Eurohealth* 5(2): 5–6.

McKee, M. 2002. "What Can Health Services Contribute to the Reduction of Inequalities in Health?" *Scandinavian Journal of Public Health* Suppl 59: 54–8.

McKee, M., and A. Britton. 1998. "The Positive Relationship between Alcohol and Heart Disease in Europe: Potential Physiological Mechanisms." *Journal of the Royal Society of Medicine* 91(8): 402–7.

McKee, M., and J. Healy, eds. 2002. *Hospitals in a Changing Europe.* Buckingham: Open University Press.

McKee, M., and B. Jacobson. 2000. "Public Health in Europe." *Lancet* 356(9230): 665–70.

McKee, M., and V. Shkolnikov. 2001. "Understanding the Toll of Premature Death among Men in Eastern Europe." *BMJ* 323(7320): 1051–5.

McKee, M., R. Adany, and L. MacLehose. 2004. "Health Status and Trends in Candidate Countries." In *Health Policy and European Union Enlargement,* eds. M. McKee, L. MacLehose, and E. Nolte, 24–42. Buckingham: Open University Press.

McKee, M., L. MacLehose, and T. Albreht. 2004. "Free Movement of Patients." In *Health Policy and European Union Enlargement,* eds. M. McKee, L. MacLehose, and E. Nolte, 157–175. Buckingham: Open University Press.

McKee, M., L. MacLehose, and E. Nolte, eds. 2004. *Health Policy and European Union Enlargement.* Buckingham: Open University Press.

McKee, M., E. Mossialos, and R. Baetens, eds. 2002. *The Impact of EU Law on Health Care Systems.* Brussels: Peter Lang.

McKee, M., V. Shkolnikov, and D. A. Leon. 2001. "Alcohol is Implicated in the Fluctuations in Cardiovascular Disease in Russia Since the 1980s." *Annals of Epidemiology* 11(1): 1–6.

McKee, M., M. Rosenmöller, L. MacLehose, and M. Zajak. 2004. "The Process of Enlargement." In *Health Policy and European Union Enlargement,* eds. M. McKee, L. MacLehose, and E. Nolte, 6–23. Buckingham: Open University Press.

McKee, M., M. Bobak, R. Rose, V. Shkolnikov, L. Chenet, and D. Leon. 1998. "Patterns of Smoking in Russia." *Tobacco Control* 7(1): 22–6.

Moller-Leimkuhler, A. M. 2003. "The Gender Gap in Suicide and Premature Death or: Why are Men so Vulnerable?" *European Archives of Psychiatry and Clinical Neurosciences* 253(1): 1–8.

Mossialos, E., and J. Le Grand, eds. 1999. *Health Care and Cost Containment in the European Union.* Aldershod: Ashgate.

Mossialos, E., and M. McKee, eds. 2002. *EU Law and the Social Character of Health Care.* Brussels: Peter Lang.

Mossialos, E., and S. Thomson. 2002. "Voluntary Health Insurance in the EU: A Critical Assessment." *International Journal of Health Services* 32(1): 19–88.

Musgrave, R. A., and P. B. Musgrave. 1984. *Public Finance in Theory and Practice.* New York: McGraw-Hill.

Musgrove, P. 1996. *Public and Private Roles in Health: Theory and Financing Patterns.* Washington, DC: World Bank.

Nanda, A., A. Nossikov, R. Prokhorskas, M. H. Shabanah. 1993. "Health in the Central and Eastern Countries of the WHO European Region: An Overview." *World Health Statistics Quarterly* 46(3): 158–65.

OECD. 2004. "Private Health Insurance in OECD Countries." Paris: OECD.

Osborne, D., and T. Gaebler. 1993. *Reinventing Government.* New York: Plume.

Peacock, A. 1980. "On the Anatomy of Collective Failure, Public Finance." *Public Finance* 35(1): 33–43.

Piha, T. 2000. "The New EU Health Strategy: Moving Forward through Communication and Debate." *Eurohealth* 6(4): 7–9.

Preker, A. S. 1989. *The Introduction of Universality in Health Care.* London: IIHS, OECD.

———. 1994. "Meeting the Challenge: Policymaking and Management during Economic Transition." *Journal of Health Administration and Education* 12(4): 433–47.

———. 1996. "Investing in People and Growth." In *World Development Report: From Plan to Market.* 123–132. New York: Oxford University Press for World Bank.

Preker, A. S., and R. G. A. Feachem. 1994. "Health Care." In *Labor Markets and Social Policy in Central and Eastern Europe,* ed. N. Barr, 288–321. Oxford: World Bank.

———. 1996. "Market Mechanisms and the Health Sector in Central and Eastern Europe," Technical Paper Series No. 293, World Bank, Washington, DC.

Preker, A. S., and A. Harding. 2000. "The Economics of Public and Private Roles in Health Care: Insights from Institutional Economics and Organizational Theory." Health, Nutrition, and Population Discussion Paper, World Bank, Washington, DC.

———. eds. 2003. *Innovations in Health Service Delivery: The Corporatization of Public Hospitals.* Health, Nutrition, and Population Series. Washington, DC: World Bank.

Preker, A. S., M. Jakab, and M. Schneider. 2002. "Health Financing Reform in Central and Eastern Europe and the Former Soviet Union." In *Funding Health Care: Options for Europe,* eds. E. Mossialos, A. Dixon, J. Figueras, and J. Kutzin, 80–108. Buckingham: Open University Press.

Reamy, J. 1998. "Managing Physician Resources: East and West." *Croatian Medical Journal* 39(3): 234–40.

Rechel, B., L. Shapo, M. McKee, and the Health and Nutrition Group of the World Bank's Europe and Central Asia Region. 2004. "Appropriate Health-Related Millennium Development Goals for the Europe and Central Asia Region: Potential Impacts and Policy Implications." Washington, DC: World Bank.

Rice, T. 1998. *The Economics of Health Reconsidered.* Chicago: Health Administration Press.

Saltman, R., and J. Figueras. 1997. *European Health Care Reform: Analysis of Current Strategies.* Copenhagen: WHO.

Saltman, R. B., R. Busse, and E. Mossialos, eds. 2002. *Regulating Entrepreneurial Behaviour in European Health Care Systems.* Buckingham: Open University Press.

Saltman, R. B., J. Figueras, and C. Sakallarides, eds. 1997. *Critical Challenges for Health Care Reform in Europe.* Copenhagen: World Health Organization/European Observatory on Health Care Reform.

Shkolnikov, V., M. McKee, and D. A. Leon. 2001. "Changes in Life Expectancy in Russia in the Mid-1990s." *Lancet* 357(9260): 917–21.

Shkolnikov, V., M. McKee, J. Vallin, E. Aksel, D. Leon, L. Chenet, and F. Mesle. 1999. "Cancer Mortality in Russia and Ukraine: Validity, Competing Risks and Cohort Effects." *International Journal of Epidemiology* 28(1): 19–29.

Stone, R. 2000. "Social Science. Stress: The Invisible Hand in Eastern Europe's Death Rates." *Science* 288(5472): 1732–3.

Valkonen, T. 1982. "Psychosocial Stress and Sociodemographic Differentials in Mortality from Ischaemic Heart Disease in Finland." *Acta Medica Scandinavica Supplementum* 660: 152–64.

Van Doorslaer, E., A. Wagstaff, and P. Paci. 1993. *Equity in the Finance and Delivery of Health Care: An International Perspective.* Oxford: Oxford Medical Publications.

Vining, A. R., and D. L. Weimer. 1990. "Government Supply and Government Production Failure: A Framework Based on Contestability." *Journal of Public Policy* 10(1): 1–22.

Walberg, P., M. McKee, V. Shkolnikov, L. Chenet, and D. A. Leon.1998. "Economic Change, Crime, and Mortality Crisis in Russia: Regional Analysis." *BMJ* 317(7154): 312–8.

Wilson, J. Q. 1989. *Bureaucracy.* New York: Basic Books.

Wolf, C. J. 1979. "A Theory of Non-Market Failure." *Journal of Law and Economics* 22(1): 107–39.

World Bank. 1993. *World Development Report 1993: Investing in Health.* New York: Oxford University Press.

———. 1996. *World Development Report 1996: From Plan to Market.* Oxford: Oxford University Press.

———. 1997. Sector Strategy for HNP. World Bank. Washington, DC.

———. 2000. *World Development Report 2000/2001: Attacking Poverty.* Oxford, New York: Oxford University Press.

———. 2003a. "Averting AIDS Crises in Eastern Europe and Central Asia—A Regional Support Strategy." Washington, DC: World Bank.

———. 2003b. "Health in Europe and Central Asia: Transition Retrospective and Business Plan." World Bank Sector Strategy. World Bank, Washington, DC.

———. 2004a. Millennium Development Goals http://www.developmentgoals.org/About_the_goals.htm. *Accessed on March 12, 2004.*

———. 2004b. "Millennium Development Goals for Health in Europe and Central Asia: Relevance and Policy Implications." Working Paper No. 33, World Bank, Washington, DC.

World Health Organization. 1993. *Health Care Reform in Europe.* First Meeting of the Working Party on Health Care Reforms in Europe, Madrid June 23–24, Ministerio de Sanidad y Consumo, Madrid.

———. 1997. *European Health Care Reform: Analysis of Current Strategies.* Copenhagen: World Health Organization.

———. 2000. *The World Health Report 2000. Health Systems: Measuring Performance.* Geneva: World Health Organization.

———. 2001. *Macroeconomics and Health: Investing in Health for Economic Development.* Geneva: WHO.

Young, P. 1986. *Privatization Around the Globe: Lessons from the Reagan Administration.* Houston: National Center for Policy Analysis.

7

EDUCATION AND TRAINING

Michael Mertaugh and Eric Hanushek

Aprevailing view at the start of the transition was that education and training systems were among the few creations of the former communist countries that did not need fixing to function effectively in the capitalist world. It became apparent early in the transition, however, that this impression was profoundly mistaken. The accession countries soon encountered problems in maintaining their relatively advanced education systems as output and revenues fell and as ideologically motivated decentralization policies made local governments responsible for managing and financing most schools. At the same time, rising unemployment of graduates signaled a mismatch of education with the evolving skill needs of the competitive economy.

In many ways the accession countries face the same challenges as all of the countries in the Organisation for Economic Co-operation and Development (OECD). Globalization and competition are forcing all countries to rethink the role of education and training. The accelerated pace of technological change and evolving markets require a more agile and more adaptable labor force if economies are to remain competitive. Education programs need to do a better job of developing students' skills in critical thinking and application across the boundaries of conventional disciplines. Opportunities for lifelong learning need to be enriched to develop job-specific skills, to help keep skills up-to-date, and to retool skills for career changes. These challenges are considerably more difficult to meet in the accession countries for two reasons: they require a more radical change from the structure and focus of the former system; and they are exacerbated by the economic and budgetary contraction that accompanied the transition.

This chapter examines the education and training challenges facing the accession countries as a result both of the transition and of the broader changes affecting all countries.[1] It focuses largely on changes in formal education at the primary and secondary levels, because it is at these levels that the equity-efficiency trade-offs are most acute and that incomplete decentralization policies are hampering reform. Questions of higher education finance are dealt with briefly in the text, and in greater detail in annex 7A.

THE LOGIC OF TRANSITION: EDUCATION

Understanding the current stresses and strains on the education systems of accession countries must begin with the systems of the past. That context coupled with the upheavals of economic transformation has pushed and distorted the evolution of the education systems and sets boundaries on the speed and direction of change.

The inherited system

Education in the accession countries prior to the transition covered virtually the entire population through the secondary level and was of high quality relative to the needs of the former system (Laporte and Schweitzer 1994). Access to higher education was, however, strictly controlled, basically limited to meeting the known needs for scientific and technical skills in the economy. Schools and universities were relatively well provisioned and maintained. The teaching profession enjoyed high prestige and attracted highly qualified candidates. The teaching process reinforced the ideological preeminence of societal needs over individual needs. As in the Soviet Union, education was intended to play an important role in creating a proletarian intelligentsia and promoting social mobility for groups that had been excluded from education and higher-level jobs under the prior order. In the process, however, it helped create a new intellectual and political elite. Preferential access to secondary and higher education for children of peasant and working-class families was an instrument of this policy (Fitzpatrick 1979). Pedagogy encouraged conformity with the established order. It discouraged personal inquisitiveness and individual initiative that might undermine the social order.

This system was no accident. The centrally planned process of economic production and directed consumption both enabled and required a close match of the education and training system with the process of economic production. Physical production targets were set long in advance and technology was relatively static, so specific skill needs could be projected with considerable accuracy. Vocational and technical training were often offered in conjunction with in-enterprise training. Upon completion of education and training, graduates were assigned to jobs—often to lifetime jobs in the enterprises where they trained. Job stability, not job mobility, was encouraged. Wages and salaries were set normatively, rather than on the basis of marginal productivity, and played no role in allocating skills to where they were most needed. Salaries for highly educated workers were often lower than for jobs with minimal skill requirements. Both the structure of the economy and the focus of education emphasized manufacturing. Service-sector production was neglected; so were the skills—including humanities, business, and social sciences—associated with the service sector. The role of education as an instrument of personal growth and enrichment did not exist.

This system was internally consistent, but inefficient—for both individual welfare and productive efficiency. Education inputs were financed on the basis of centrally established norms. Input-based financing provided neither the opportunity nor the incentive to improve efficiency, resulting in gross overcapacity in facilities and staffing by comparison to OECD standards. The process of financing inputs was also ineffective as a quality control mechanism in comparison to approaches that more directly address program outputs such as enrollments, graduates, learning achievement, and labor-market relevance of skills. The broad coverage and relatively high quality of compulsory education masked the inequities of a system that remained highly elitist at higher levels, and that focused inordinate attention and resources on the most highly performing students.

The impacts of transition

The transition involved numerous changes in the economy that led to a major reconfiguration in the composition and types of skills needed in the labor market. Fundamental reforms were needed if education programs were to respond to those changes. However, it was difficult for education programs to reform effectively because the transition also led to a collapse of the traditional sources of financing for education programs. Political changes that accompanied the transition also affected education programs. A major motivation for the transition was the desire for more responsive government with greater input at the local level. In all of the accession countries, one of the first acts of the transition governments was to decentralize responsibility for finance and delivery of basic education. As discussed below, the manner in which decentralization occurred seriously affected the quality and equity of education programs in the accession countries.

Impacts on economic output

The economies of the accession countries were deeply affected by the breakup of the Soviet Union and the dissolution of the Soviet economic block. Output levels fell sharply at the start of the transition in most of the accession countries, which led to a collapse in the revenues available for education. Although the output declines were not as steep or as prolonged as in the Commonwealth of Independent States,[2] they were nonetheless significant (figure 2.2). In most of the accession countries, the cumulative decline in output was at least as large as the fall in output in Europe and the United States during the Great Depression of the 1930s (see chapter 2 of this volume, and World Bank 2002). The decline in production and income in the accession countries and the even steeper declines in the former Soviet Union compelled enterprises to find new markets for their products and to compete more vigorously with other suppliers in selling to those markets. Public revenues fell even more steeply than national output, as the formal-sector tax base bore the brunt of the output decline.

Impacts on labor markets and skill requirements

The transition launched three broad trends with mutually reinforcing effects on labor markets and skill requirements:

- First, market liberalization meant that production was driven by consumer choice rather than by central production targets. Prices of outputs and inputs were freed from administrative control. Wage and salary levels were no longer normatively set but were free to reflect differences in productivity and to signal emerging scarcities and redundancies in specific labor-market skills. Market liberalization led to a major reconfiguration of the structure of production and the creation of entirely new industries, especially in the service sector. It also led to major adjustments in the returns to skills: earnings in most low-skill occupations, especially in the manufacturing sector, fell sharply relative to salaries in occupations requiring higher skill levels.
- Second, the opening of the accession economies and the disappearance of subsidies and guaranteed markets required that enterprises compete to survive. This created powerful new incentives for efficiency in production. Inefficient enterprises—including many of the largest employers—closed or were restructured. Efficient enterprises and enterprises that responded to

long-stifled consumer demand prospered. Market stability was replaced by more rapid succession of economic specializations or "niches."

- Third, freer flows of trade, of financial resources, of information, and of human capital interacted with an acceleration of technological change throughout the global economy, reinforcing the other demands for change in the accession economies. New applications such as the replacement of mechanical control with digital control in manufacturing; the substitution of robotics and production teams for repetitive, assembly line tasks; miniaturization; substitution of lighter, cleaner, and cheaper materials; and the proliferation of web-based information, communications, and marketing lowered the value of "old" skills. Improved information and communications technology contributed to these changes in various ways. It accelerated technological change by speeding the diffusion of new technologies. It also accelerated the evolution of markets by enabling just-in-time provision of inputs to production, thereby reducing the need for inventories of inputs, and, as a result, reducing the buffering effect of inventories.

These fundamental changes in the economy introduced less predictability in labor-market skill requirements. The immediate consequences were dramatic. The shrinking of many traditional activities (often in the manufacturing sector) and the growth of other activities (often in the service sector) transformed the demand for skills, making many skills redundant and creating excess demand for others. Open and sizable unemployment appeared. Lifetime employment became the exception rather than the rule. The more typical pattern that appears to be replacing it is a need to change jobs—and often occupations—several times in the course of one's working life.

Impacts on education budgets

At the same time that the transition brought with it the need for these fundamental changes in education programs, it also made funding education more difficult. Real GDP declined early in the 1990s in all of the accession countries (figure 2.2), but there was considerable variation in the degree of recovery at the end of the decade (table 7.1). In 2000, real GDP remained seriously below its 1990 level in Bulgaria, Estonia, Latvia, Lithuania, and Romania, but had recovered to at least its 1990 level in the Czech Republic, Hungary, Poland, the Slovak Republic, and Slovenia. The impacts on education budgets were even more diverse. In some cases, the allocations of public budget compensated for the effect of falling GDP on governmental resources; in others, it reinforced that effect. In Bulgaria, budget allocations accentuated the decline in GDP and contributed to the most severe decline in education expenditures in the acces-

TABLE 7.1 Real changes in GDP and public expenditures on education,
1990–2000

	Real GDP in 2000 as % of 1990 GDP	Real expenditures on education as % of 1990 level	
		1995	2000
Bulgaria	82.1	52.6	40.3
Czech Republic	99.9	118.3	96.0
Estonia	86.1	91.2	108.5
Hungary	108.0	93.5	98.6
Latvia	62.3	86.5	116.1
Lithuania	68.4	69.1	70.1
Poland	143.2	154.6	211.0
Romania	82.9	154.8	128.9
Slovak Republic	105.1	90.1	81.3
Slovenia	120.1	117.8	139.5

Source: World Bank database.
Note: Expenditure figures refer to consolidated (central plus local) general budget.

sion countries: real education expenditures in Bulgaria in the year 2000 were just 40 percent of their 1990 level. In Estonia, Latvia, and Romania, budget allocations played a strong compensatory role: real public outlays for education rose in spite of falling GDP over the decade. In Poland and Slovenia, budget allocations reinforced the effect of rising GDP: real education expenditures increased even more than GDP. In Lithuania, increasing budget allocations protected education expenditures from falling as deeply as GDP over the 1990s. In the Czech Republic, budget allocations protected real education expenditures in the first half of the decade, then moved to other priorities leaving lower real spending for education during the second half of the decade. In Hungary and the Slovak Republic, GDP grew over the decade, but real public outlays for education fell; falling budget shares more than offset the effect of growing GDP. (Note, however, that the student population in most the accession countries also declined over the period, so the declines in spending per pupil are not as sharp as seen in the declines of total real expenditure. These declines, discussed below, are generally insufficient to reverse the decreases in spending in table 7.1 with the possible exception of Hungary, but they reinforce the spending growth in Estonia, Latvia, Romania, and Slovenia).

The accession governments' initial response to collapsing revenues and collapsing education budgets at the start of the transition focused on reducing expenditures and diversifying financing sources. Reduced expenditures occurred largely through sharply reduced budget outlays for preschool education, suspension of expenditures for renewing educational materials, arrears in teacher salary payments at the start of the transition, and falling real salary levels thereafter. Sources of financing were diversified through five sets of actions:

- Decentralizing the responsibility for financing and managing most primary and secondary education programs from central to regional and local governments
- Introducing student fees and other user charges (including "contracted" provision of secondary and higher education within public schools and universities for students with entry scores below the threshold for budget-financed admission)
- Requiring parents to purchase textbooks and other educational materials that had formerly been provided free by schools
- Expanding private education
- Allowing schools to raise and retain funds through actions such as rental or sale of unneeded facilities and provision of paid extracurricular courses.

In addition, many teachers and school principals generated income through paid tutoring and solicitation of informal payments from students and parents.

These actions led to a number of adverse consequences for education programs, including the closure of many preschools and a decline in preschool enrollment early in the transition. The increased reliance on financing from local governments and households with different capacities contributed to the emergence of large differences in education quality. This may have contributed to the declines in coverage that were observed for primary and secondary education in Bulgaria and for secondary education in Romania. Reliance on extra-budgetary sources of financing often created perverse incentives, such as the incentive for teachers not to cover the complete curriculum in class to create a demand for paid, extramural tutorial instruction; and the incentive for production activities in vocational schools and service provision in general secondary schools—such as offering computer classes to the community—to displace educational activities. Although it is difficult to document, corruption in the form of solicitation of informal payments for better examination scores and for admission to university programs also became (and remains) a serious concern in some of the accession countries.

Changing education quality

Student assessment provides the best indication of changes in education quality with regard to learning achievement. For the accession countries, the most inclusive source of internationally comparable data on what students learn is the Trends in International Mathematics and Science Study (TIMSS), which was carried out for a nationally representative sample of eighth-grade students in 24 countries in 1995, 39 countries in 1999, and 45 countries in 2003.[3] Seven accession countries—Bulgaria, Hungary, Latvia, Lithuania, Romania, the Slovak Republic, and Slovenia—participated in all three assessments, and the Czech Republic participated in both the 1995 and 1999 surveys. As shown in table 7.2, four of the accession countries had mean math and science scores above the international—largely OECD—average in 1995. By 1999, the pattern of performance was changing. Only two countries were above the international average in both subjects (the Slovak Republic and Hungary), while the Czech Republic remained above the international average in science. Latvia's and Lithuania's average math and science scores improved significantly in 1999, but not enough to take them above the international average. The international average fell sharply in 2003, because of the inclusion of a number of low-scoring developing countries in the assessment. Thus, the comparison to the average is not as meaningful in 2003, but the fact that Bulgaria and Romania are close to the new, lower average level is telling. Estonia, which first participated in 2003, outscored all of the accession countries.

TABLE 7.2 TIMSS eighth grade student assessment results for science and math for eight accession countries, 1995, 1999, and 2003

	Mathematics mean score			Science mean score		
	1995	*1999*	*2003*	*1995*	*1999*	*2003*
Czech Republic	546	520	n.a.	555	539	n.a.
Slovak Republic	534	534	*508*	532	535	*517*
Hungary	527	532	529	537	552	543
Bulgaria	527	511	*476*	545	518	*479*
International Average	519	521	466	518	521	473
Slovenia	494	n.a.	493	514	n.a.	**520**
Latvia	488	505	**505**	476	503	**513**
Romania	474	472	475	471	472	470
Lithuania	472	482	**502**	464	488	**519**

Source: International Association for the Evaluation of Educational Achievement 2000a, 2000b; National Center for Education Statistics 2004.
Note: Scores for 2003 in **bold** indicate significant increases and in *italics* indicate significant decreases between 1995 and 2003. n.a. = Not available. The Czech Republic did not participate in 2003 and changes in schooling ages make the 1999 scores for Slovenia not comparable to the 2003 scores. The significantly lower international average for 2003 reflects the addition of many low-scoring developing countries during that year.

Tracking the changes over time is illuminating. Latvia and Lithuania showed very significant gains between 1995 and 2003 in both subjects, and Slovenia had significant science gains. In contrast, the Slovak Republic and Bulgaria showed significant declines over the 1995–2003 period. The Czech Republic, which did not participate in the most recent testing, dropped sharply between 1995 and 1999.[4]

Because Bulgaria experienced the largest real decline in public budgets for education during the decade and the largest drop in combined math and science scores, it is tempting to suspect a direct relationship between education expenditures and student assessment results. However, the data in tables 7.1 and 7.2 show, as do many other studies, that there is no simple relationship between education expenditures (or changes in education expenditures) and average levels of student achievement (or changes in average student achievement). In contrast to Bulgaria's experience, Lithuania achieved dramatically improved average scores despite lower expenditures on education, and scores in Romania remained constant even with significant increases in expenditure from 1990.

Increases in educational inequality

As chapter 2 describes, the economic dislocation of transition and the policy actions to respond to it led to a sharp increase in income inequality in the accession countries. Income inequality among households worsened during the decade in all of the accession countries, with the average Gini coefficient[5] rising from 0.23 at the start of the decade to 0.32 by 2000 (World Bank 2002). Increasing reliance on financing from households and local communities led to greater between-school differences in the availability of teaching and learning resources. Local governments vary widely in their capacity to mobilize resources from local taxes and other sources (including parental contributions). Thus, the shifting of financing responsibilities to local communities and to parents has meant that schools in poor communities are often poorly maintained and poorly equipped with teaching and learning materials, while schools in more prosperous communities are often well maintained and well equipped.

These transition-related differences in the objective aspects of teaching and the learning environment may well have exacerbated differences in student learning achievement, particularly between urban and rural areas. The most systematic differences in educational performance in the accession countries are the differences between urban and rural schools. In Romania, for example, fourth grade students in rural areas consistently perform below their urban counterparts (table 7.3). This gap is consistent with not only the poorer resource endowment of rural communities and rural schools, but also the generally lower

TABLE 7.3 Urban-rural differences in fourth grade assessment in Romania

Subject	Location	Share at each level of performance (%)			
		Low	*Medium*	*Good*	*Very good*
Mother tongue	Urban	3.5	6.9	18.8	70.8
	Rural	17.0	17.1	29.9	36.1
Mathematics	Urban	4.5	7.4	28.0	60.2
	Rural	17.2	19.6	32.0	31.2
Sciences	Urban	1.2	6.3	31.8	60.7
	Rural	8.2	17.9	40.3	33.6

Source: Stoica 2002.

qualifications and experience of teachers in rural areas, the poverty of rural households that makes it hard for them to afford education-related purchases, the lower educational status of rural parents, and the relative lack of educational stimuli in the rural environment. Cost differences exacerbate the resource differences between urban and rural areas. Costs of education are higher in rural areas than in urban areas because dispersion of population leads to uneconomically small class sizes, large transport costs, or both. Dispersed rural population complicates the task of school rationalization. In Lithuania, for example, 13 percent of rural comprehensive schools have an average of 5 students per class in grades six through nine, 23 percent have 7 students per class, and 31 percent have 10 students per class—class sizes that appear too small to be rational (Economic Research Centre 1999). Heating and utility costs also tend to be higher for rural schools. Because these intrinsic sources of higher unit costs of education are most prevalent in areas with the smallest revenue base, they tend to reinforce the differences in educational quality that result from urban-rural differences in household income and local revenue capacity.

One of the few other sources of international comparative data on education quality differences within the accession countries is the Programme for International Student Assessment (PISA) for 2000.[6] This study was carried out by the OECD for a sample of 15-year-olds in 31 countries (including Bulgaria, the Czech Republic, Hungary, Latvia, Poland, and Romania) in 2000. By comparison to the TIMSS surveys, the PISA surveys make a particular effort to assess students' skills in application and synthesis of concepts—the generic skills that are most relevant to the needs of the global economy. Mean scores for the six accession countries represented in the survey are all below the OECD average, ranging from the Czech Republic (2 percent [eight points] below the OECD average) to Romania (14 percent [72 points] below the OECD average) (table 7.4). In all the accession countries except Hungary, there is greater

TABLE 7.4 PISA Student assessment results for literacy for 15-year-olds for
OECD and six accession countries, 2000

	Mean score	Total variation in student results[a]	Percentage of total variation resulting from between-school variation[a]
OECD average	500	100.0	36.0
Czech Republic	492	100.0	51.9
Hungary	480	95.0	71.2
Poland	479	107.3	67.0
Latvia	458	112.5	35.1
Bulgaria	430	112.1	66.1
Romania	428	n.a.	n.a.

Source: OECD and UNESCO Institute of Statistics 2003.
Note: n.a. = Not available.
a. expressed as a percentage of the average variation in student performance in OECD countries.

dispersion of student assessment results than the OECD average. In all but Latvia, much more of the variation in student assessment results is explained by between-school differences than is true for the OECD average. These greater between-school differences in student achievement in Bulgaria, the Czech Republic, Hungary, and Poland may reflect greater between-school differences in financing that have emerged under the transition. Unfortunately, there are no time series data that would allow confirmation of these results over time. There is a strong suspicion, for example, that many of the urban-rural outcome differences have existed for some time—since before transition. Regardless of their time trends and their causes, these sizeable between-school differences in what students learn should be a cause for concern—for reasons of both economic performance and equity—in countries that aspire to educate all students to international standards.

Another international study that sheds further light on education and skill requirements in the accession countries is the survey carried out by the International Adult Literacy Survey, the OECD, and Statistics Canada in the mid-1990s (OECD and Statistics Canada 1997). This study examines adults' understanding of concepts and their ability to apply them effectively in 11 OECD countries and Poland. It finds that 75 percent of the Polish population ages 16 to 65 years performed below the level judged necessary by labor-market experts and employers to function effectively in an information-rich workplace—far below the level recorded for the OECD countries. The same study found much lower levels of unemployment and higher levels of earnings among workers of higher functional literacy proficiency in all the countries surveyed.

Follow-up work supported by Statistics Canada documented the deterioration of functional literacy skills over time unless these skills are maintained through subsequent training or work experience in an information-rich work environment (Coulombe, Tremblay, and Marchand 2004). An implication of these findings is that the education system of Poland—and presumably of the other accession countries as well—does a better job of imparting concepts than the ability to apply concepts. It also suggests that whatever practical skills the education system does manage to impart deteriorate more rapidly than they would in a more information-rich working environment and an environment that offers more opportunities for lifelong learning.

Reform directions

The impacts of transition implied that the inherited education and training programs, however appropriate they may have been for the former system, were unlikely to meet the skill requirements of the new market economy. This, in turn, implied a need for urgent reforms in two broad areas: content and structure; and finance and management. This section describes what reforms are needed in both these areas as result of the transition. It also explains the main reasons the transition requires these reforms.

Reform of content and structure

Transition implies a need for change in the content and structure of education and training programs to respond to the economic changes described above— the instability and unpredictability of labor-force skill requirements, the higher technical content of occupations in all branches of economic activity, the more rapid succession of technologies and market niches, and the changing nature of work itself.

EDUCATION AND TRAINING CONTENT. To survive in this dynamic new world, individuals need not only to keep their technical skills up-to-date but also to fundamentally change their approach to work. Increasingly, labor-market success requires that individuals become inquisitive, flexible, adept at working as members of teams, knowledgeable about sources of reliable information, and alert to evolving opportunities (OECD 2001; World Bank 1999, 2003). Getting and keeping a job is no longer assured; it requires initiative. Education programs need a fundamental reorientation to respond to these needs. The inherited education systems in the accession countries were generally strong in conveying factual knowledge—especially in mathematics and natural science programs. They were not as good at developing critical thinking skills and skills of application and synthesis. The content of education programs needs to be changed to give more attention to higher-order skills of application and synthesis and critical thinking. This calls for a different approach to teaching, and for access to a richer environment of educational resources for students and teachers.

EDUCATION AND TRAINING STRUCTURE. The structure of education and training also needs to change to become more responsive to evolving needs of the economy. Several types of changes are called for. The emerging demand for skills in areas such as foreign languages and computer applications means that the traditional distinction between academic and vocational or technical specializations is increasingly obsolete, because many of the most highly demanded skills in labor markets are typically offered in structured academic programs. The streaming or tracking of students into specialized vocational and technical programs and the highly selective admission into higher education need to be softened and made less ultimate. To the extent that specialized programs of vocational and technical education are offered in secondary and higher education, they need to be developed in ways that provide generalizable skills—skills that will not become obsolete immediately with changes in technology and industrial structure. The transition of the educational structure will be facilitated by providing better information to parents and students about the career implications of alternative educational choices and by promoting more student involvement in decisions about the changing structure of education and training programs.

Specialized training programs also need to be developed to provide relevant adult training opportunities for people in and out of the labor market. Adult training and continuing education are important for three reasons: to upgrade skills to keep workers competitive in occupations with changing technology, to provide occupational mobility by equipping workers with new skills to change occupations, and for personal enrichment. In view of the nonexistence of such programs under the inherited system, responding to this need constitutes a major challenge, involving the development of a framework for training providers and of appropriate incentives and financing mechanisms for delivery of training by a diverse range of providers.

Reform of finance and management

Reform of education finance and management is needed for two reasons. First, efficiency in the use of education resources (staff, facilities, materials, and budgets) must be improved. While not a new problem, the budget pressures of the transition made it more urgent, and the decentralization measures that were expected to bring improved efficiency failed to do so. Second, reform was needed to correct the problems of declining education quality and increasing educational inequality described above.

The manner in which the accession countries decentralized the responsibility for delivery of primary and secondary education had major effects on budget resources for education. Decentralization in the accession countries typically involved financing teacher salaries from the state budget but devolving responsibility for school maintenance and provision of educational materials (and often even teacher training) to local governments. In principle, the decentralization of responsibilities for education finance and management to local governments offers the potential to make the management of education more efficient and the content of education more responsive to local needs. It could also encourage the mobilization of additional resources for education. However, fundamental problems in the design of decentralization policy in the accession countries have blocked the attainment of these benefits.

Teacher and classroom utilization in the accession countries was low at the start of the transition by comparison to the OECD countries and deteriorated further during the 1990s (table 7.5). Fertility declines led to declining school-age population—and often enrollments—in all the accession countries except Poland and the Slovak Republic. Rather than using this opportunity to reconfigure schools to improve school efficiency, local and central governments tended to cooperate in maintaining existing teaching positions, schools, and classrooms—letting adjustment come through decreases in student-teacher ratios. (The same pattern was also apparent, but to a lesser degree, in the OECD countries.) Country norms on minimum teaching hours in the accession countries are also low by OECD standards. For example, teaching hours in primary schooling average 583 hours per year in Hungary and 724 hours in the Czech Republic compared with 958 hours in the United States, and 788 hours in the OECD as a whole (OECD 2000). These problems of persistent inefficiency in use of education resources reflect a lack of incentives in the financing and management formula for schools, and are discussed later in this chapter.

Shortcomings in financing and management contributed to quality and inequity problems in higher education, where rapid enrollment growth and declining budgets early in the transition led to a serious deterioration of teaching and learning conditions, including the obsolescence and nonrenewal of educational equipment and materials of all kinds. Mobilization of additional resources and more selective use of existing resources are clearly needed to improve the quality of higher education. Changes in financing and management of higher education are also needed to address problems of equity and efficiency, as described later in this chapter and in annex 7A.

TABLE 7.5 Changes in student-to-teacher ratios, accession countries and OECD comparators

	Average annual population growth in %, 1990–97	Student-to-teacher ratio in primary education	
		1990	1997
Bulgaria	−0.7	14.8	13.9
Czech Republic	−0.1	19.6	14.5
Estonia	−1.2	10.5	11.7
Hungary	−0.3	12.5	12.2
Latvia	−1.1	—	12.0
Lithuania	−0.1	12.0	11.3
Poland	0.2	16.7	15.4
Romania	−0.4	16.7	14.8
Slovak Republic	0.2	19.4	17.1
Slovenia	−0.1	15.4	13.5
OECD average	—	20.9	17.1
Japan	−0.2	—	21.4
Republic of Korea	0.6	—	31.0
United Kingdom	0.4	—	22.0
New Zealand	1.3	—	24.7

Source: Population growth from World Development Indicators. Accession country student-to-teacher ratios from UNICEF-ICDC database, as provided in Berryman 2000.
Note: — Not available.

EDUCATION UNDER ACCESSION

European Union (EU) accession conditionality consists of three parts:

- Specific legislation addresses education and training only in terms of inclusiveness goals, because the EU has consistently treated education as falling under the competence of the member states.
- Other relevant legislation under the Growth and Stability Pact affects education and training only indirectly through fiscal conditionality.
- Nonbinding coordination includes three specific targets for education and training programs in member states, including the accession countries. These are: to increase the percentage of 22-year-olds who have completed at least upper secondary education to 85 percent in each member state by 2010; to increase the number of working adults (ages 25 to 64) receiving training and continuing education to an EU-wide average of 12.5 percent by 2010; and to reduce the number of students who drop out of school before completing compulsory education to 10 percent in each member

state by 2010 (European Union 2003). These targets are monitored in the annual Joint Assessments of Employment Priorities as part of the Open Method of Coordination exercise.

This section first describes the challenges involved in meeting current EU conditionality affecting education and training. Next, it examines whether and to what extent broader EU conditionality has been helpful in addressing the reform needs summarized earlier.

Meeting EU accession conditionality

Meeting the formal requirements of accession involves (a) filling the remaining gaps in enrollments and school attendance (largely a matter of devising more effective strategies for addressing the educational and noneducational causes of early drop outs) and (b) beginning to develop an effective capacity for adult training. However, the older EU members themselves are finding that maintaining competitiveness in the global knowledge economy requires considerable changes in their own education systems. These changes and their implications for the accession countries are discussed later in this chapter.

Closing the gaps in school enrollment

Despite the difficulties experienced by the accession countries during the 1990s, official data on school enrollments generally show improved coverage of preschool, primary, and, especially, higher education (expressed as a percentage of the relevant age group enrolled in school) in the accession countries (table 7.6). Registered enrollments actually declined as a percentage of the age group in two countries at the preschool level (Lithuania and the Slovak Republic), in four countries at the primary level (Bulgaria, the Czech Republic, Hungary, and Latvia), and in five countries at the secondary level (Bulgaria, the Czech Republic, Latvia, Lithuania, and, especially, Romania).[7] Most of the registered decline in secondary enrollments occurred in vocational and technical education. In Romania, for example, the enrollment in secondary vocational and technical education declined from 78 percent of the age group in 1990 to 44 percent in 1999, while enrollment in general secondary education increased from 12 percent of the age group to 26 percent in 1999.[8] Where it occurred, the decline in secondary enrollments—especially in secondary vocational enrollments—reflects both the weakened links with enterprises during the transition and a perception that vocational secondary education no longer ensures jobs for graduates. (Many of the enterprises that had traditionally recruited secondary vocational students at the completion of their training

TABLE 7.6 Enrollment ratios through the transition

	Preschool net enrollment ratio (%)		Primary gross enrollment ratio (%)		Secondary gross enrollment ratio (%)		University gross enrollment ratio (%)	
	1990	1999	1990	1999	1990	1999	1990	1999
Bulgaria	66	66	99	95	77	76	26	35
Czech Republic	75	85	99	98	79	76	17	26
Estonia	67	74	95	98	57	72	34	45
Hungary	85	87	99	99	73	99	12	29
Latvia	45	61	95	92	70	69	21	46
Lithuania	56	52	93	96	70	65	27	39
Poland	47	50	98	98	89	100	17	43
Romania	53	66	93	99	90	70	9	23
Slovak Republic	72	70	98	108	78	80	14	23
Slovenia	56	70	95	97	—	93	23	51

Source: UNICEF 2001.
Note: — Not available. Figures shown are gross enrollment ratios, which tend to overstate actual coverage because they include over-age students in the numerator but not in the denominator.

closed or reduced their staffing and no longer recruited graduating students.) Part of the decline, however, may also reflect the pressure for some students to enter the labor market at an early age to augment falling household income. The expansion of higher education enrollments during the 1990s was striking, amounting to more than a doubling of enrollments in many of the accession countries. This rapid growth came about both through a liberalized university admission process (especially for fee-paid contract courses) and through rapid development of private higher education.

Although the figures in table 7.6 do not specifically show compulsory education enrollment rates or completion rates, most of the accession countries have reached the 90 percent completion goal for compulsory education. Three accession countries (Hungary, Poland, and Slovenia) have already surpassed the EU secondary completion goal. The other seven accession countries, however, face a considerable gap in secondary enrollments. Closing this gap will require sustained effort and imaginative policies to achieve the 85 percent completion goal by 2010. This will need to include both educational initiatives (such as counseling and tutoring for students with learning difficulties) and economic initiatives (such as targeted subsidies to poor students to defray the cost of school transport and purchase or rental of textbooks and school supplies). One specific and important schooling challenge in the accession countries is to raise the low completion rates and low performance levels of Roma children (box 7.1).

BOX 7.1 A Special Dimension of Education Coverage: Education of Roma Children

An important dimension of the problem of education coverage in the accession countries is the widespread phenomenon of low school attendance among Roma children. Roma children often start school, but drop out during the initial grades of primary schooling. Language is one of the problems that Roma children face in school. Although all of the accession countries offer minority-language instruction for other ethnic groups, Roma students do not benefit from these programs because there is no consensus on an appropriate version of the Romany language. In addition to the linguistic problem that Roma children face in school, there are other handicaps of Roma families that contribute to low school attendance.[a] Parents are often illiterate and do not appreciate the importance of education. Low income makes it difficult for most Roma households to purchase the textbooks and other school supplies that parents are expected to provide. Roma children often work in the informal sector to supplement meager family income. Many Roma children do not have a reasonable command of any of the languages of instruction in schools. Many Roma families lack legal status and are therefore denied access to schools, health care, and other services. Roma often marry and start childbearing as early as age 12. Of those Roma children who do complete primary school, few attend secondary school or go on to university education. Recent survey data show that school attendance among primary-school-age Roma children is 61.5 percent in Bulgaria, 86.2 percent in Hungary, and 72.0 percent in Romania.[b] Another problem is that Roma children who do attend primary school are often stigmatized by being assigned to schools for the handicapped, because of their lack of command of the national language and other educational handicaps resulting from their environment.

A number of approaches to improving the educational performance of Roma children and other at-risk groups have proven successful in the region, including preschool education in the Romany language or in a multilingual environment, parental education, assistance in legal registration, and assistance in job placement or self employment at completion of schooling. The experience with Roma-targeted programs in the region shows that an inclusive approach that combines these dimensions of support offers the best prospects for raising school participation and school performance among the Roma population—especially when it involves child-centered learning methodologies and the commitment of the Roma community. Other successful measures to improve Roma school attendance and educational performance include provision of financial incentives to schools that attract and

(continued)

BOX 7.1 A Special Dimension of Education Coverage:
Education of Roma Children (*Continued*)

retain Roma students, provision of catch-up classes for Roma drop-outs and tutoring for Roma students, special training for teachers of Roma children and provision of linguistic and cultural mediators in schools with Roma students, and offering of optional Romany language and culture classes. At a July 2003 international conference, the accession countries with the largest Roma minorities committed themselves to developing and implementing a 10-year action program to improve the social inclusion of their Roma minorities through better education, health care, housing, and job opportunities. The countries and agencies that sponsored the conference agreed to develop a Roma Education Fund to help finance educational interventions under this initiative.

a. The challenges for integration of the Roma population in Central and Eastern Europe and some of the successful approaches for doing so are summarized in Ringold, Orenstein, and Wilkens 2003.
b. Data from six-country study on living conditions carried out by Yale University Department of Sociology.

Providing adult training

Considerable effort will be required on the part of the accession countries to meet the goal of providing training for 12.5 percent of the adult labor force each year. The Beyond Accession section below argues that meeting this goal is not so much a matter of providing financing or incentives for adult training as it is of providing a supportive legal and regulatory framework.

Has EU accession conditionality helped motivate needed reform?

EU accession conditionality does address reform needs for education and training in the accession countries and it helps motivate improved coverage of primary and secondary education and the initial development of adult training. However, this section argues that the potential benefit of these measures is likely to be less than intended for three reasons: first, the conditionality misses the crucial distinction between registered enrollments and actual attendance (see box 7.2); second, it does not address the need to reverse the decline in education quality in the accession countries; and, third, the quantitative target for adult training does not provide guidance regarding the appropriate content of training or the most viable means for achieving it. The fiscal constraints

BOX 7.2 School Attendance and School Enrollments

Although official enrollment data show generally improving coverage of education in the accession countries, household survey data consistently show that actual school attendance is well below enrollment ratios based on administrative data and is often declining. Survey data also reveal significant gaps in attendance in rural areas, in areas with ethnic minorities, and among the poor. For example, recent survey results show average attendance rates in primary education of 87 percent in Bulgaria, 90 percent in Hungary, and 88 percent in Romania—all well below the enrollment ratios based on official enrollment data. Enrollment estimates based on administrative data tend to overstate actual education coverage because there are incentives to overstate enrollments to increase budget resources and maintain existing teaching positions. Aggregate enrollment ratios based on administrative data also do not reveal the often sizeable differences in school attendance among different groups. In Bulgaria, for example, survey data show that

- school attendance rates are lower for rural population than for urban population, especially for secondary education (where remoteness of schools is often a constraint);
- school attendance rates for the poor are much lower than for the nonpoor at all levels of education;
- Roma have much lower rates of school attendance than either ethnic Bulgarians or Bulgarian ethnic Turks for all levels of education (see table).

Bulgaria: Rates of school attendance by level, 1995, 1997, and 2001
percent

	Preschool education			Primary education			Secondary education		
	1995	1997	2001	1995	1997	2001	1995	1997	2001
Total Population	44	14	22	87	88	90	47	55	46
Males	42	12	21	88	88	90	49	54	46
Females	46	15	24	85	88	89	45	56	46
Urban	46	13	24	88	90	92	52	63	53
Rural	40	14	20	83	84	84	31	32	22
Nonpoor	47	16	26	89	93	94	49	60	52
Poor	8	11	10	54	81	70	20	46	13
Bulgarians	44	15	26	90	93	94	55	66	56
Turks	53	10	19	88	93	90	10	30	34
Roma	25	5	16	55	58	71	3	5	6

Source: Bulgaria Integrated Household Survey, 1995, 1997, 2001 data.

imposed by the Growth and Stability Pact could have hindered an appropriate budgetary response to the problem of declining education quality. The information presented in previous sections and table 7.1 suggests that this was not generally the case, with the possible exceptions of Bulgaria, Lithuania, and the Slovak Republic. On balance, then, it appears that EU accession conditionality did little either to help or hinder the accession countries in pursuing the education and training reforms required both by the transition, and by the challenges that they face as members of the EU.

BEYOND ACCESSION: THE NEW DEMANDS ON EDUCATION

As described earlier in the chapter, the central reforms in education and training required by the transition involve changes in the content and structure of education programs to respond to new skill requirements of the competitive market economy, and reforms in finance and management of education programs to respond to the collapse of public revenues, and to improve quality, efficiency, and equity of education and training programs. It was argued above that EU accession conditionality makes little contribution either to advancing or hindering these reforms. This concluding section argues that the main challenge facing the accession countries in the education and training sector is to successfully complete these reforms in three broad areas:

- Making education and training programs responsive to the needs of a global economy
- Addressing issues in finance and management
- Making education and training programs more inclusive

Because many countries in the EU and elsewhere are moving aggressively to make their education systems more responsive to the needs of the global knowledge economy, the accession countries need to make considerable progress just to keep even with their competition. Improving their relative competitive position will require an even greater effort.

Responding to the needs of the global economy

Education reforms launched in the accession countries during the transition focused on devising a new financing and governance structure that

- was consistent with the (politically-driven) decentralization policies pursued in all of the accession countries;

- offered the prospect of reversing the sharp fall in education finance experienced in all the accession countries during the early years of transition;
- would provide the right internal incentives to make education programs efficient and responsive to changing needs of the economy.

Reforms also aimed to address the content and pedagogy needs of the global market economy, but these substantive aspects of reform were largely displaced by the urgent need for reform of education governance and finance. As they complete the reforms in management and financing of their education systems during the next decade, the accession countries will need to give greater attention to substantive reforms that are needed to make their education systems more responsive to the needs of the global economy. No longer is it a question of the accession countries simply catching up to education programs in the older EU countries. Instead, it is a question of the EU countries and the accession countries together struggling to respond to the needs of a global economy.

Education plays a key role in supporting the process of development from low-income, resourced-based economies to high-income, knowledge-based economies. A recent study of global competitiveness (Schwab, Porter, and Sachs 2001) identifies three successive stages of economic development—factor-driven growth, investment-driven growth, and innovation-driven growth—and characterizes the role of education in each of those stages, as shown in table 7.7.

Together with supportive macroeconomic and financial policy and infrastructure investments, education plays a key role in developing the necessary human capital at each of these successive stages of development. Regarding educational coverage, the accession countries appear to have reached the highest level of educational attainment at the start of transition (although, as we have seen, there are concerns about school attendance by at-risk groups). The TIMSS results presented in table 7.2 support this conclusion. But why, then, do the PISA assessment results (table 7.4) show them performing so poorly? The TIMSS assessment tests students' mastery of the formal curriculum. Test questions follow the material as it is typically presented in class. In this limited application, the discipline and pedagogy of the inherited education programs led to impressive results. The PISA test instrument specifically aims to assess students' mastery of higher-order skills such as synthesizing knowledge across disciplinary boundaries, integrating uncertainty into analysis, monitoring their own learning progress, and knowing where to access relevant information. These are exactly the skills that are needed for most of the fastest growing jobs in the global economy, as revealed by the experience of the OECD countries and the accession countries themselves (World Bank 2003). These skills were

TABLE 7.7 The role of education in the stages of economic development

Development stage	Key economic challenges	Focus of economic production	Education and labor-market requirements
Factor-driven growth	Get factor markets working properly to mobilize land, labor, and capital.	Natural resource extraction, assembly, labor-intensive manufacturing. Primary sector is dominant.	Basic education, low-level skills, disciplined work habits.
Investment-driven growth	Attract foreign direct investment and imported technology to exploit land, labor, and capital and begin to link the national economy with the global economy.	Manufacturing and outsourced service exports. Secondary sector is dominant.	Universal secondary education, improved secondary vocational and technical education, life-long learning to retool and update skills, flexible labor markets (easy entry, easy exit).
Innovation-driven growth	Generate high rate of innovation, and adaptation and commercialization of new technologies.	Innovative products and services at the global technology frontier. Tertiary sector is dominant.	Highly developed higher education, especially in science and engineering specializations; high rates of social learning, especially science-based learning; dynamic R&D sector linking higher education programs and innovating firms.

Source: Adapted from Schwab, Porter, and Sachs 2001.
Note: R&D = Research and development.

also deliberately neglected in the former communist education systems. A clear message in the low PISA scores for the six accession countries that participated—and probably for the other accession countries as well—is that education systems need to do a much better job in developing higher-order skills of synthesis, problem solving, application, and "thinking outside the box." This will require changes in teaching methods, and more reliance on supplementary sources of information other than the textbook and the teacher's presentation of the approved curriculum.

Although the Czech Republic and most recently Estonia have performed well, the less impressive PISA assessment results in 2000 and 2003 for Latvia, Poland, and Hungary—three of the more progressive accession countries—indicate a problem in how students learn and what students learn. A fundamental reorientation of education is needed to support global competitiveness in the accession countries. As highlighted in a recent presentation to the OECD Governing Board,[9] effective education systems will require developing a much more refined ability to deal with new technologies and new knowledge along with the distinct possibility of more frequent individual changes in careers and job activities. This ability to deal with "disequilibria," cited long ago by Nobel Laureate Theodore Schultz, has become the clear reality of today (Schultz 1975).

Two key features of change that future policies will need to address—in both the accession countries and the OECD countries—are the information explosion and the changing structure of work, and how these changes require changes in teaching and learning approaches so as to remain competitive. The challenge posed by the diversification of sources of information is not so much how to access information, but how to discriminate among sources of information to determine which are most relevant to immediate needs, and how to judge the quality and significance of information from various sources. Providing skills of selectivity and judgment in use of information in an environment of overabundant information of varying quality is one of the key educational challenges faced by all advanced countries. A second key challenge of education systems is how best to provide the skills for effective teamwork in the workplace—increasingly a feature of high-productivity employment. Effective educational approaches to provide teamwork skills for the workplace may also promote the goal of social cohesiveness in the expanded European Union.

Reforms in finance and management

A number of reforms in financing and management of education are needed in the accession countries, both to complete the reform measures already launched and to make education programs more efficient and responsive to the evolving skill needs of the global economy. These include resolving inconsistent roles in delivery of education, improving the financing formula for primary and secondary education, and diversifying the financing of higher education.

Resolving inconsistent roles

In all of the accession countries, local governments are meant to be accountable to the local community for managing basic education effectively and efficiently. They lack the authority to do so, however, because the bulk of financing for teachers' salaries and benefits remains centrally financed and controlled, and because Ministries of Education retain control over key decisions affecting education delivery. Ministries of Education in the accession countries are responsible for curricula; recruitment, evaluation, training, and promotion of school principals and teachers; and for establishment of norms governing minimum and maximum class size and teaching hours. These constraints make it impossible for local governments to carry out actions to improve efficiency, such as school consolidation, unless the Ministry of Education agrees. In most of the accession countries, the Ministry of Education must approve any proposals for teacher dismissals, school closure, or school consolidation.

In designing decentralization measures, the legislatures in the accession countries have retained these functions for Ministries of Education as an instrument of education quality assurance; but the experience of the past decade shows that these input controls are not effective instruments for quality assurance. Quality differences among schools appear to have grown as a result of decentralized financing of education and as a result of differences in the capacities of communities and households. The decentralization models in the accession countries need to be refined to better align responsibilities and accountabilities for managing primary and secondary education. In general, this means empowering local authorities to carry out actions such as staff reduction and school consolidation that are necessary for improved efficiency. Quality assurance should be carried out through assessment of teaching practices and classroom results, rather than through imposing central norms on class size and teaching loads.

Improving the financing formula

Because teacher salaries account for by far the largest component in per-student costs of primary and secondary education, improved efficiency of teacher use is the most important action for improving the efficiency of public expenditures in primary and secondary education. The current financing formula for primary and secondary education in most of the accession counties finances educational inputs—teachers, and sometimes textbooks, other educational materials, and in-service teacher training. It ensures financing for all current schools and teachers, as long as the class size and minimum teaching hour standards established by the Ministry of Education are met. These statutory minimum class sizes and minimum teaching hours are well below OECD norms (see table 7.5 for average class sizes). Moreover, Ministry of Education inspectors can, and often do, provide exceptions that do not meet even these low standards. Additionally, Ministries of Education must approve any proposals to consolidate or close schools, raising a serious third-party payer problem: staffing and school consolidation decisions are made by Ministry of

Education authorities with the involvement of local government authorities, but the central budget pays.

This model provides no incentive either for local governments or for Ministry of Education authorities to pursue more efficient ways of providing education. Not surprisingly, little school optimization or system rationalization to promote efficiency has been carried out in the accession countries under this model. What little system rationalization has occurred, as in the Czech Republic,[10] has tended to occur only within schools, not across schools. Organized opposition can easily thwart local governments' attempts to consolidate schools and to use resources better, as it did in the Czech Republic. To proceed, school rationalization needs to have the right financing incentives, needs to reflect unavoidable differences in costs of providing education (due, for example, to dispersion of population in rural areas), needs to be carried out at a level of aggregation large enough to capture the potential efficiency gains, and needs solid and visible backing of central government authorities to help overcome the resistance of teacher trade unions and other opposition groups. A perception persists in the accession countries that central budget financing of salary costs of basic education is a temporary expedient that will eventually be replaced by local governments assuming full responsibility for at least the recurrent costs of primary and secondary education. The major risk is that such a move to complete reliance on local financing for basic education would lead to negative consequences for poorer communities—including closure of schools, and emergence of unacceptable quality differences in education. It may be preferable that teacher salaries and benefits and other essential recurrent costs of primary and secondary education remain centrally financed, at least until it is established that all communities can afford to assume these costs. Even then, decentralization of these expenditures could entail risks of underfunding in poorer communities and may not be the optimal policy. An inevitable trade-off will have to be faced between the potential efficiency gains from greater local decision making and the possible adverse distributional impacts that this implies. This trade-off suggests, among other things, that funding schools entirely from central or local sources is unlikely to be the best approach.

The need for efficiency improvements in financing primary and secondary education will become more acute in the coming years, especially if the projections of a continued shrinking of the school-age population in the accession countries (table 7.8) prove true. By the beginning of the transition, most of the current accession countries had attained less-than-replacement fertility. Throughout the decade, fertility continued to fall and the size of the school-age cohort contracted at rates formerly seen only in cases of war, famine, or pestilence. The rate of contraction in most of the accession countries will taper off and the size and structure

TABLE 7.8 Shrinkage of the school-age population, 1990–2000, and projected change, 2000–2015

	Size of 0–14-year-old cohort (thousands)			Annual change (%)	
	1990	*2000*	*2015 (projected)*	*1990–2000*	*2000–2015*
Bulgaria	1,781	1,279	916	−3.3	−2.2
Czech Republic	2,223	1,695	1,273	−2.7	−1.9
Estonia	349	254	184	−3.2	−2.1
Hungary	2,098	1,705	1,303	−2.1	−1.8
Latvia	573	418	280	−3.2	−2.7
Lithuania	841	723	546	−1.5	−1.9
Poland	9,574	7,462	6,185	−2.5	−1.3
Romania	5,468	4,112	3,154	−2.9	−1.8
Slovak Republic	1,351	1,070	824	−2.3	−1.7
Slovenia	381	318	243	−1.8	−1.8

Source: World Bank WDI and demographic databases.

of the population will eventually stabilize, but the size of the school-age cohort will continue to shrink significantly for at least another decade. By 2015, the school-age cohort in the accession countries will be from one-third to one-half less than it was in 1990, and about 25 percent less than it was in 2000. These population dynamics imply a further need for downsizing staff and facilities in many primary and secondary schools throughout the accession countries.

The continued use of input-based financing formulas for primary and secondary education is the main reason there has not been more progress in improving efficiency of teacher use in the accession countries. A preferred method for financing education is capitation-based financing, which determines the amount of a local government's educational subsidy based on the number of students it is educating at each level—differentiated to reflect different costs of different programs of education, and possibly other sources of cost variation. This approach, used in the Czech Republic and Lithuania, is preferred for two reasons: first, because the basis of financing—enrolled students—is much closer to the educational objective than are school inputs such as numbers of classrooms and teachers; and second, because it provides an incentive for providers to rearrange inputs to provide education more efficiently. This approach assumes, however, that central authorities no longer constrain local governments' decisions on teacher recruitment and teacher assignment through imposition of class size and teaching load norms and through direct involvement in hiring, firing, and assignment of teachers.

The capitation approach is not perfect. It does not, by itself, provide safe-guards to ensure education quality or teaching effectiveness. It also does not necessarily reflect cost differences among different programs, place-specific cost factors, or cost differences arising from special learning needs of students. Finally, it does not provide for improvements in curriculum, teaching materi-als, and teaching practices—all of which are needed in the accession countries. Nonetheless, such cost differences can be built into a modified, or cost-based, capitation system without compromising the positive efficiency incentives that such systems provide.

Table 7.9 shows how a composite financing formula can provide for these needs. The most advanced applications of this approach are in the primarily

TABLE 7.9 A composite formula for education finance

Component	Dimensions	Indicators
Basic per-student allocation	Total enrollment, differentiated by grade and program	Full-time equivalent (FTE) enrollments by grade and type of program
School site needs	School size	Primary < 200 FTE Secondary < 600 FTE
	School remoteness	Kilometers to town of 50,000 or more persons
	Operations and maintenance costs	Interior area of school in square meters
Student supplementary educational needs	Socioeconomic hardship	Percentage of students from households receiving social assistance
	Low educational achievement	Number of students below 20th percentile assessment results
	Nonfluency in national language	Percentage of students below cutoff score in national lan-guage test
	Disabilities and special learning needs	Number of students formally assessed with special learning needs
Educational quality improvement	Specialized curriculum	FTE enrolled in specialized pro-gram
	Specialized school	Total FTE (if special curriculum school)

Source: Adapted from Levačić and Ross 1999.

English-speaking countries: the United States, Canada, the United Kingdom, Wales, Australia, and New Zealand (Ross and Levačić 1999). Among the accession countries, the Czech Republic, the Slovak Republic, and Lithuania are the most advanced. They finance primary and secondary education through capitation formulas with some of the elements recommended in table 7.9 to reflect cost variations. The Czech Republic also uses a capitation formula to finance lifelong learning courses offered by universities. Romania and Bulgaria calculate per-student costs, but do so after the fact; the actual financing formula remains input-based. In the accession countries that have not yet adopted capitation-based financing, financing formulas for education at all levels should be based on the number of students rather than inputs. Per-student allocations should be differentiated to reflect intrinsic differences in the costs of education delivery, such as the higher cost of technical specializations and greater population dispersion in rural areas.

The details of how the formula reflects cost differences do matter. If financing formulas simply mirror the current unit costs of different localities, the resulting schedule of coefficients will legitimate an inefficient delivery model. The same considerations apply to differentiation of costs for different programs of studies. In the Slovak Republic, for example, per-student recurrent costs are 100 percent higher for upper secondary vocational education and sports education schools than for *gymnasia* (upper-secondary academic schools). Per-student costs in professional art schools are almost four times as high as in *gymnasia*. These unit costs differ largely as a function of class size and teaching loads, not factors that should necessarily be encouraged to continue. Secondary art schools in the Slovak Republic typify the problem of unsustainably high costs that result from too-small class sizes. The recurrent-cost financing formula for upper secondary and higher education should encourage these institutions to rationalize course offerings, perhaps by moving toward more affordable class sizes, or reconfiguring course offerings—for example, by providing art education as one of several options in comprehensive secondary schools rather than in free-standing art schools.[11]

The basic concern throughout is providing support for cost differences without introducing perverse incentives that lead schools to act inappropriately. For example, while extra programs are generally needed to help students who come to school with learning deficiencies, language problems, or other special needs, the finance system should encourage working to eliminate these problems rather than retaining them because of the promise of added funding. Along these lines would be a formula financing educational results rather than enrollments.[12] Some of the charter school contracts in the United States, for example, condition the payment to private education providers on the achievement of agreed on educational targets for learning achievement. Similarly, some state accountability systems reward schools for large gains in student achievement. The Czech model for subsidizing private education embodies the same approach. It finances a higher proportion of recurrent costs for schools that meet higher quality standards. This approach is likely to grow in use as the tools for assessing school performance improve and quality can be directly measured by student outcomes.

Financing higher education

Several EU member states have moved to mixed public-private financing of higher education, but there is considerable diversity in the form and extent of public financing. The introduction of student fees has been a highly political issue in some of the EU states, in some cases causing the government to revoke student fees or abandon proposals for student fees. The more common model in the accession countries is the introduction of fee-paid, "contract education" within public universities, which accounts for as much as two-thirds of higher education enrollments.

Because budget-subsidized places in public universities are awarded competitively and because faculty salaries are supplemented by income from contract students, the practice of selective cost recovery through contract places in public universities has led to the ironic and inefficient result that the most capable faculty are often diverted to teaching the least capable students. It has also exacerbated educational inequities, because poorer students are less likely to win budget-financed places because their primary and secondary schools are more likely to be of inferior quality and because they have less access to paid tutorial instruction to prepare them for the university entrance exam. They are thus more likely to have to pay for their higher education than are more affluent students.

A preferable model is the mixed financing formula—the UK model, for example—in which all universities can receive public financing on a per-student basis, subject to meeting explicit performance standards. This model has important advantages of flexibility (combining cost recovery with public subsidization) and focusing on educational outcomes (in terms of students, graduation rates, and academic achievement). It can also easily accommodate the EU's inclusiveness goal by incorporating affirmative action indicators among the eligibility or performance criteria for financing. Equity concerns can be addressed with student loan schemes. Another approach is the new student fee policy approved by the cabinet of the Slovak Republic in February, 2005, and planned to take effect in September 2005. Under this policy, each university will be free to set fees within a specified range,[13] and income-contingent loans will be available to students to help cover tuition costs.

Private universities have also developed rapidly in most of the accession countries during the transition. For the most part, however, governments have not developed regulatory mechanisms to ensure that private higher education is of acceptable quality. Instead, they have relied on market mechanisms—student demand—to determine the appropriateness of these new schools. However, the absence of reliable information about the quality of private programs makes this an ineffective mechanism of quality assurance. Improved information about program quality would improve the process.

The same argument that justifies public instead of private financing of education (box 7.3) applies to the level of government that finances education. If most of the external benefits of education accrue to the immediate community, it is appropriate for local governments to finance education. This rationale applies to local government financing of skill training in, for example, US community colleges and UK municipal training centers. To the extent that education provides external benefits that accrue to society more broadly, central government financing, at least proportional to the nonlocal benefits, may

---

BOX 7.3 Financing of Education and Training: Public or Private?

Although there are many reasons for governments to finance education and training, there are just three *economic* reasons for them to do so. The first is an efficiency rationale, which rests on the principle that education provides externalities, that is, benefits to society beyond the benefits that it provides to individuals. In this situation, reliance on private financing of education would lead to a level of provision lower than is efficient for society as a whole. Public financing of education is generally seen as most appropriate for initial education, because it conveys skills (such as literacy) and values (such as good citizenship) that are crucial to the proper functioning of a democratic society. This is also the reason that initial education is compulsory and free in most countries of the world. The second reason rests on technological, cost grounds. If there is a minimum scale for efficient operation of a school, as may exist in low density rural areas, competition may not be appropriate. In this case the government would want to fund a monopoly school so as to capture the economies of scale. The third reason is an equity rationale that acknowledges that public financing of education is necessary to reduce the inequities that would result if education were fully financed by individuals.

Source: See Friedman 1962; Barr 2004a.

be appropriate. Central government financing of basic science education and scientific research is often justified on this basis.

The typical pattern of public financing in the accession countries makes local governments responsible for financing initial education and central governments responsible for financing higher education—the opposite of the financing pattern that the economic argument in box 7.3 implies. It would be more efficient and more equitable for central governments to finance initial education, and for higher education to be financed by a combination of private financing, local public financing, and central public financing.

Similar concerns apply to adult training. In a liberal economy, firm-specific productivity gains should motivate employers to finance training; more broadly applicable earnings gains should motivate individuals to acquire and finance training. An approach that is well-established in some EU member states is central government incentives for employers to provide training for their employees—for example, in the form of vocational training levies. Vocational training levies are equivalent to a payroll tax combined with a tax credit for firms that provide approved training. Such levies are costly instruments for promoting training. As described in chapter 3, such initiatives to protect the rights of workers add significantly to the cost of employment and thereby discourage job creation and worker mobility. Training credits are also a blunt instrument for motivating employers to provide training that is relevant to their employees' long-term training needs. Instead, training credits provide an incentive for employers to provide job-specific training that reduces rather than enhances their workers' mobility. Finally, it is questionable whether they lead to workers receiving more training. In the presence of minimal public incentives for training,[14] employers in the United States provide far more training to their employees than employers in countries with vocational training levies.

Improving the inclusiveness of education programs

Education was accorded a high priority in the accession countries during the communist period as was evident both in the resources devoted to education and in the impressive gains achieved in education coverage and quality prior to the transition. The attention given to education was consistent with an egalitarian socialist ideology. Despite this orientation, education policy retained important elitist aspects. Examples include the highly restricted access to higher education (not always based purely on merit), and the practice of streaming the bulk of students into terminal, occupation-specific courses relatively early in their studies. Another was the tendency to judge the quality of the entire education system by the performance of the best students in the system. In education, as in athletics, the former system gave disproportionate attention to developing its highest performers. Extraordinary efforts and resources were devoted to ensuring impressive performance by the most gifted students, who were selected to compete in the equivalent of the academic Olympics and groomed for optimal performance. Ironically, this approach stands in stark contrast with the more common approach in capitalist countries, in which the quality of education systems is usually judged by the average performance of all students, and particular effort and resources are often concentrated on raising the performance of the least-able students.

Even today, a tendency prevails in the accession countries to judge the quality of education systems by the performance of the best students in the system. This Olympic mentality is not suited to the needs of the global economy. Evidence derived from comparing growth of different countries indicates that all segments of the population need high-quality and relevant education if the economy is to prosper and grow (see Hanushek and Kimko 2000). Educational policies that leave some groups of students behind would further lead to social fragmentation and would risk social cleavages that could undermine the core principles of the expanded EU.

Concerns over the possibility that education could lead to greater social fragmentation are not limited to the accession countries. Table 7.10 shows PISA 2000 mean mathematical literacy scores and the differences in mean scores that are attributable to difference in socioeconomic status for the OECD countries and three accession countries, starting with the highest level of mathematics proficiency. Some education systems achieve quality and equity together; others achieve quality at the expense of equity; some achieve neither quality nor equity. Japan, the Republic of Korea, and Finland are representative of the first group, with high average performance and relatively small differences in performance by socioeconomic status (SES). Switzerland, the United Kingdom, Belgium, and France achieve relatively high performance, but at the cost of significant inequity. Germany, Hungary, the United States, and Luxembourg are in the unenviable situation of below-average performance and high inequality, with a particularly strong quality-equity trade-off in Germany. This situation—in which education systems are achieving neither quality nor equity—is a cause for serious concern and immediate corrective action. Poland, Italy, and Mexico are examples of systems with low (but relatively equitable) performance in the 2000 survey. The findings of the 2003 PISA survey are broadly consistent with this finding, except that Poland improved its average mathematics literacy score by 20 points (to 490), and very significantly reduced the SES gradient associated with its mathematics literacy

TABLE 7.10 PISA 2000 results: Mean mathematical literacy scores, and score gradient attributable to difference in socioeconomic status

	Mean score in mathematical literacy	Score gradient[a]
Japan	557	24
Korea, Republic of	547	23
New Zealand	537	45
Finland	536	30
Australia	533	46
Canada	533	37
Switzerland	529	49
United Kingdom	529	49
Belgium	520	48
France	517	48
Austria	515	41
Denmark	514	42
Iceland	514	24
Sweden	510	36
Ireland	503	38
OECD Average	500	41
Norway	499	42
Czech Republic	498	49
United States	493	48
Germany	490	60
Hungary	488	54
Spain	476	32
Poland	470	38
Italy	457	32
Portugal	454	41
Greece	447	38
Luxembourg	446	46
Mexico	387	35

Source: OECD 2004b.
a. Score difference associated with a one unit increase in socioeconomic status (on a six-point scale).

scores. This outcome may reflect recent policy reforms in Poland that result in a more integrated education program and delay differentiation of content until after the age of 15 (OECD 2004a).

One of the implications of the strong quality-equity trade-off in Germany is that education tends to perpetuate and reinforce socioeconomic differences rather than mitigate them. In part, this outcome may reflect the early streaming of students into academic and vocational programs under Germany's dual system of vocational and technical education. This system is already under threat from the growing unwillingness of German employers to provide training for apprentices. German policy makers have responded to this development by exhorting employers to accept more apprentices. These findings on the equity outcomes of education suggest, however, that this approach may be misguided. In fact, Hanushek and Wößmann (2005) suggest, based on international evidence, that early tracking in schools not only generally leads to wider variation in student outcomes but also does not offer clear gains in terms of the overall level of achievement. The above recommendations to improve the relevance of education to the learning needs of the global economy also suggest that the appropriate response may be to move away from the dual system and its dichotomous distinction between academic and vocational education, and to move instead toward a more integrated approach to secondary education.

Two basic approaches may be used to address problems of inequality arising from the different financial capacities of households and localities and place-specific differences in unit costs. The first approach involves identifying a minimum set of essential educational inputs, and financing them uniformly for all schools from central government resources. While varying in detail, this essential approach is being applied in all of the accession countries. Specialized secondary education, higher education (apart from the retained income from student fees and other sources), and education for children with special needs are financed centrally in most of the accession countries, as are capital investments for schools. In general, the formula provides for central budget financing of more educational inputs in the more prosperous accession countries than in the less prosperous accession countries. In the Czech Republic, the Slovak Republic, and Lithuania, for example, the central government budget finances not only teachers' salaries, but also school utilities, textbooks, in-service training for teachers, and teacher salaries and benefits for private schools that meet stipulated quality standards. This broader central financing helps reduce, but does not eliminate, spending inequality in education.[15] On the other hand, in Bulgaria, for example, the poorest of the accession countries, parents are required to purchase textbooks. Limited central funding can clearly maintain resource inequities across poorer and wealthier areas.

The second approach to the regional inequality problem is to rely upon more local resources to finance essential educational inputs, and to provide compensatory support through targeted central subsidies to localities. This targeting approach is used, for example, in the United States, where the federal government provides limited support for schooling—largely for disadvantaged or special-need students.[16] Categorical funding goes even further to ensure that localities have funding for and provide minimal resources for essential education programs, although as discussed above it is important to get the incentives for good performance right.

It is clear not only in the accession countries but across the OECD countries that it is easier to equalize education resources and expenditures than it is to equalize educational outcomes. Central government financing, particularly for specific inputs, is generally accompanied by central government regulation over such things as teacher hiring and retention, teacher-to-pupil ratios, and the provision of textbooks and educational supplies. These regulations ensure minimum provision but it is less clear how they relate to efficiency of the system or to student outcomes. These matters cannot be assumed and must be considered in the design of the financing system.

Annex 7A. Financing Higher Education

Nicholas Barr

With the fall of the communist regime, universities in István's country started to enjoy the fruits of academic freedom. They revised courses, adopted western textbooks, translated books, and energetically set about writing new ones. As this chapter makes clear, these changes took time, and the journey—as in the older member states—is a continuing one. Nevertheless, changes in content were fairly rapid.

In contrast, the finance and organization of universities continued largely unchanged. In the latter days of communism, and even more during the fiscal crisis of the early transition, universities became increasingly underfunded; they also exhibited the familiar inefficiencies of more conventional state-owned enterprises: buildings were underused, and in some subjects student-to-teacher ratios were extremely low. These problems created worries about the quality of university education. Separately, there was little financial support for students, creating worries about access to higher education for those from poorer backgrounds.

Under communist ideology, basic commodities were subsidized, and goods such as health care and education were free—at least in principle. Thus it was natural to provide schooling largely free and hence, by analogy, to provide higher education free. István, it was argued, could go to university even though his parents were poor, because he would not have to pay fees.

As the 1990s unfolded, the government became increasingly worried about the quality issue: EU accession, and hence a single European market, was a real prospect; wider global competitive pressures intensified; and human capital grew in importance as a determinant of national economic performance. Both the need to expand higher education and the need to improve its quality became increasingly salient.

Here, however, the government was caught between conflicting imperatives: the constraints of the Stability and Growth Pact, and the demands of other parts of the public sector—unemployment benefits, active labor market policies, poverty relief, and policies to address social exclusion, pensions, health care, and school education. The resources to finance mass, high-quality higher education from taxation were simply not there. The government therefore proposed a policy with two elements: the introduction of tuition fees; and the parallel introduction of student loans to pay those fees and contribute to living costs.

Specifically, the government proposed to allow universities to set their own fees, up to a ceiling, simultaneously increasing their resources and introducing some competition. Loans were to have income-contingent repayments: that is, repayments were not a certain amount per month, but a certain percentage of the borrower's subsequent earnings, collected as a payroll deduction along with income taxes until the loan had been repaid. In addition, loans were to be large enough to cover tuition fees, plus contribute toward realistic living costs.[17]

The reaction was instant. How could a socially progressive government introduce such a right-wing policy? Fees and loans would make it impossible for István to go to university, but would not harm Anna, whose family had been substantial property owners until the communist takeover, and had remained well-connected. Such a policy, therefore, was regressive, socially divisive, and incompatible with the tradition of free higher education. People, increasingly well-informed through the Internet, knew about the demonstrations against the introduction of loans in Australia and the United Kingdom in the late 1980s (although by the later 1990s both countries had income-contingent loans). Some lurid newspaper headlines talked about huge student debts, typically based on data from U.S. medical schools.

Students in Central and Eastern Europe, however, had a different starting point from those in OECD countries, who typically had had access to a range of tax-funded student support; in the OECD countries loans took away the grants and scholarships students had previously enjoyed. Students in the former communist countries had nothing. Thus, loans covering at least part of their living costs improved their position during their student days. In addition, students were very aware that the quality of their degrees would be instrumental in shaping their life chances. This is true everywhere, but with particular weight in post-communist countries where incomes increasingly came to reflect a person's education and training (Rutkowski 1996). In sharp contrast with western countries, therefore, students, being supreme realists, made common cause with government.

Were the students right? They were right to recognize that the reforms would benefit them. What they, like most politicians and political commentators, failed to realize was the extent to which the proposals were not regrettable necessity but deeply progressive social policy, a view shared by many western experts but not yet absorbed by many politicians or the wider public. They failed to recognize that "free" higher education had remained a largely middle-class activity: what stopped István's parents from going to university was not tuition fees but the fact that in those days there were few university places, and they had never even thought of going to university.

Different elements of the package are in place in the accession countries. Poland has tuition fees for some students, and a system of student loans.[18] Hungary has introduced income-contingent loans,[19] and the Slovak Republic is actively considering such arrangements. Why is the package the right one?

The first element, tuition fees, although controversial in Europe, is taken for granted in countries like the United States. Fees give universities more resources to improve quality; and variable fees (where each university sets its own fees), through competition, improve the efficiency with which those resources are used. That is not an argument for law-of-the-jungle competition, but for regulated markets.[20] Variable fees not only increase efficiency; they are also fairer. Because the majority of students are from better-off backgrounds, undue reliance on taxation means that the taxes of the truck driver pay for the degrees of people from better-off backgrounds, degrees that will further increase their economic advantage. It is supporters of the old system who are protecting middle-class privilege, not the advocates of the new one.

Thinking on fees can be muddled. People may agree that higher education is a right, but it does not follow that it must be free. Food is a right, yet nobody demonstrates outside supermarkets or restaurants. Another confusion is between social elitism, which is abhorrent, and intellectual elitism, which is both necessary and desirable. There is nothing inequitable about intellectually elite institutions. The access imperative is a system in which the brightest students can study at the most intellectually demanding institutions, irrespective of their backgrounds.

The obvious argument against fees is that they deter students from poor backgrounds. That is true if the student has to write a check at the start of each semester, but not if students go to university free and make a contribution to fees only after they have graduated. This brings us to the second element in the package: well-designed student loans.

The two features of the loan—income-contingent repayments, and loans large enough to cover fees and at least part of living costs—have profound implications. They eliminate upfront fees (the student loans administration makes the fee payment directly to the university). Thus higher education is free at the point of use; and student poverty is reduced, because students have at least some support for their living costs.

If loans are large enough to cover fees and all realistic living costs, the package is equivalent to free higher education. Students pay nothing at the time they go to university. Income-contingent repayments differ from tax in only two ways: they are paid only by people who have been to university and benefited financially from a degree; and they do not go on forever. Higher education is largely free for *students*—it is *graduates* who make repayments, and then only if their earnings warrant. Put another way, student support is targeted not on the basis of parents' income (that is, where a person starts), but on each person's own income after graduation—where he or she ends up. István repays his loan if he becomes an international financier; Anna does so only partly if she becomes a social worker.

BOX 7A.1 The Design of Student Loans

The theoretical case for organizing student loans around income-contingent repayments rather than as conventional loans is that borrower and lender both face significant uncertainties about the financial benefits from an academic degree, because future earnings are uncertain, and (unlike home loans) there is no security. Once the decision to adopt income-contingent repayments has been made, however, important design elements remain: What interest rate should borrowers pay? How should nonrepayment be financed? Should loans have a fixed duration of repayments or a variable one?

What interest rate? It is widely supposed that a subsidized interest rate helps poorer students. That argument is false: a more appropriate interest rate is broadly equal to the government's cost of borrowing, and a more appropriate strategy has targeted subsidies rather than a blanket subsidy. Interest subsidies, like many price distortions, cause inefficiency and inequity: they are costly (in the United Kingdom, where borrowers pay a zero real interest rate, about one-third of all lending to students is not repaid because of the subsidy); they impede quality because student support, being politically salient, crowds out the funding of universities; and they impede access because loans are expensive, therefore rationed and therefore too small. Finally, interest subsidies are deeply regressive: the main beneficiaries are successful professionals whose loan repayments cease after, say, 10 years with a subsidized interest rate rather than, say, 12 years with a market rate. It is more progressive to charge an interest rate broadly equal to the government's cost of borrowing (the risk-free rate), combined with targeted interest subsidies of the sort described below.

How are losses financed? Suppose that loans charge the government's cost of borrowing. If all students repaid in full, the scheme would stand on its own. In practice, however, there will be losses because of low lifetime earnings, early death, and so forth, such nonrepayment being well-targeted social spending and a deliberate design feature of income-contingent loans. These losses could be covered from general taxation, as in Australia and the United Kingdom. Alternatively, the cohort of borrowers could cover at least some of the loss through what is, in effect, a form of social insurance.[a] There is also a case for interest subsidies targeted at low earners.

How long should repayments continue? With a conventional loan, monthly repayments and the duration of the loan are both fixed, the variable being the fraction of a person's income absorbed by repayments. With income-contingent repayments, in contrast, the fraction of a person's income absorbed by repayments is fixed and the duration of the loan variable. In a pure scheme, if a person dies before repaying,

(*continued*)

BOX 7A.1 The Design of Student Loans (*Continued*)

outstanding debt (like any other debt) is a claim on their estate. In practice, the duration of the loan is always capped: in some countries
repayments cease at retirement; in others, any loan that has not been
repaid within a specified period (25 years, for example) is forgiven.
Establishing a maximum duration, albeit a deviation from a pure loan,
does not raise major problems. In contrast, having a fixed duration of
repayments for everyone is difficult. It means that low earners do not
repay in full even though, with a longer repayment duration they
might; analogously, high earners repay more than they have borrowed.
Each of these features can be regarded as inequitable. A fixed repayment duration also causes inefficiency. It creates incentives to adverse
selection (people who are "good" risks, expecting high earnings, but
realizing that they will have to repay more than they have borrowed,
will opt out). It also creates a situation in which loan repayments are
identical to a tax, with the potential for adverse incentives; with a loan,
in contrast, an increase in earnings increases loan repayments but also
hastens the day when the loan is paid off and income-contingent
repayments cease—with very different incentive effects than a tax.

a. In New Zealand in the 1990s, the interest rate on student loans was set about
1 percent above the government's cost of borrowing, thus, according to official
estimates, covering about half the loss on the portfolio; the taxpayer covered the
remaining loss.

The introduction of a third element into the package—active measures to
promote access—makes it even more socially progressive. There are two causes
of exclusion: financial poverty and information poverty. Any strategy for access
needs to address both.

Problems of access cannot be solved entirely within the higher education
sector. More resources are needed earlier in the system: growing evidence indicates that the roots of exclusion lie in early childhood. Measures to address
financial poverty should reach back to schools, for example through targeted
financial assistance to encourage young people to complete school. There
should also be a system of scholarships for students from poor backgrounds
once they reach university. Both policies could be supported by financial incentives to universities to widen participation, and by extra resources to provide
additional intellectual support at university for students from disadvantaged
backgrounds.

A second set of measures supports access by offering assistance for people
with low incomes after graduation. People with low lifetime earnings could be

protected by writing off any loan not repaid after, for instance, 25 years. The loans of workers in the public sector could be progressively written off (in the United Kingdom, 10 percent of the loan of new teachers in shortage subjects is written off for each year in the state system). People caring for young children or elderly dependents could be granted loan remission.

Information poverty, the second strategic impediment to access, is inadequately emphasized. Action to inform school children and raise their aspirations is critical. The saddest impediment to access is someone who has never even thought of going to university.

The three elements—variable fees, income-contingent loans, and active measures to promote access—are a genuine strategy in which each reinforces the others. The resulting strategy simultaneously enhances quality and increases fairness.

NOTES

1. This chapter draws upon one of the author's work on education policy issues in the context of World Bank collaboration in several of the accession countries (the Slovak Republic, Bulgaria, Romania, and Hungary), as well as a number of published sources. In addition to sources cited in the text, the following works were particularly valuable: Godfrey 2002; OECD 2001; World Bank 1999; World Bank 2003; and the various OECD annual economic reviews for the accession countries.
2. The countries of the former Soviet Union excluding Estonia, Latvia, and Lithuania.
3. TIMSS was renamed in 2003. Previously it stood for the "Third International Mathematics and Science Study."
4. Although not completely comparable, the Czech Republic did participate in the 2003 PISA tests and scored significantly above the OECD average in mathematics (OECD 2004a). On those mathematics examinations, the Slovak Republic was approximately at the OECD average, while Poland, Latvia, and Serbia were below the average.
5. The Gini coefficient measures how much the income distribution diverges from full equality of incomes. Larger values indicate more unequal distributions.
6. Note that PISA was repeated in 2003 with a change in focus to performance in mathematics (OECD 2004b). The Czech Republic, Latvia, Poland, Serbia, and the Slovak Republic participated.
7. Note that gross enrollment rates compare school enrollment with population numbers for the age groups that should be attending school. Because of grade repetition, late entry to school, and other factors, these enrollment rates can exceed 100 percent.
8. Data provided by Romanian Ministry of National Education.
9. Presentation by Professor David Hargreaves, Cambridge University, to the OECD CERI Governing Board, March 24, 2000.
10. The Czech school rationalization program successfully consolidated 159 schools and reduced 4,000 jobs, but was suspended due to opposition of teachers and local communities.
11. In the Czech Republic, per-student allocations in upper secondary schooling range from about CZK 24,000 (slightly over US$1,000) for *gymnasia* and business academies, to

about CZK 29,000 (US$1,250) for technical schools. This relatively narrow spread encourages more efficient delivery of technical education. Because any additional costs would need to be financed from local sources, it also encourages local authorities to consider carefully whether technical education programs that cost more than this amount are providing good value to the local community.

12. Note that treatment of low achievement presents special problems. Some low achievers enter schools less well prepared and in need of extra help to obtain high levels of achievement. Other low achievers are in that position because the schools themselves are ineffective. It is important to deal with problems of need without rewarding schools for failing to educate children. Thus, for example, the incentives are clearer when funding goes with observable, prior conditions (economic disadvantage of families, language handicaps, and so forth) as opposed to simple low achievement.

13. The initial proposed range is Sk 3,500 (US$120) to Sk 21,000 (US$700) per year, representing from 5 percent to 30 percent of total average costs per student.

14. Employers in the United States can deduct training costs as a business cost—a far weaker incentive than a tax credit for training.

15. Lithuania provides a textbook allocation of LTL 20 (US$7.50) per student, but the actual cost of secondary textbooks is about LTL 150 (US$57.50) per year (OECD 2002).

16. The United States is actually a hybrid system because it operates at three levels: local, state, and national. The state governments, which have the primary responsibility for organizing schools, typically delegate considerable authority to local governments and require local governments to share the financing role. Although it differs somewhat across states, the state governments typically compensate local governments for low ability to raise educational funds in setting the general funding for core operations of schools.

17. For fuller discussion, see Barr (2004b) and Hanushek, Leung, and Yilmaz (2004).

18. The constitution does not allow tuition fees for "regular" students, but they are permissible for "evening" students, the definition of which is flexible. Poland's loans do not have income-contingent repayments.

19. Although a huge advance, work remains both to ensure that the scheme qualifies as private finance and to organize the collection of repayments through the tax authorities.

20. Although the issue of fees is generally treated as ideological, the core of the argument is technical. Fees (that is, prices) contribute to the efficient use of resources in well-understood circumstances including—centrally—well-informed consumers. Thus it is consistent to argue against fees for school education but to support them for higher education on the grounds that university students are better-informed than school children. The two cases are contrasted in Barr (2004a, chapters 13 and 14).

REFERENCES

Barr, Nicholas. 2004a. *The Economics of the Welfare State,* 4th edition. Oxford and Stanford, CA: Oxford University Press.

Barr, Nicholas. 2004b. "Higher Education Funding." *Oxford Review of Economic Policy* 20(2): 264–283. http://oxrep.oupjournals.org/cgi/content/abstract/20/2/264?ijkey=20GIFCugfcjFz&keytype=ref.

Berryman, Sue. 2000. *Hidden Challenges to the Education Systems in Transition Economics.* Washington, DC: World Bank.

Bulgaria. 1995. "Bulgaria Integrated Household Survey." Administered by Gallup International for Bulgarian Ministry of Labor and Social Affairs.

———. 1997. "Bulgaria Integrated Household Survey." Administered by Gallup International for Bulgarian Ministry of Labor and Social Affairs.

———. 2001. "Bulgaria Integrated Household Survey." Administered by Gallup International for Bulgarian Ministry of Labor and Social Affairs.

Coulombe, Serge, Jean-François Tremblay, and Sylvie Marchand. 2004. *Literacy Scores, Human Capital, and Growth across Fourteen OECD Countries.* Ottawa: Statistics Canada.

Economic Research Centre. 1999. "Effectiveness and Efficiency of Public Expenditures in the Education Sector, Summary." Vilnius. Cited in OECD, 2002, *Lithuania, Education and Skills: Review of National Policies for Education,* OECD, Paris.

European Union. 2003. "Council Decision of 22 July 2003 on Guidelines for the Employment Policies of the Member States (2003/578/EC)." *Official Journal of the European Union, 5/8/2003.*

Fitzpatrick, Sheila. 1979. *Education and Social Mobility in the Soviet Union 1921–1934.* Cambridge: Cambridge University Press.

Friedman, Milton. 1962. *Capitalism and Freedom.* Chicago: University of Chicago Press.

Godfrey, Martin. 2002. "Quality of Learning: Towards 'Unilateral Educational Disarmament.'" In *Social Monitor 2002: Social Trends in Transition, HIV/AIDS and Young People, Quality of Learning in Schools.* Florence: UNICEF Innocenti Research Centre.

Hanushek, Eric A., and Dennis D. Kimko. 2000. "Schooling, Labor Force Quality, and the Growth of Nations." *American Economic Review* 90(5): 1184–208.

Hanushek, Eric A., Charles Ka Yui Leung, and Kuzey Yilmaz. 2004. "Borrowing Constraints, College Aid, and Intergenerational Mobility." NBER Working Paper No. 10711, National Bureau of Economic Research, Cambridge, MA.

Hanushek, Eric A., and Ludger Wößmann. 2005. "Does Educational Tracking Affect Performance and Inequality? Differences-in-Differences Evidence across Countries." NBER Working Paper No. 11124, National Bureau of Economic Research, Cambridge, MA.

International Association for the Evaluation of Educational Achievement. 2000a. "TIMSS 1999: International Mathematics Report." Chestnut Hill, MA: Boston College.

———. 2000b. "TIMSS 1999: International Science Report." Chestnut Hill, MA: Boston College.

Laporte, Bruno, and Julian Schweitzer. 1994. "Education and Training." In *Labor Markets and Social Policy in Central and Eastern Europe: The Transition and Beyond,* ed. Nicholas Barr, 260–287. New York and London: Oxford University Press.

Levačić, Rosalind, and Kenneth Ross. 1999. "Principles for Designing Needs-Based School Funding Formulae." In *Needs-Based Resource Allocation in Education via Formula Funding of Schools,* eds. Kenneth Ross and Rosalind Levačić, 25–55. Paris: International Institute for Education Planning, UNESCO.

National Center for Education Statistics. 2004. *Highlights for the Trends in International Mathematics and Science Study (TIMSS), 2003.* Washington, DC: NCES.

OECD (Organisation for Economic Co-operation and Development). 2000. *Education at a Glance, 2000.* Paris: OECD.

———. 2001. *Education Policy Analysis: Education and Skills.* Centre for Educational Research and Innovation. Paris: OECD.

———. 2002. *Lithuania, Education and Skills: Review of National Policies for Education.* Paris: OECD.

———. 2004a. *Learning for Tomorrow's World:* http://www.pisa.oecd.org/dataoecd/1/60/34002216.pdf

———. 2004b. *Message from PISA 2000.* http://www.pisa.oecd.org/dataoecd/31/19/34107979.pdf

OECD and Statistics Canada. 1997. *Literacy Skills for the Knowledge Society: Further Results from the International Adult Literacy Survey.* Paris: OECD.

OECD and UNESCO Institute of Statistics. 2003. *Literacy Skills for the World of Tomorrow: Further Results from PISA 2000.* Paris: OECD.

Ringold, Dena, Mitchell A. Orenstein, and Erika Wilkens. 2003. *Roma in an Expanding Europe: Breaking the Poverty Cycle.* Washington, DC: World Bank.

Ross, Kenneth, and Rosalind Levačić, eds. 1999. *Needs-Based Resource Allocation in Education via Formula Funding of Schools.* Paris: International Institute for Education Planning, UNESCO.

Rutkowski, Jan. 1996. "High Skills Pay Off: The Changing Wage Structure during Economic Transition in Poland." *Economics of Transition* 4(1): 89–112.

Schultz, Theodore W. 1975. "The Value of the Ability to Deal with Disequilibria." *Journal of Economic Literature* 13(3):827–46.

Schwab, Klaus, Michael Porter, and Jeffrey Sachs, eds. 2001. *The Global Competitiveness Report, 2001/2002.* Geneva: The World Economic Forum.

Stoica, Adrian. 2002. *Rural-Urban Differences in Student Assessment Results, 1999, 2000, and 2001,* Working Paper commissioned by the World Bank, Bucharest.

UNICEF. 2001. *A Decade of Transition: The MONEE Project, CEE/CIS/Baltics.* Florence: UNICEF Innocenti Research Center.

World Bank. 1999. *World Development Report 1998/99: Knowledge for Development.* Washington, DC: World Bank.

———. 2002. *Transition, the First Ten Years: Analysis and Lessons for Eastern Europe and the Former Soviet Union.* Washington, DC: World Bank.

———. 2003. *Lifelong Learning in the Global Knowledge Economy: Challenges for Developing Countries.* Washington, DC: World Bank.

INDEX